The Development of Methodism in Barbados
1823 - 1883

Noel F. Titus

The Development of
Methodism in Barbados
1823 - 1883

PETER LANG

Bern · Berlin · Frankfurt a. M. · New York · Paris · Wien

Die Deutsche Bibliothek – CIP-Einheitsaufnahme

Titus, Noel F.:
The development of methodism in Barbados 1823 - 1883 / Noel
F. Titus. - Bern ; Berlin ; Frankfurt/M. ; New York ; Wien ;
Paris : Lang, 1993
ISBN 3-906752-08-9

Printed in Germany

PREFACE

This work constitutes the first detailed attempt to look at Methodist work in Barbados in the nineteenth century. It makes extensive use of unpublished archival materials, especially the manuscript records of the Methodist Missionary Society. By using the Methodists as an example, it seeks to highlight the problems some dissenting groups faced in West Indian societies, in which there were "state" or "established" churches, and where religious intolerance, though not as rife as in the previous century, nevertheless was a noteworthy characteristic of these societies.

By the beginning of the eighteenth century, the Church of England was firmly established in Barbados. The Quakers of the previous century had all gone, due largely to the intolerance of members of the Established Church. Moravian missionaries arrived in the latter half of the century to work among the slaves. They existed on sufferance, and were able to survive by pandering to the prejudices of the planter class. The Methodists who arrived in 1788 were to have a different experience. Unlike the Moravians, they were a dissentient offshoot from the Church of England, and this fact, plus their uncompromising attitude in an already hostile plantation society, contributed to the way in which they were treated.

This dissertation seeks to examine the development of Methodism in the closing years of slavery, and the years which followed the abolition of the slave system. It will seek to show that religious intolerance in the Barbadian society, especially as that was linked to the existence of a church establishment, was a major obstacle for the Methodists to overcome. This intolerance affected them in several aspects of their development – their right to function, their relations with the Established Church, their quest for public financial support, and their operation of schools. It will show that they themselves were not without blame for some of the problems which they encountered. It will also show that internal problems regarding discipline in one congregation, and class or colour distinction among the ministers, created further difficulties for them. This was particularly the case when efforts were made to establish an autonomous West Indian Conference.

Noel F. Titus, August 1991

ACKNOWLEDGEMENTS

In the preparation of a work of this magnitude one is naturally in-debted to a large number of persons. I wish to acknowledge my debt to Mr. Alvin Thompson, who served as my supervisor throughout my time as a research student at the University of the West Indies. He gave very generously of his time, advice and encouragement to enable the completion of the work. My thanks are also due to Dr. (now Sir) Keith Hunte for valuable assistance in the early stages of writing, and to Dr. Hilary Beckles for encouragement and criticisms. I also owe a debt of gratitude to various members of the History Department for comments and advice on different points as I progressed. From all of these persons I derived great benefit, though the responsibility for the work is my own.

I wish also to acknowledge the valuable assistance from various institutions: from the staff of the School of Oriental and African Studies (SOAS) in London; from the staff of the University Library at Cave Hill, particularly Mrs. J. Carnegie; from Mrs. Christine Rocheford and staff of the Archives Department, and Mrs. J. Ward and colleagues in the Reference Section of the Barbados Public Library. Thanks are also due to the Barbados Board of Tourism for permission to use the map of Barbados. Lastly, I wish to express thanks to Mrs. Velma Newton of the Caribbean Law Institute at Cave Hill for very valuable assistance in the final stages of production, and to Triumph Publications for typing the dissertation.

TABLE OF CONTENTS

TABLE OF CONTENTS

LIST OF TABLES

LIST OF FIGURES

LIST OF ABBREVIATIONS

S.P.G.   Society for the Propagation of the Gospel in
Foreign Parts

C.M.S.   Church Missionary Society

MMS   Methodist Missionary Society

x

Map Showing Location of Methodist Churches in Barbados

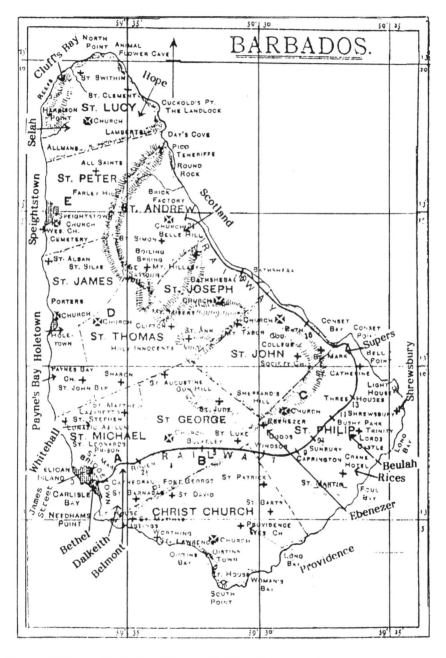

Source: J. Fraser, Barbados Diamond Jubilee Directors, 1907–1908.

Chapter 1

INTRODUCTION

Methodist missions were introduced into the West Indies in circumstances in which the plantation formed the vortex of the entire social structure. The plantation dominated the social landscape, as it did the economic and political ones, and determined the nature and characteristics of the social institutions which existed. The church was unquestionably the dominant social institution during the period under review, divided, however, into various segments or denominations. Chief among these was the Anglican denomination, or the Established Church, as it came to be known. It was the state church and the only one for a long time which was recognised by the colonial authorities as having the right to exist legally in the colonies. Other denominations, referred to variously as sects or dissenting churches, such as the Moravians, existed from time to time on sufferance; a few, such as the Quakers and the Roman Catholics, were actively persecuted in the English-speaking Caribbean. However, whatever the church or denomination, both ministers and laity were acutely aware that religion was part of the politics of the age and that tolerance towards or persecution of a given denomination related not so much to its theological orthodoxy as to the perceived relevance of its dogma and practice to what were regarded as the imperatives of plantation society. So that, those denominations which did nothing to disturb the social status quo and, even more so, those which upheld it, were the ones most likely to receive the blessings of the planter class. In order to understand more clearly the place and the role of the church in plantation society, as perceived by the plantocracy, it is necessary to deal in some detail with the social structure and organisation of that society, particularly at the time that Methodism was introduced into the island of Barbados.

Plantation Society

The main social characteristic of plantation society was its rigid stratification into three major categories: whites, free coloureds and slaves. These categories corresponded largely to colour differences. Phenotypic differences were legal in Jamaica but conventional in Barbados and some other islands. In Barbados, however, the distinctions were as rigid as if they had been buttressed by law. Social divisions were characterised by separation of the groups, except where the necessities of plantation labour demanded interaction. They were also characterised by the subordination of the free coloureds and the slaves. For example, the Assembly in Jamaica, referring in 1797 to the social divisions in the island, added in a report:

> all these classes, when employed in the public service, have, as far as it has been practicable, been kept separate. [1]

John Poyer, an ideologist for white supremacy in Barbados, regarded a system of subordination as "absolutely necessary" to preserve distinctions which either were natural or had evolved in the colony. [2] Poyer's attitude reflects the kind of thinking that was prevalent in Barbados during his time. It was the attitude of those whites who had become the dominant class in the society, and which included planters as well as professionals such as doctors, lawyers, and even members of the clergy.

The proprietary class of Barbados was largely composed of residents of the colony, many of whom had been born in the island. Several of their families had remained in the island and some family names persisted in the Assembly, the Council, and the militia of the island. Such was the extent of endogamy [3] that, even if a name disappeared, it did not necessarily entail the cessation of a particular family connection.

To these proprietors Barbados was home. In this regard the island seems to have escaped that inclination, noticed in Jamaica, for many of the resident planters and some of those born there to think of England as "home". [4] The intensity of insular pride which they displayed led them on the one hand to see their island as pre-eminent in the region and almost indispensable to England, and on the other hand to resent any challenge to those traditions which they had built up. [5] Watson may be correct in criticising the failure to empathise with the Barbadians' pride in their native island. However, other groups within the society were not so free as to participate in the island's institutions, nor to share the pride of the white elite to the same extent. It was the pride of a small group.

At the base of the society were the slaves themselves, constituting with the whites what Edward Cox labelled polar opposites. The number of slaves in the West Indies had grown rapidly as sugar production offered the opportunity of wealth. In 1786 for example, Barbados had some 62,115 slaves to 16,167 whites. In 1788 the Leeward Islands had approximately 81,000 slaves to 8,000 whites, and Jamaica in 1787 had 237,000 slaves to 23,800 whites. By the year 1809 Barbados had 69,369 slaves and 15,566 whites compared with Jamaica's 260,000 slaves and 30,000 whites in 1807. [6] The size of the slave population posed a serious threat to the ruling class, especially since there had been a large-scale and successful servile revolt in Haiti. It was, therefore, not simply their superiority in numbers which was the problem, though that in itself was disturbing. The fact of enslavement had always been unpalatable to the slave population, who sought freedom by death or by revolt.

In an intermediate position in the slave society stood the free coloureds and free blacks. These were persons who had either been manumitted by their owners, or who had been born free. The group included blacks descended directly from slave parents, as well as persons who were the result of planter-slave miscegenation, and showed a wide range of complexional differences. This group constituted the smallest element in Barbados during the pre-emancipation period. But the group was growing through manumissions and natural births. In Barbados in 1801 there were 2,209 of them; in 1811 the number had grown to 2,613, and by 1829 it was 5,146. [7] In Barbados, as in St. Kitts and Jamaica, these free people were concentrated in the capital and its suburbs. They avoided work on the plantations, preferring what little freedom they had to the harsh conditions of life in the plantation setting. With whites dominating the supervisory positions on the estates, they would have found little to do besides field work. In the vicinity of Bridgetown, however, they were able to engage in trades, and in business as shopkeepers, merchants, keepers of taverns and hotels, as well as to become owners of houses. Thus, the free coloureds and blacks became owners of significant property in the town, and some of them even became owners of plantations. [8] These persons would have been owners of slaves as a result. Some of them actually considered the ownership of slaves an indispensable mark of their status. So that when early in the nineteenth century a bill was introduced to restrict their ownership of property, especially in slaves, a group of them regarded the change as a prospect worse than death. [9] A sign of their division appeared in 1823 when a group of them petitioned for the end of disabilities, while another group presented a loyal address to the Assembly. [10] This group could not be expected to have a community of interests with those in the lower stratum of the free coloured class, especially those who had recently been manumitted. By extension they could not be expected to have a community of interests with the slaves.

Plantation society was also arbitrary and dehumanising. The grim reality of chattel slavery was that the slave was regarded as cargo on the ships which transported them, quite unlike the sailors. [11] Moreover, the slave on the plantation was subject to the control of the owner, who dealt with that slave kindly or otherwise as he felt inclined. The prevalence of absenteeism in some islands contributed, to a certain degree, to cruelty in the treatment of slaves. This in turn created the conditions which favoured insurrection among the slaves. On the other hand, some resident proprietors were inefficient, and were themselves guilty of overworking their slaves. [12] Even where religion was concerned, the arbitrary control of the proprietors ensured that ministers could not have access to the slaves without the approval of the planters.

The system was essentially exploitative, not only as regards the extraction of labour, but also as regards the cruel punishment which could be capriciously inflicted on the slaves. Such brutality was seldom punished as the evidence of slaves was not acceptable against white persons. In Barbados in the eighteenth century the murder of a slave was not a capital offence, and indeed was punishable only by a fine. It was only early in the nineteenth century that a law was passed making the murder of a slave a capital offence. But as Jerome Handler has observed, when the Speaker of the Assembly expressed his support for the bill, he was more concerned with its applicability to the free coloureds. [13]

Early in the nineteenth century, the cases of certain planters in the Leeward Islands served to show the extent to which planter inhumanity could go. Edward Huggins of Nevis had a number of his slaves severely beaten, one of whom died while others were maimed. Rev. Henry Rawlins similarly caused some of his slaves to be whipped, and actually participated in the whipping. Arthur Hodge, a Tortola planter, was charged with murdering some of his slaves. Huggins was fortunate to be acquitted, and Rawlins was fined and imprisoned. Because of the Governor's insistence on seeing justice done, Hodge was found guilty and hanged. [14] Planter juries were not very keen to convict other planters even for established cases of cruelty.

Plantation labour was time consuming to the extent that Sunday was the only day the slaves had to themselves; and this day was spent in two ways. One of these was in working on their plots of ground or going to the market. [15] The other was as a day of recreation – usually in dancing to the accompaniment of singing and drumming. Such activities did not meet with approval for various reasons. As will be shown later, missionaries were critical of them because they regarded such activities as inconsistent with what they considered behaviour proper to a Christian. The ruling class saw in these activities opportunities for clandestinely plotting the destruction of the white population. In this context every effort was made to control the slaves, including the passage of legislation to prohibit both their drumming and their assembling together. The legislators themselves were not particularly concerned about the religious observance of Sunday, since their own conduct was not exemplary in this regard. On the contrary, they seemed concerned to control what they could not or did not understand. Dr. George Pinckard, on a visit to the island, thought that the fatigue which the slaves usually underwent in dancing was greater than that involved in labouring for four days per week. [16] His assessment cannot be taken seriously, though the publication of it might well have lent support to the prejudices already ingrained in the white population. In itself it betrays a certain degree of prejudice on the part of that author.

Burial rites for the deceased played an important part in the life of the slaves. In a sense death meant merciful release from the oppressive system, and this can be regarded as providing encouragement for suicides. It meant more, however, in that there was an understanding that the departed would journey back to Africa to be united with their ancestors. For this purpose, proper disposal of the deceased's body was a major concern. Various articles were placed in the grave to help the departed on the journey home to Africa. [17] This explains a feature which was open to misunderstanding by the non-African. Pinckard, for example, expressed the disappointment of some Europeans at the absence of any semblance of grief among members of a funeral procession he witnessed. He complained of the lack of a hymn or dirge, observing that there was only a song in the pattern of a chant and response between a solo voice and the crowd. [18] Yet a funeral did not mean the same thing to the slave as it did to the white creole or European. A funeral could have been a form of protest against an act of injustice, as when a slave was executed for attempted murder, or when a slave was murdered. [19] Such funerary protests are still usual in South

Africa today, and tell us something of the mood of those involved. Grief could have been superseded by bitterness – the bitterness of slavery, the bitterness of an unjust execution, the bitterness of a murder.

Another important area in the culture of the slaves was the practice of obeah. Obeah is best defined as a "system of magico-religious beliefs and practices." [20] As a means of social control it had both a positive and a negative aspect. In its positive aspect obeah was used to prevent, detect and punish crimes among slaves. Thus a variety of practices evolved, as shown by Orlando Patterson, both to deter the larceny of crops and to discover the perpetrator of a crime.

Obeahmen sometimes functioned as medicine men, using their knowledge of herbs to the benefit of fellow-slaves. In its negative aspect, obeah might involve the poisoning of other slaves or one's enemy. In addition, the obeahman was sometimes used to administer oaths of secrecy, thus involving him in the planning of slave rebellions. These factors, when taken together, show that the obeahman was a person of influence, feared as much by the white population as he was by the slaves. [21] As was the case elsewhere in the West Indies, the Barbadian legislature passed laws against those identified as obeahmen.

Plantation society also involved a restriction of the popular franchise. The whites in Barbados, as elsewhere in the West Indies, were the ones from whose ranks the bi-cameral legislature was drawn. A number of the principal planters and professional persons were chosen to form the Council. As a Privy Council, they were the Governor's advisers; but they sometimes functioned as a legislative body. Twenty-two persons were elected annually to form the House of Assembly, two representatives from each of the eleven parishes. The qualifications necessary for the franchise were: a minimum of ten acres of land, or a house having an annual taxable value of £ 10 currency. To this one should add that the person had to be a white male and a Christian. As in other parts of the West Indies, these qualifications ensured that a large part of the population was deprived of the franchise. [22] The same qualifications, with the same general effects, applied to membership of the parochial vestries. The vestries were responsible for administration at the parochial level, collecting parish taxes and rents, providing poor relief, and looking after the church establishment and such schools as they administered. What was said of the vestries in Jamaica could with justice be said of the vestries in Barbados: "they were useful and obedient instruments of Assembly policy". [23] And because of the community of interest on the part of those who constituted both bodies, the net result was that a small body of whites effectively controlled the entire island.

Not only did the legislators and vestrymen come from this class, but so too did the magistrates and judges in the various courts. As a rule these functionaries could not lay claim to any kind of legal training, so that judgments tended to be based on common sense or on self-interest. It was customary for the Governor to appoint any member of the Council to be Chief Justice of the Grand Sessions to hear murder trials. And Helen Manning has shown that as late as 1820 the Chief Justice of Barbados was a medical practitioner. [24] This situation persisted until 1825, when H.N. Coleridge observed that none of the more than twenty planters and merchants who formed the judiciary had been legally trained. [25]

The subordination of free coloureds and blacks meant the exclusion of members of that group from holding public office, or from either voting or being elected to the vestries or the House of Assembly. This experience was one which they shared with their counterparts elsewhere, except that in Antigua the free coloureds were allowed to vote even though they were not legally entitled to do so. [26] What made this restriction disturbing to the injured group in Barbados was the fact that several of their members easily met the franchise qualifications.

The growth of a propertied free coloured class in St. Kitts and Grenada, had led its members to chafe at similar restrictions. They protested the fact that "any transient white foreigner" could have been enfranchised while, as permanent residents, they were excluded from the franchise. A similar situation existed in Barbados, and the legislators were not disposed to change it. In fact, such was the intransigence of the legislators towards the concerns raised by the free coloureds in 1823, that in response to their petition the Assembly resolved that they were not entitled to any rights and privileges except those granted to them by the Colonial Legislature, the continuance of which must depend on their good conduct. [27]

Change in the franchise law in Barbados, when it did come, was intended to benefit only a few of them. The so-called "brown privilege bill" did not alter the franchise qualifications for whites. For free coloureds it retained the ten acres property qualification, but raised the annual taxable value of a house to £30. Since the property of the free coloureds was mainly in housing, the bill in effect granted to only a small number of them the right to vote. Governor Smith estimated that only seventy-five persons benefitted from it. [28]

The atmosphere of division in the West Indies was further complicated by growing humanitarian concern about the slaves in the West Indies. As early as 1671 George Fox had urged his fellow Quakers in Barbados to relinquish their title to slaves. [29] These Quakers also followed the unusual practice of allowing their slaves to attend their worship, and of actually sitting with the said slaves. The Barbados legislature responded with two pieces of legislation making their action illegal. [30] Such liberalism as the Quakers practised, since it might have created among the slaves a feeling of equality with the whites, was not tolerated.

In 1783 it was a group of Quakers who initiated the debate against the slave trade when they presented to Parliament a resolution calling for the abolition of that trade. The resolution was defeated, but a Society for the Abolition of the Slave Trade was formed nearly two years later, which had in its membership Quakers and Evangelicals known as the Clapham Sect. Led in Parliament by William Wilberforce, this group kept up a steady agitation for the abolition of the trade. In Parliament, resolutions, petitions and examinations of witnesses testified to their commitment. So, too, did the collection of evidence and the production of books and pamphlets on the part of dedicated supporters. Success in their objective was not achieved until 1807. [31]

The debate was viewed with concern by West Indian planters and merchants in London, and by the agents of the colonies. In the West Indies the legislators did not look with toleration on the activity of the abolitionists. Not only did they consider the autonomy of their assemblies to be threatened, they feared for their property as well. They were therefore opposed to those who seemed to hold out a threat to their livelihood. The Methodists probably became natural targets because of their association with prominent members of the Clapham Sect, and later on of the Anti-Slavery Society. When this Society was formed in 1823, it had as its Secretary Richard Matthews, a Methodist and a lawyer. Not only this, but at a later stage, prominent Methodist ministers became members of that Society. These included the Rev. Richard Watson and the Rev. Jabez Bunting, both of whom served as General Secretary and President of the Methodist Conference. [32] While it cannot be said that the Methodist missionaries in the West Indies were agents of the abolitionists, the association between the leadership of both organisations would have encouraged the accusation.

When in 1760 the Methodist Society began its work in Antigua, through the efforts of Nathaniel Gilbert, the parent body in England was less than twenty-two years old. For, while this new body traced its birth to John Wesley's conversion in 1738, it was some years before there evolved a distinct religious group called the Methodists. So, too, when Thomas Coke visited Barbados in 1788, he arrived on the island about four years after the first Methodist ministers had been ordained in England. In addition, his arrival long ante-dated the formation of the Methodist Missionary Society. Indeed, it was not until some twenty-five years after that there occurred that famous meeting in Leeds which gave rise to the Missionary Society. [33]

A number of reflections follow from this. The first is that the Methodist Society bore very largely the characteristics of a sect. It had been a movement of religious protest which had separated itself, or become separated, from the Church of England. Like any other sect, it showed all the vigour that is characteristic of a new movement. Its membership was by choice, since separation from an established body always involved risks; and continuance in membership was based on sustained evidence of commitment. [34] The second reflection is that the missionary work in the West Indies was being administered by a Missionary Committee that was itself younger than the missions over which it presided. While Methodist missions in the West Indies formally started in 1786, it was not until 1813 that the Wesleyan Methodist Missionary Society was formed. Prior to 1813, missionary work was overseen by a Committee headed by the President of the Conference; but Thomas Coke was the one who effectively organised everything. After 1804 a special Committee of Conference supervised missions, and after 1813 there was a Missionary Committee. [35] While there was among them undoubted zeal for missionary work, the directors of the work in England were ignorant of real conditions in the West Indies. Missionaries' letters, therefore, are replete with requests for reconsideration of decisions made. Thirdly, the Methodist Society [36] in the West Indies was in the process of growth and change at the same time that its juvenile "parent" was growing to maturity in England. The result is that there was no time to assess changes in England before they were applied in the West Indies. Fourthly, the Methodist Society insisted on certain norms of behaviour in religion and in general conduct which were more appropriate to settled communities. In the case of the West Indies, the nature of estate management and of planter fear ensured that the black population remained unstable. Families could not be maintained as such, since planter caprice alone could permanently divide them.

Quite apart from all this, the experiences of this body in contemporary England will throw some light on their experience in the West Indies. In the late eighteenth and early nineteenth centuries, this Society functioned under a cloud of suspicion. A minority organisation, their loyalty had been suspect for some time. It became even more so as the eighteenth century neared its close, perhaps because the French Revolution had encouraged suspicion of any movement popular among the lower classes. This is not altogether surprising when it is noted that the father of Jabez Bunting, a prominent Methodist leader, had been an ardent supporter of the French Revolution in its early days. Indeed, Jabez Bunting worked hard to remove from Methodism the stigma of Jacobinism. [37] At the beginning of the nineteenth century, therefore, one of their major concerns seemed to have been to establish their loyalty to the Crown. It is in this context that we learn of Thomas Coke's informing the Duke of Portland of suspected seditious activity in the Yorkshire-Lincolnshire area. It is also in this context that we learn of Methodist preachers successfully undermining a projected brotherhood of pitmen in Northern England, or opposing the Luddite Movement in the East Midlands. [38]

To make matters worse, in some parts of England, magistrates were refusing to grant Methodist ministers licences to preach. [39] And this was happening at about the same time that they were being refused licences in Jamaica and elsewhere in the West Indies. The Methodist historian, Smith, has argued that the refusal was based on a misunderstanding of the Toleration Act. He referred to a decision of the Court of King's Bench to the effect that:

> a man to entitle himself to a licence for preaching, was bound to show that he was the acknowledged teacher or preacher of some particular congregation. [40]

And he suggested that this was being misunderstood to mean a parish. Wearmouth takes the discussion further and demonstrates that the refusal of the magistrates was based on their suspicion of Methodist loyalty. This suspicion persisted until the 1840's, some missionaries being arrested and even imprisoned whenever disturbances occurred.

During his life time John Wesley had clung, somewhat tenuously, to his connection with the Church of England. It was a slender thread based on the fact that he had been ordained a minister in that body. However, his own activities tended to undermine that connection in four significant ways. In the first place, he established what he called preaching-houses where his supporters gathered for worship. In the second place, he arranged for the vesting of this property in Chapel Trustees, who had no connection with the Church of England. In the third place, he himself ordained a number of ministers to go to the United States in furtherance of his own missions. And finally, before his death, he established a Conference to administer the affairs of Methodism. In short, Wesley had done a great deal towards severing the link between his organisation and the Church of England. Within five years of his death, the Conference he established had taken the process to its logical conclusion and established Methodism as an independent body. Hence Methodism came to be viewed as a schism from the Church of England.

In the eighteenth century some of the clergy were poor representatives of the Church of England. These were often ignorant, superstitious and bigoted, becoming involved in the harassment of the Methodists. But among the body of the bishops and clergy, "perhaps not the majority" were of this baser type. Referring to them, a Methodist historian wrote:

> This class of eighteenth century cleric loved his country, her laws, her ordinances, institutions, State religion and government. He abhorred the troubler of the State, the spurious reformer, the obstreperous, tyrannic demagogue, and the disorganising sophist. He disliked the irregular or abnormal in anything, and hated exaggerated feelings, uncurbed eccentricity, peculiarity in thought, or mannerism in its expression. [41]

In a further criticism of these clergymen he said: "they did not realize that the Christian faith is not a creed to defend but a Gospel to preach..." These men, he said, were "excellent clerics" who nevertheless held themselves aloof from Methodism. [42]

The writer's criticisms of these "excellent clerics" suggests that they differed from Methodism less in terms of doctrine and more in terms of social outlook. The clergy were defenders of the existing institutions and the mechanisms by which they were preserved. When therefore such clergy began to work in the West Indies, they were able to make common cause with the plantocracy and the latter with them. Some of them became planters, thus causing an identification between the two groups. Since some of the West Indian clergy were members of the plantocracy, the link between clergy and planter was further strengthened.

In the closing years of the eighteenth century, the religious situation in the West Indies was one in which the established Church of England was the dominant group. It was an accepted part of the English system that English settlers were members of that Church. In the West Indies they were normally members of that body, even though many of them proved not to be active members. As the monarch in England was head of the Church there, so the Governor, as representative of the Crown in the West Indies, was head of the church. The Governor was the one who made appointments to parishes, and recommended persons for ordination. Parishes were demarcated in each territory as a matter of course. These varied in size from a few thousand acres in the smaller islands, to as many as 100,000 acres in Jamaica. [43] Each parish was expected to have a church and rectory, and to provide a stipend, glebe lands and fees for the rector. This placed the incumbent of the office in a secure position, at least on paper. These benefits were not always paid to the incumbents.

The rector of a parish was expected to function within his parish, caring for the spiritual needs of his parishioners. Rectors were frequently not diligent in the performance of these duties; indeed the quality of rectors was as varied as their performance. Some were well educated English clergy, who graduated from one of the English universities; others were the sons of West Indian planters or professionals, who were educated in England; and still others were Englishmen or West Indians favoured by a particular Governor. Some of the clergy were persons of good character, others were of poor quality. Often, as Long observed, the defects of the poor ones tainted the characters of them all. [44] On the whole the clergy were not very active in evangelising the slaves, though, as Prof. Goveia pointed out with respect to the Leeward Islands, they did not prevent the slaves attending church. [45]

As was the case in the other parts of the West Indies, the clergy-planter nexus in Barbados was strong and enduring. Ideologically, these clergy could not fail to reflect the views of their planter connections. A good example of this was the Rev. H.E. Holder. Writing in 1788, the very year Methodism was introduced into the island, he described slavery as part of the scheme of divine government. While defending the system, he nevertheless conceded the need for a more humane regulation of it. He recognized that the wide diffusion of the gospel was an indispensable duty, but he could find no way of adjusting christian principles to the "Licentious Negro". He also conceded the need for missionaries to establish Sunday Schools for instructing the slaves, since nothing had been done up to that point. [46] With slight variations, Holder's views were reproduced by clergy in other parts of the West Indies. Some were unwilling to venture into the evangelization of the slaves, but a few of them were critical of slavery and slave owners. [47]

Active work among the slave population needed to be carried on by bodies that were not dependent on local support. However the Established Church was entirely dependent on the plantocracy either directly through the vestry, or indirectly through the legislature which stipulated those provisions which the vestries administered. This dependence involved the clergy in such a struggle to maintain themselves that they often failed to give due attention to their pastoral duties. [48] The populace were not ardent churchgoers; and though Dickson found a wide cross-section of the Barbados population represented in church, he nowhere indicated that the numbers were large. On the contrary, he asserted that not much encouragement was given to the clergy. [49]

The planter-clergy nexus and the dependent state of the church served to suppress any interest there might have been in active work among the slaves. The planters were unwilling to accommodate the views of the clergy even for the minimum the latter were prepared to do. [50] They had always been afraid that by making a slave a Christian they were automatically making that slave free. Hence they were resistant to any effort directed towards evangelising their slaves. [51] Preceding the Methodists by over twenty years was the group known as the United Brethren or Moravians. As its name implies, it was a union of different forms of Protestantism. Principal among these were the Lutheran form to which the leader Count Zinzendorf belonged; [52] and the Moravian form, which had its roots in a Province of Czechoslovakia. This coming together of various persuasions made tolerance one of the principal characteristics of the Moravians. One of the chief aims of this body was the attainment of inward piety, in the cultivation of which they took great care to supervise the development of each member. [53] To facilitate this task, they evolved a network of helpers as part of their organisation. When they established themselves in the West Indies, the Moravians often appointed slaves to be helpers. [54] In so doing, they made leaders of those slaves who had held positions of responsibility on the estates.

The Moravians devoted most of their time to the slaves. They were also painstaking in their discipline for the admission of new members and in the organization of their congregations. Personal honesty in all their dealings was enjoined on them, as well as a renunciation of their former way of life. This did not only involve actions that were wrong in themselves, but also certain marks of their old culture. [55] With respect to their masters the slaves were expected to be obedient, diligent, faithful and submissive. They were not to demur if they received unjust punishment, or if they were punished excessively for any fault of theirs. [56]

At first the Moravian missionaries were not well received in the West Indies. They began by earning their living on estates in St. Thomas and Jamaica, and this left them very little opportunity for effective missionary work. The planters seem to have regarded them with suspicion, because of their association with the slaves. In fact some planters accused them of being too familiar with the slaves, and resented the visits of the missionaries to the slave huts. In Barbados the planters showed little disposition to support the missionaries in the early years. One local resident, who was sympathetic towards the mission, warned a missionary that "the conversion of the negroes would not be generally approved of in the island." [57] This reluctance only changed when it became apparent that instructed slaves were better characters than those who were not instructed. [58] In St. Thomas the Moravians were subjected to harassment by the pastor of the Dutch Reformed Church, and only with great difficulty won the right to function. [59]

The early policy of owning slaves proved to be something of an embarrassment for the Moravians. The slaves in Jamaica, for example, were reluctant to respond to them, even when they were ordered to attend meetings. At that time the plantation was owned by the missionaries, and the slaves were therefore the property of the Moravians. [60] In Barbados the slaves began to respond well at first, but their interest eventually waned. So that in the late 1780's, by which time the Methodists had arrived in the island, the Moravians were experiencing considerable discouragement. [61]

Methodist Beginnings in Barbados

Before entering properly into a discussion of this topic, it is necessary to say a word about Methodist organisation insofar as it respects lay leadership. This should help the reader to understand developments which follow. The Methodist church was so organised as to make extensive use of lay leaders. [62] The ordained minister, in his capacity as itinerant preacher, was responsible for a number of stations grouped together to form a Circuit. Within each Circuit there were lay persons, called local preachers, whose preaching activity was restricted to a specific locality under the direction of the itinerant preacher. The minister or itinerant preacher depended on these local preachers to ensure that regular worship was maintained at each station.

Each Methodist congregation was divided into classes, with each class having its own leader. The office of class leader was one of some importance, and was sometimes combined with that of local preacher or Sunday School teacher. Each leader was expected to hold a weekly meeting of his or her class so as to assess the development of the members and "to advise, reprove, comfort, or exhort", the members. [63] The leaders were also to meet regularly with the ministers so as to be instructed by the latter. They were to bring to his attention any members who were sick, or whose conduct merited discipline. The leaders themselves were to meet regularly, weekly in the urban areas and fortnightly in the rural areas. These leaders' meetings had the right to approve the admission of new members as well as the appointment of leaders, and had to approve the dismissal of any leader.

In December 1788 a Methodist mission was formally established in Barbados by Dr. Thomas Coke, a Methodist missionary on his second visit to the West Indies. His first visit was accidental, the result of difficulties with the ship on which he was travelling to North America. The accident allowed him to support the work which had been started in Antigua, and to initiate missionary work in other islands of the Leewards group. Following his visit to Barbados, Coke travelled to the Windward Islands and Jamaica, where he started missions before continuing his journeys to the United States.

On his arrival in Barbados Coke found the nucleus of a Methodist congregation in members of a detachment of Irish soldiers. These persons had been converted to Methodism and had kept regular meetings on premises furnished by a merchant called Button. Button himself had come under Methodist influence in the United States, with two of his slaves having been baptised by Coke. This merchant furnished Coke with the first hall in which the missionary preached. Coke and his colleagues had also brought with them an introduction to a planter called Trotman. Even though they did not find the planter to whom they had been referred, the openings given them by others served to encourage in them hopes of success. [64] This pattern would repeat itself in other islands, such as St. Vincent, where they also received invitations from planters.

[65] These were not many, and most likely would have placed the planters under considerable pressure.

Coke left as missionary in the island the Rev. William Pearce, with whom the Irish soldiers had been acquainted. Pearce was able to procure a plot of land in Bridgetown and, by means of a public subscription, to start construction of a chapel. Those persons who were unable to make a financial contribution offered their services in labour. Even so the Methodists had a large debt on the chapel when it was opened in August 1789. [66] While the chapel was being built, the missionary had to endure vilification and threats. This did not cease when the chapel was opened for worship. On the contrary, within a period of seven months their services were disturbed on several occasions. The missionary took the offenders before the courts on two occasions. On the first occasion, the judge declared his incompetence to handle the case because the offence had been committed against God. On the second occasion the magistrates placed the offenders on a bond. [67] This beginning did not augur well for the future.

In the first few years their membership was not only small, but consisted of a large number of white persons. In 1789, there were 40 members all of whom were white; in 1790 of the 50 members 16 were white, the rest being free coloured; in 1792 no less than 34 of the members were white, seven being free coloureds and ten slaves. [68] This small membership continued into the early 1820's when the slave amelioration programme began. Methodist work was not confined to Bridgetown by any means. Matthew Lumb, who succeeded Pearce as missionary, was also called upon to visit estates. In 1791 he was attending seventeen estates on an occasional basis; in 1792, by which time he had a colleague, John Kingston, some twenty-six estates had been accessible to them. They visited these estates fortnightly in addition to the duties they performed in Bridgetown. But Lumb found the slaves apathetic, and the town people self-opinionated and contemptuous of religion. [69] By 1798 the mission was temporarily closed by the withdrawal of the missionary, and the station remained without a missionary until 1801. After the resumption of the mission in 1801, the Methodists in Barbados continued to experience slow growth. In 1804 there were only twenty-four full members; by the following year the membership had grown to forty-five, of whom eighteen were slaves. In 1810 there were only thirty members, while in 1818 there were thirty-three. [70] The pattern which we saw earlier persisted for a long time, leaving this island as the only "failure" in the West Indies.

By contrast with Barbados, other missions appeared to be doing well. For instance, at Tortola in 1793 there was a membership of 1496 after some four years. In the same year Kingston, Jamaica, founded a few weeks after the Barbados mission, had 170 members, and had increased to 600 by the year 1798. In St. Vincent in 1797 there were 1000 members at the end of nine years. Attitudes towards the Methodists tended not to be as harsh in the Leeward Islands as they were in Jamaica or Barbados.[71] In addition to this, Jamaica operated a system of licensing which often restricted a missionary to a single parish. So that a missionary did not only experience considerable difficulty in obtaining a licence, but found that his licence conferred on him no authority to function in another parish. [72] Even so the Methodists were gaining successes in Jamaica.

One possible reason for the lack of success was the lack of support which the Methodists experienced from the white population generally. Except for the few planters who had previous connection with the Methodists, the bulk of the white population seems to have kept aloof. The planters were not amenable to any interference in the slave system from any external source. They viewed with suspicion the experiments which were being undertaken on the Codrington estates, notwithstanding the limitations of the efforts there. In fact, managers on those estates were reluctant to carry out the S.P.G. policy, because that policy ran counter to the general course of things in the island. The planters in the island therefore did not as a body constitute a strong source of support for the missionary work.

Other elements of the white population were responsible for the harassment of Methodists – a circumstance which was not conducive to their success. This harassment was blamed by the missionaries on persons of poor character, under the influence of strong drink, and usually took place during their night services. This practice of holding night services for the benefit of the slaves was characteristic of the missionary bodies in the West Indies. The nature of the plantation routine was such that slaves were forced to work from dawn till dusk. In homes and commercial establishments the pattern of labour was unlikely to be different. The only time when the slave was likely to be available for instruction was therefore after dark. Planters in the West Indies were not generally in favour of any gathering of slaves, and tended to regard such gatherings as opportunities for plotting rebellion. They were doubly suspicious when the assembly of slaves took place at night. As a result, laws were passed to prevent the assembling of slaves at night for religious purposes – but only as a means of frustrating the missionaries. Restrictive acts were also passed against missionaries in St. Vincent in 1793, and in Tortola in 1799. [73]

The poor showing of the Methodists among the slaves is surprising. Coke himself had found this circumstance bewildering, and offered the explanation that "the Negroes of Barbados are much less prepared for the reception of genuine religion than those of any other island in the West Indies." [74] Some thirty years earlier the Moravian missionary, Samuel Isles, had made a similarly discouraging remark about the slaves in Antigua. Yet Isles' successor, Peter Braun, had positive things to say about the slaves in the same island, and in a patient ministry of some twenty-two years had greatly increased the Moravian membership among that group. [75] Findlay and Holdsworth surmised that the large number of whites in the early Methodist membership deterred the slaves. [76] Yet why this should have been so they did not say.

One reason for the paucity of slave members may have been the fact that, since the late seventeenth century, there were laws prohibiting planters from having their slaves in worship. These laws had been passed to dissuade the Quakers from engaging in what was seen to be an offensive practice. And even though the laws might have fallen into desuetude, the habit of exclusion would have been sufficiently ingrained not to require enforcement. Southey suggests that slaves were forbidden to attend the Methodist chapel on pain of corporal punishment. [77] This serves at least to show that there was some measure of personal restriction on the part of some of the slave owners.

As has been noticed earlier, the opening of the Methodist chapel was greeted with some hostility. They were subject to harassment by persons who entered and disrupted their services. The harassment which the Methodists encountered was spasmodic rather than organised or consistent. Night services had ceased during the vacancy at the turn of the century, and were only re-introduced about the year 1805 by the Rev. Isaac Bradnack. He experienced considerable inconvenience in that the services of the mission were frequently disturbed by a number of young persons. Several years later a similar experience befell a missionary, the Rev. James Whitworth, who gave to Governor Beckwith the names of four of the culprits. They were Roland Gibson, William Brook, and John Gibson, all of "Quaker Meeting Street", as well as Richard King, "a writer in the Secretary's office and an old offender." [78] The last named offender can be described as a civil servant, but of the others nothing is known. Legal action was instituted against them, the missionary being persuaded that it was necessary to make an example of them.

The Governor's attitude was that previous missionaries might have had similar protection had they sought it. But it could also be said that the Governor could have requested the legislature to frame a law to deal with the nuisance. However, one gets the impression that legal protection was by no means automatic for those missionaries who functioned in the island. On at least one previous occasion the magistrates of the town had refused to give redress to the injured missionaries. The Governor's position also assumed that other Governors would have acted with the same integrity he displayed. That was not necessarily the case.

By the following year, a new missionary spoke of the cessation of the disturbances and of the large congregations which attended their services. But this situation was hardly better than a truce.

The persistence of local prejudices against the Methodists greatly influenced the extent of the hostility which was directed at the group. Methodist teaching had given offence in England, where they had a reputation for promoting ideas of equality. The words of the Duchess of Buckingham best express the offence of the Methodists:

> their doctrines are most repulsive and strongly tinctured with impertinence and disrespect towards their superiors, in perpetually endeavouring to level all ranks and do away with distinctions. It is monstrous to be told you have a heart as sinful as the common wretches that crawl on the earth. [79]

These were the "tenets" to which, presumably, Schomburgk was referring when he wrote of their offensive teaching. The Methodists had been greatly influenced by the Moravians, who used to address individual slave members as "brother" or "sister".

That the attitude of the missionaries, as much as their actual teaching, was a cause of offence can be seen from the following extract from the Demerara Royal Gazette:

> It is dangerous to make slaves Christians, without giving them their liberty. He that chooses to make slaves Christians, let him give them their liberty. What will be the consequence, when to that class of men is given the title of 'beloved brethren', as is actually done? Will not the

negro conceive that by baptism, being made a Christian, he is as cred-
ible as his Christian white brethren? [80]

In Demerara from which this extract emanated, missionaries were the victims
of severe harassment even at the hands of the highest civil authority. In 1805
Governor Beaujon ordered a Methodist missionary to leave the country, as
soon as he had ascertained the missionary's purpose. When a planter called Post
invited the London Missionary Society to minister among his slaves, he became
the victim of the hostility of other planters and was even accused of causing an-
archy and disorder among the slaves. [81]

The prejudices which the Barbadian populace harboured against the
Methodists did not decrease with the passage of time. Moses Rayner, who arrived in the island in 1818, referred to "prejudicial reports and erroneous views"
as two factors which contributed to the unfortunate atmosphere in which the
missionaries had to function. [82] This prejudice might have been compounded
by the quality of persons who were appointed to lead the mission. One layman
observed in 1818 that these prejudices were not generally held, but that the better classes would not have harboured them "had they seen in all the Preachers
a conduct correspondent to the Doctrines they Preached." [83]

Some years previous to this, the Methodist correspondence indicated the
presence of some disquieting characteristics involving the missionaries serving in
the island. For instance, William Gilgrass alleged that some missionaries owned
and hired out slaves for their profit. He gave no indication as to whether any former missionary in Barbados had been a slave owner. His successor, Whitworth,
did become one by virtue of marriage and was temporarily removed from missionary service. The Methodists had long frowned on their missionaries having
property in slaves. Such persons were either removed or were required to relinquish such property. So that when in 1823 William Shrewsbury married into a
slave-owning family, his wife relinquished her share of the property. [84] A slave-
owning missionary could be regarded as compromising the Methodist mission.

The conduct of Gilgrass himself came under investigation towards the
end of 1813. That investigation was instituted because he was accused of frequently spreading damaging gossip about his colleagues. The reports submitted
by four laymen, pursuant to a request from the District Meeting, not only show
Gilgrass to have been unscrupulous, but raised questions about other missionaries as well. These include Isaac Bradnack and Richard Pattison, who had pre-

viously served in Barbados, and whom Gilgrass alleged to have been dishonest and drunken respectively. One of the laymen, a trustee of the chapel, considered it his duty to declare the truth – however painful – because "the improper conduct of the preachers has bin the Principle obstacle to the spread of the Gospel in the Island." [85]

In 1820 the District Meeting identified another source of concern. A letter from that body to the Missionary Committee set out the Meeting's views with respect to the salaries and allowances of the missionaries. In the course of doing this, the letter added serious criticisms of some missionaries. Some, it stated, were in the habit of hoarding their own funds while taking "advantage of the generosity of their friends by receiving presents, and living at their tables... Such a mode of proceeding as this has given rise to reflections on our conduct, if not to a suspicion of our motives." [86] If they were inclined to be spongers, then it is conceivable that planters might have lost respect for them; and that, in turn, would have been detrimental to the cause of the mission. The difficulty which the letter poses for the reader is that it is impossible to identify any of those criticised, or to determine whether the individual had served in Barbados. Some missionaries did frequent the tables of planters; and even William Shrewsbury had sharp encounters in the homes of planter hosts. [87] However, the letter seems to be reflecting on a problem in the District as a whole, which means that the situation in Barbados was part of a wider problem. The Methodist mission, therefore, was likely to suffer on a much greater scale.

Further questions could be raised about the attitude of the Methodist missionaries on the issue of colour prejudice. In 1814, a coloured local preacher called Beck complained in a letter to a correspondent called Samuel Thomas of the disparaging way a missionary was prone to speak of coloured people. He alleged that the abusive conduct of Jeremiah Boothby had caused several persons to leave the Methodist body, and that the preacher had advised coloureds and blacks to recognise the difference between themselves and the whites – a difference presumably of social status as against the obvious one of colour. Beck, who had spoken to the missionary, posed two questions to his correspondent: were the missionaries sent primarily to the coloureds and blacks? And, secondly, "how will the work progress among the Coloured and Black people... Is not this an affliction"? [88] Beck's second question was clearly rhetorical; his first must have been an embarrassment to the Missionary Committee in London. The missionary was injudicious: even if he harboured no feelings of prejudice against the coloured and black population, his ministry was compromised. Fortunately for all concerned, he was hastily removed.

Another incident relates to a couple who were allowed to retain their membership although they had been living together and had not been married. The missionary – Moses Rayner – believed them willing to be married but thought no clergyman of the Established Church was likely to perform the marriage. His letter concluded:

> I have not united the man and woman, as my friend and I thought it might create a noise that would prevent our obtaining subscriptions towards our chapel...[89]

Rayner's reluctance to perform the ceremony was based on his concern not to risk the financial support he expected to receive. As a further indication of his willingness to conform to local prejudice, we note that when he built the new chapel in 1818, he reported providing a "Gallery large and commodious for the Whites who may attend." [90] He was not alone in his reluctance to go beyond the patterns of behaviour in the colony. William Shrewsbury on one occasion showed considerable caution when dealing with a coloured aspirant to the ministry. From the look of it his caution was not merely concerned with the requirements for the ministry, but with the colour of the person who came forward as an aspirant. Thus in writing to the Missionary Committee, he stated:

> One young man possesses some talents for public speaking, and had mentioned to me twice his thoughts with regard to the work of the ministry, but hitherto I have not thought it my duty to give him much encouragement: I am afraid lest being a novice, he should be lifted up with pride, and fall into the condemnation of the devil. Young men of Colour, when possessing talent, are in great danger of falling into this snare. As a local Preacher, I have no doubt but he will become useful, if he be not thrust forward too soon. [91]

What all these indicate is that some Methodist missionaries, like some clergy of the Established Church, were influenced by the prevailing colour prejudice in their dealings with their flocks.

One of the criticisms made of Methodist activities in the West Indies was that the missionaries were transferred from one circuit to another so rapidly that one had little opportunity to get to know them. [92] At the root of this criticism, however, was the Methodist practice of itinerancy. The principle of itinerancy was enunciated in the Deed of Declaration executed by John Wesley in 1784. In that document it was explicitly stated that the Conference was not to appoint or nominate any person to a chapel for more than three consecutive years. After Wesley's death, however, the Conference reduced the period a preacher was allowed to stay in a Circuit, and imposed a condition for extension. Thus the Conference of 1791 resolved:

> No preacher shall be stationed for any Circuit above two years success-
> ively, unless God had been pleased to use him as the instrument of a re-
> markable revival. [93]

The position was modified only slightly by the Conference of 1818 whereby it was required that, before a man could be stationed in the same place for a third year, the reasons for so doing had to be clearly stated to the Conference. A tradition of regular movement was therefore part and parcel of the life of a Methodist missionary. His appointment was for one year, renewable as indicated above; and he moved from one Circuit to another. In the West Indies a Circuit was part of an island or large colony such as Jamaica or Guyana, or it was a whole island such as Antigua, Barbados, or St. Vincent. When a missionary changed Circuits in the West Indies, he was also liable to change islands.

The result of the policy of itinerancy was that between 1788 and 1823 no fewer than twenty missionaries served in the island. During the thirty-five year period there were vacancies totalling approximately ten years. This pattern of regular movement might well have created a sense of impermanence in the minds of some inhabitants, though one cannot attribute to it the hostility Methodists encountered in Barbados. But the question may well be asked whether such frequent movement contributed to instability and ultimately to lack of growth. In the view of this writer it did. Methodist itinerancy contrasted with the course followed by the Moravians. The tendency in their case was for missionaries to remain at a station unless removed by sickness or death. It was therefore unusual, and a matter of great regret, when Benjamin Brookshaw and John Bennet were removed after only three years each in the island. Later in the nineteenth century, J.Y. Edghill and J.G. Zippel stayed for lengthy periods in the island. In the late eighteenth century Peter Braun had stayed in Antigua for twenty-two years.

The practice of itinerancy was questioned from time to time by several of the missionaries, who seemed to think that it was too rigidly applied. Isaac Bradnack, for example, was reluctant to move after spending just one year in the island. In his opinion, "Neither Preacher nor People in the Western Isles can be say'd to have a fare trial under two years having a variety of Places to Preach at..." Representatives of his congregation pleaded in vain that at "this critical moment" a new pastor was not what they needed. [94] They praised Bradnack's good work and spoke of the new opportunities facing the mission in Barbados; but to no avail. Bradnack's successor faced a peculiar difficulty in not being able to give an account of the financial state of the mission, because Bradnack had gone with the books.

The deleterious effects on the mission of such frequent changes was the subject of complaint from time to time. Moses Rayner stressed in 1818 the is-land's need for a regular supply of missionaries and for a fair trial if any good was to be expected. He referred to the lack of a resident preacher for the three years prior to his arrival. His suggestion that the mission be abandoned only if such trial proved to be of no avail, [95] might indicate an awareness that such a course was being contemplated by the Missionary Committee. One layman put the issue succinctly when he observed that without a pastor new converts lapsed and old ones became frustrated. [96] William Shrewsbury and John Lar-com in 1820 noted the absence of preachers at times, alleging that "each mis-sionary began just where his predecessor began before him." [97]

The itinerant process was keenly felt in Barbados where the missionary staff amounted as a rule to one person. Only occasionally was there a second missionary in the island, and in each such case only for a very short period. By contrast, Antigua with a large Methodist membership had three missionaries annually between 1797 and 1807. The same was true of the island of St. Vincent in the late eighteenth and early nineteenth century, where there was a growing Methodist membership. This had risen so rapidly that by 1820 it had exceeded 3,000 members. [98] Where there were more than one missionary, unless both were removed simultaneously, no serious problems were likely. Where there was only one, the constant removal created a hardship as some of the missionaries complained. And where vacancies occurred for a lengthy period, it is a reason-able assumption that some rebuilding needed to be done.

We now pass on to consider one of the critical issues with respect to the operation of the mission. Every missionary society functioning in the West Indies gave to its missionaries instructions for the conduct of themselves and the affairs of the mission. All Methodist missionaries were furnished, as from 1818, with the instructions drawn up by the Missionary Committee in December 1817. [99] Principal among these instructions was that the missionaries were to concentrate on religious matters and were not to meddle in "political parties and secular disputes". Citing Wesley's loyalty to his country and to the monarch, the instructions reminded them of the motto: "Fear God and honour the King." They were therefore to submit to all local Governors and thereby gain their protection. More in optimism than in confidence, the Instructions urged that such protection would be forthcoming as long as the missionaries conducted themselves as they ought, and anticipated their being free "to instruct and promote the salvation of those to whom they were sent."

Addressing specifically those who were being appointed to the West Indies, the Instructions expressed the need for "peculiar circumspection and prudence" among other things. Their specific task was to instruct the "ignorant, pagan and neglected black and coloured population", using the catechism with which they had been provided. They were neither privately nor publicly to "interfere" with the civil condition of the slaves. The most crucial clause, as far as the region was concerned, read in part as follows:

> You are in no case to visit the slaves of any plantation without the permission of the owner or manager: nor are the times which you appoint for religious services, to interfere with their owner's employ; nor are you to suffer any protracted meetings in the evenings, nor even at negro burials... In all these cases you are to meet even unreasonable prejudices, and attempt to disarm suspicions, however groundless, so far as you can do it consistently with your duties as faithful and labourious Ministers of the Gospel. [100]

The final part of the section urged that, where there was opposition to their ministry, they were to adopt "a meek and patient spirit." Their only other course was to refer that problem to the Missionary Committee, and not to engage in acrimonious disputes.

Given the prejudices of planters and governments in the West Indies, these latter instructions created a hardship for the missionaries. In the context of the West Indian slave system, it was impossible to reconcile the demand for zeal with the requirement restricting them to fixed times of meeting. At the time these Instructions were framed, the Missionary Committee would have been aware of the subterfuges employed by the planters to ensure that the missionaries could not evangelise the slaves. One can only assume, at this distance, that the Instructions were so framed as to give as little cause of offence to the planters as possible.

Access to the slaves on the plantations was never an easy task for missionaries of any persuasion. Proprietors or their attorneys exercised the right of absolute control over their slaves, and often stood as stumbling blocks in the way of the religious instruction of those slaves. On the Codrington estates, for example, the efforts of S.P.G. missionaries were often frustrated by un-cooperative plantation officials. [101] Even if the clergy of the Established Church were able, they evinced little interest in instructing the slaves. In the very year that Methodism was introduced to the island, these clergy were complaining to the Bishop of London about their lack of success with the slaves. Some had been baptised, but the clergy did not consider them reliable in their religious observance. [102] Not many of the clergy could have laid claim to any vigorous effort in this regard, and their letter gave no indication of a desire on their part to persevere. In some cases the clergy were planters, and were unable to take a line independent of others of that class. The clergy-planter nexus was well represented by the Rev. H.E. Holder, who himself was an apologist for slavery. Writing in 1788 he described slavery as part of the scheme of divine government, but conceded the need for a more humane regulation of it. He recognised the wide diffusion of the Gospel as an indispensable duty, but could find no way of adjusting christian principles to the "Licentious Negro." [103]

Unlike the Anglicans, the Moravians showed a willingness to undertake work among the slaves from the inception of their mission. In the Danish islands and Jamaica they had the benefit of estates on which they either were established, or which they had bought. However, in Antigua and Barbados they had no ready access to slaves on the estates. The planters in Antigua were more favourably disposed to missionary efforts than those in Barbados. So that John Baxter, the Methodist local preacher, was able to visit slaves regularly and to gather a large slave congregation; and Peter Braun also achieved success in this area. In Barbados the opportunities were few, the most encouraging being in the parish of St. John. Here the Moravians received the cooperation of a planter called Haynes. In 1819 Charles Harding of Buttall's in St. George had so supported Methodism that he became a trustee of their chapel. By the early 1820's William Reece of Christ Church had also become an active supporter of missionary work, he himself having been a convert to Methodism. [104] At that time, Reece was among a small band of persons who showed open support for the Methodist missionaries.

The unwillingness of the planters to support the Methodists in Barbados was fuelled by the slave revolt of 1816. This revolt came about as a consequence of the opposition of slave proprietors to the process of the registration of slaves. The abolitionists had been able to persuade the British government that extensive importation of slaves had been taking place in the West Indies. The government therefore sought to curb this practice by a process of registration, which would indicate the number of slaves a proprietor had at different periods of registration. The new policy had two objectives: the first of these was to ensure that slaves were not being smuggled into the colonies. Any unusual increase after the first registration was viewed as an indicator that smuggling was taking place. The second objective was to monitor the physical condition of the slaves so as to ensure that they were not being ill-treated. This objective was to be achieved by comparing, after each period of registration, the detailed descriptions of the slaves. Any adverse difference was considered likely proof of the ill-treatment of the slaves. The programme was introduced into Trinidad in 1812 by an Order-in-Council. In 1815 the British government called on the older colonies to pass slave registration acts. [105]

The attitude of the planters and the response of the slaves have been dealt with by various writers, and more comprehensively by Dr. Hilary Beckles. Here one may ask the question: why was there such a harsh reaction to the slave uprising of 1816? One possible answer is that the plantocracy intended to suppress effectively the spirit of rebellion which manifested itself. This rebellion was the "Hydra" which had been "engendered" in the minds of the blacks, and which had allegedly "well nigh deluged our fields with blood". Another possible reason was that the plantocracy wanted to erase any hopes of freedom from the minds of the slaves. One notes that the Assembly's Report pointed to the slaves' mistaken interpretation of the Registration Bill as implying their manumission. That Report also referred to their hope (of freedom) being "strengthened and kept alive" by promises that the abolitionists were working towards emancipation of the slaves. [106] They were not simply concerned with ending the rebellion. Beyond that, the plantocracy wanted to destroy the hope

of freedom which the slaves cherished. And they went about it with a delibera-
tion that was calculated.

As was to be the pattern in the case of slave risings in other places, the
missionaries were held responsible for what took place. Such accusations were
not specific either as regards the missionaries being blamed or the nature of their
alleged complicity. The Moravians very quickly denied any involvement on the
part of slaves instructed by themselves; the point was unnecessary since the Moravians had not been active in any of the parishes in which the rebellion had taken place. [107] Hutton has indicated the conclusion to which all of this led,
which is that the planters befriended the mission because Moravian slaves had
not been involved. [108] By the same token, the Methodists had no involvement
in any of those parishes. Their activity was confined to Bridgetown where they
had their only chapel, and where, because of lack of staff, they were not able to
do more. One of the General Secretaries of the Methodist Missionary Society
was sufficiently moved by the accusations against Methodists in general and
those in Barbados specifically, to write a defence of Methodist work in the West
Indies. [109] His work did not deal with the accusation against the Methodists
in Barbados, though it defended Methodist work in the West Indies. The development shows that, in the minds of the Barbadians, the Methodists were the
villains.

In the period leading up to 1823, Methodist involvement in the instruction of slaves fluctuated considerably. The interest which led to their having
twenty-six estates to visit in 1792, changed so that by 1820 they only had access
to three estates: Lammings, Quinton and Buttals. The last named was owned by
a planter called Charles Harding, who at that time was a Trustee of the Methodist chapel. By 1821 they had access to four: Buttals in St. George, Searles in Christ
Church, Carleton in St. Michael and Kendal in St. John. Three of these were
new, which means a loss of two of those to which they previously had access.
Shrewsbury and a colleague found that the proprietors of slaves were unwilling
to have their slaves instructed "by any person, and in any matter whatever: their
sage maxim is : 'To make the Negroes wise, is, to teach them to rebel'." [110]
This saying, when viewed against the background of the 1816 slave rebellion,
helps to explain the opposition to the Methodists in Barbados, and the support
which the destroyers of the Methodist chapel in 1823 found in the wider community. This will form the subject of discussion in the next chapter.

Chapter 2

TRAGEDY AND RECOVERY

The period 1823 to 1834 was destined to be an important one for Barbados, and for the Methodists in particular. For the island it would witness the efforts of the British Government to have a satisfactory amelioration programme introduced, and the stubborn resistance of the Barbadian legislature to this programme. This process would culminate in the abolition of slavery, with the Barbadian legislature again displaying its unwillingness to pass the necessary legislation. For the Methodists, it would witness the destruction of their chapel in 1823 and the flight of their missionary. These events served to draw the attention of the Colonial Office to the experiences of dissenting missionaries in the West Indies, a factor which contributed to the general improvement of the conditions under which those missionaries laboured. The re-instatement of the mission in 1826 raised questions regarding their right to function. These questions engaged their attention almost up to the eve of Emancipation.

The most prominent and controversial Methodist in the island at the time of the destruction of the chapel was the missionary, William Shrewsbury. At the time of his arrival he was still a very young man. Born on February 16, 1795, he had just passed his twenty-fifth birthday when he reached his third station in the West Indies. [1] Tortola was his first, and Grenada his second. He was, as his son and biographer observes, one who had a "high and enthusiastic regard for old Methodism and all its belongings." When it is remembered that a missionary usually spent four years as a probationer, it becomes clear that Shrewsbury was entering the island in his first appointment as Superintendent of the Circuit. One does not know what special qualities recommended him to the Missionary Committee for such a sensitive position, given the tendency of the colonists to harass the Methodists. What we can say is that he got on even less amicably with the slave owners than did his more cautious predecessor, Moses Rayner.

Shrewsbury was a forceful character, very energetic in his missionary duties. He was also inclined to be forthright in his criticisms of things he observed and considered wrong. As a result, he sometimes came into conflict with planters who entertained him. Within four weeks of his arrival in the island, he collaborated with a colleague, William Larcom, in a very strong letter to the Missionary Committee in London. This was the letter of March 28, 1820, which was to be projected as the cause of popular annoyance in 1823. While in general their letter pointed to some very glaring evils in Barbados, it can also be said to have indulged in some exaggerations. For them to say that "Swearing, Drunkenness, Fornication, and every other species of immorality like an overwhelming torrent, overspreads the land" was far too sweeping and exaggerated. To censure the upper and middle classes as vain and dissipated, and inflated with pride to the extent that they "consider themselves as wise as the wisest, and as good as the best of Christians" only partially conceals the writers' own self-righteousness. The real problem was the attitude which the missionaries projected. With respect to the same two classes, they continued: "Reprove for sin; and you touch their *honour* (of which every ignoramus amongst them boasts) you offer them an insult not to be endured." One is led to wonder if their haughty attitude, especially in the administration of rebuke, might not have caused some retort which led to the anger that is evident in their letter. For they were dealing with the experiences and observations of a few weeks, by which time they could not be said to have known the people well. We note that in another letter, just three months later, Shrewsbury complained that older members of the Methodist Church were unwilling to accept rebuke from them because of their youth. [2] It is difficult to escape the conclusion that the haughty attitude of the young men proved to be an obstacle to their progress.

Shrewsbury's tendency to use strong language can be seen in several pieces of correspondence, in which he sometimes, along with a colleague, denounced the Barbadian population. He found the people depraved, ignorant, intemperate, and suffering from an "incurable malady" of which they were unaware. [3] Slaves, Jews, Redlegs – everyone was indicted in letters to the Missionary Committee between 1821 and 1823. [4] Speaking of slaves in one of his sermons in Barbados, he stated: "Little superior to the beasts that perish, the only end they seem to answer in creation is *to prove how deeply man has fallen by sin*." [5] To him they were excessively superstitious. He appeared convinced that:

> tormented by the chimeras of a disordered mind, they often suffer more from imaginary evils than from afflictions that are real. Having no just ideas of God, it is impossible that their minds can be impressed

with a sense of those duties that belong to their station in life: If they be obedient, it is merely owing to constraint, and not to any conviction that obedience is a duty. [6]

This passage, preached obviously to an audience including slave owners, concluded that the slaves needed instruction.

In two other sermons, preached to slave audiences, he was critical of the belief that they returned to Africa when they died. That belief to him was one of the devil's delusions to keep them from "seeking that heaven where all good people dwell." He was critical of their native religion to the extent that he concluded: "God has...by bringing you to this land, punished you for worshipping devils, and trusting to gree-grees..." He criticised their polygamous practices, counselled them against running away, stealing, or speaking ill of their master – even if that master ill-treated them. They were also to forsake dances and similar sins. [7] In all of this one notices no criticism of the dehumanising excesses of the masters; indeed there was no censure of such persons. Only twice in the first of these sermons was there any mild reproof of his audience. This was to warn them against being influenced by polluted sources as to what Methodists stood for. On the other hand, while urging worship on the Sabbath, he noted that the slaves were not to blame if "established customs" required them to work on Sundays; the accumulated guilt must lie upon those who require it at their hands." [8]

Shrewsbury's sermons indicate that his teaching was no different from what one might be led to expect from any missionary in the West Indies. He was adhering to the terms of the Instructions given to missionaries which required that they did not interfere with the relations between masters and slaves. Even his observations about those who caused slaves to work on Sundays did not have much force. Rather, it comes across as something of an aside. He did have sharp words with some planters, one of whom he told that God would strike him dead before morning because of his offensive attitude to the missionaries. [9]

In his three years as missionary Shrewsbury had laboured with fluctuating fortunes, complaining at one time that he was in the wrong place. He reached this conclusion because he could see no satisfactory fruits of his labour. [10] However, by 1823 when he was forced out of the island, Methodist membership had grown to some 90 persons. Judging by earlier figures, the mission was beginning to show signs of improvement. These were difficult years, coming not long after the slave revolt of 1816. The atmosphere would already have been charged by that event, and whites in the islands were on tenterhooks, fearing assassination in their beds. One suspects that Wilberforce's toast to King Henri Christopher might have led some of them to believe, rather irrationally, that Anti-Slavery ideology was a threat to their lives as well as their livelihood. [11] They took seriously every allegation of plots by the slaves. One such allegation in 1821 was only dismissed because the source of the information was an individual whose mental stability was suspect. Even Governor Warde harboured reservations about gatherings of slaves, confident that "their whole thoughts would be directed to plans and plots for insurrection and murder." This was the background against which the amelioration programme was to be played out.

Slave Amelioration

The year 1823 was destined to be a fateful one for the Methodists in Barbados and their missionary, William Shrewsbury. In this year Earl Bathurst, the Colonial Secretary, put forward for adoption by the old West Indian colonies a new policy towards slaves in keeping with a resolution passed by Parliament. In the recently ceded territories of St. Lucia and Trinidad the policy was implemented by Orders-in-Council. Among the chief characteristics of this programme of amelioration were the following: the whip as a badge of authority was no longer to be carried by drivers; punishment of offenders was to be regulated and monitored, and women were to be treated differently in this matter from the men; the slaves were to have Sundays free; legal provision was to be made for the admissibility of slave evidence against whites; manumissions were to be encouraged; slave marriages were also to be encouraged and the separation of slave families brought to an end. [12]

The British Government's amelioration policy met with a mixed response in the West Indies. The assemblies of Grenada, St. Vincent and St. Kitts were amenable to the proposals from London. For the most part, however, the response was hostile, with Jamaica and Barbados leading the way. The basis of the opposition was the belief that the programme constituted an interference with the authority of the master over his slave. The Jamaica assembly not only avowed its readiness to resist the programme, but went so far as to threaten independence. [13] Similarly there were protests from the Council of Advice in

Trinidad, as well as protest meetings in various parts of the island. On this show-ing, things did not augur well for the programme in the West indies. Not every-one might have called openly for war against the Methodists, or described them in the derogatory terms used by the Rev. George Bridges in Jamaica. But there were many who wished to be rid of all missionaries.

As a counterfoil to the activities of the dissenting missions in Barbados, the clergy of the Established Church were instrumental in forming an Associa-tion for the purpose of affording Religious Instruction to the slave population of Barbados. In forming this Association in August 1823, the clergy acknowl-edged their own inactivity in previous years, but thought that the success of three of their number held out hope for the others. In addition, they noted the abso-lute control of the masters whose cooperation was necessary for success, and whose favourable disposition at that time they regarded as auspicious. [14] The timing of the meeting suggests that it was a response to Bathurst's letters to the West Indian governors indicating the new policy towards slaves. An important element of that policy – the admissibility of slave evidence – was dependent on religious instruction. This was to ensure that the slaves understood the nature of the oath and the need for truthfulness. And this in turn was dependent on the religious instruction of the slaves.

The role which the clergy intended to adopt in this joint endeavour was a very limited one. The moving figure among the clergy was J.W. Orderson, rec-tor of Christ Church. In his introductory remarks to the assembled body, he dis-claimed any interest on their part in interfering with the "necessary and imperi-ous duties of estates." Rather, he explained, they aimed to teach the importance of moral virtues with a view to promoting the happiness of masters and slaves. The limitation of their programme was further emphasised by the fourth reso-lution passed by the meeting which indicated that instruction was to be strictly oral. The exclusion of reading and writing suggests a perception that instruction of that nature was dangerous; it was therefore pointedly omitted. The at-tempt justly merited William Shrewsbury's observation that the clergy had been "shamed...out of their negligence." [15]

About the same time that this organisation was being formed, news be-gan to filter into Barbados about the slave revolt in Demerara that August. Like the uprising in Jamaica in 1832, this one was based on the notion that free-dom had been granted by the British government but was being withheld by the local plantocracy. Not only had the Court of Policy [16] in Demerara been dilatory in dealing with Bathurst's proposed reforms, but the planters had themselves discussed the matter openly. The slave revolt which ensued had as one of its leaders, a deacon from the chapel operated under the auspices of the London Missionary Society. The Rev. John Smith, the missionary, was charged with treason in that he knew of the revolt and had failed to report it. Smith was subsequently tried for this crime by a military tribunal. There were other white persons who had heard the rumours, but had taken no action. It was Smith's teaching however, on which attention was focussed. The most that one can say of his teaching is that he discussed highly sensitive topics without grasping their implications for his converts. Nothing could be more explosive than the story of Moses leading the Israelites out of slavery in Egypt. [17] Yet, the missionary cannot be blamed for the conclusions drawn by the leaders of the revolt. They were taking the discussion beyond the point at which the missionary stopped. A court martial convicted and sentenced the missionary to death, and he died in prison before news of the reversal of the court's decision reached Demerara. The incident served to highlight the hostility encountered by dissenting missionaries in the West Indies, and the persecuting tendencies of the plantocracy. It was to become the subject of debate in the House of Commons in June 1824, and was instrumental in rousing public opinion against slavery.

To the prejudiced mind of the Barbadian slave owner, the Demerara rebellion served to confirm their fears that any discussion of amelioration would lead to violence against themselves. Misinformation and prejudice combined to make them focus on the Methodists as being implicated in the Demerara crisis. It was a short step from this to the conclusion that Methodism, and especially the missionary William Shrewsbury, was a threat to the island's security. The missionary quickly became the object of invective, and one of his detractors even suggested that he be hanged. At this stage, his letter of March 28th, 1820 was published in the Barbados Mercury by way of inciting further hostility towards him. Shrewsbury himself had made the letter available in a public hall, not by way of defiance, but in order to establish his innocence of the charges against him. [18] In this regard his efforts were unsuccessful. After two attempts at disrupting his services, one of which could have resulted in fatalities, he was advised by a friendly clergyman of the Established Church to close his chapel. Accepting his advice, and attending instead the service at the parish church of St. Michael, Shrewsbury escaped injury to himself. On that very Sunday, a body of people in Bridgetown assembled at the chapel in the evening and began the demolition of the chapel. By next day, they had completed the demolition of the dwelling-house as well. No effort was made by the civil authorities to control the rioters, or to arrest any of the perpetrators. They were never subsequently brought to justice.

The immediate aftermath of the Methodist catastrophe in 1823, demonstrated the weakness and ineffectiveness of the Governor, Sir Henry Warde. Available evidence points to the fact that some days before the destruction of the chapel, [19] Shrewsbury had sought the protection of the Governor. At just about the same period, the missionary had been summoned before a magistrate called Moore to explain his failure to enrol in the militia. Ironically, it was to the magistracy, including Moore, that the Governor had referred Shrewsbury for protection, noting that he himself could not intervene unless the magistrates had refused to help. After the destruction of the chapel, Warde convened a meeting of the Privy Council to ask their "advice and opinion as to what steps (could) be taken by the Magistrates for his protection, and for the prevention of outrages of a similar nature..." Two courses of action were proposed by the Privy Council. Inspired by Renn Hamden, the Council advised the Governor to issue a proclamation and to request of the Assembly the passage of a Riot Act. [20] Quite predictably, the latter was flatly refused by the Assembly; the former was greeted by an audacious proclamation offering a reward for the identity of anyone who should inform the Governor of the identity of the perpetrators. No one was likely to brave the hostility of the perpetrators under such circumstances, even if he did not condone the act.

On two separate occasions Warde sought to institute an investigation into the conduct of the magistrates, and the fact that he was thwarted was partly the result of his own weakness. On the first occasion, October 24, 1823, the Council objected to any discussion of the magistrates' conduct. [21] On the second occasion, January 21st, 1824, no decision was recorded, even though the Legislative Council agreed to the investigation on February 3, 1824. [22] Eventually, the Council looked into the matter and a report of their investigation, dated February 11, was formally tabled on March 10th. [23] This report revealed that, of the six magistrates for Bridgetown, four had been in the town on one or both of the nights of rioting. These four magistrates acknowledged having heard or dismissed "rumours" concerning the destruction of the chapel. One claimed to have gone to Chapel Street, and to have retreated after being threatened by the mob. Another went home after having been advised to do so by two coloured persons. None of them made any effort to intervene authoritatively in the disturbance, and all six admitted to having made no attempt to communicate with the Governor who, in this case, had conveyed no instructions to them. In short, the magistrates who lived in the town and were in a position to help, had chosen to turn a blind eye to the disturbances. The Legislative Council, for their part, did nothing better. Despite the fact that the magistrates were considered guilty of "very culpable dereliction of duty", the episode ended simply with the Governor being advised by the Council to express his displeasure. [24]

Writing to the congregation from St. Vincent, to which he had fled, Shrewsbury urged his readers to persevere in their fellowship and to accept their suffering cheerfully. He also called on the leaders to avoid any struggle for precedence, but instead to co-operate for the good of all the members. [25] The pacific tone of his letter seems to have had a good effect on the members, with the result that they were able to withstand the hostility which lingered on for several months.

The departure of Shrewsbury from Barbados in 1823 left his congregation without a pastor, his colleague Nelson having left sometime previously. At the time of his departure, there were about 90 full members, two-thirds of whom Shrewsbury estimated to be free. His total congregation would have numbered several hundreds. This gathering of members and hearers was left under the oversight of some eight or nine leaders. The names which have come down to us are those of Thomas Exley, John S. Thomas, Ann Gill, Jane McCarty, Ann Packer, Christian Gill, John I. Bovell, Mary Roach, Thomas E. Dummett and James W. Goring. [26] The majority of these leaders are likely to have been free coloured persons, reflecting the composition of the Methodist membership at this time.

In the years which intervened between 1923 and until the re-establishment of the mission in 1826, Mrs. Ann Gill became the person around whom the remnants of the Methodists gathered. Like the Moravians, the Methodists depended heavily on lay leadership. It was through a layman that the mission began in Antigua, and through laymen that a nucleus of methodism was established in Barbados. As part of their supervision of members, the Methodists developed a system of classes similar to that in the Moravian church. They do not appear to have appointed slaves as class leaders, but a large number of their leaders was from the free coloured class. Such coloured leaders can be dated back to the early 19th century, when one of them held the responsible position of steward. Such a development was not likely to be disturbed where there was missionary supervising the members. In the absence of the missionary, and with a coloured person assuming leadership, the white inhabitants were unlikely to view the matter with favour. Members of the Assembly and others could not fail to recall that the free coloureds had only recently petitioned for an improvement in their condition. Coloured leadership in a church was suspect, especially when that church involved the hated and much maligned Methodists. The same general observation could be made about Jamaica where the Baptist Church suffered. As the only mission started by blacks, it failed to receive any encouragement from the planter class in Jamaica. In the early 19th century, when a court ruling upheld the rights of a magistrate to question the credentials of missionaries, a severe blow was dealt to the Baptists. Consisting of blacks and coloureds, and with a leadership of comparatively uneducated persons, they were virtually closed down. [27] It was not until the arrival of a missionary in 1814 that the mission revived.

The members of the Methodist Church in Barbados were unable to meet publicly for some time after the departure of Shrewsbury. This was largely due to fear, which in itself sprang from tension which had persisted long after the destruction of the chapel. The leaders complained of an atmosphere of persecution which was alive for almost a year after the destruction of the chapel. [28] However, members were able to meet regularly in the house of Mrs. Ann Gill for the purpose of prayer, study, and encouragement from the leaders.

To say that Ann Gill was a tower of strength to the remnants of the mission hardly provides an adequate assessment of her role, or of the difficulties which she had to overcome. At a very early stage she was singled out as the target of harassment, which continued intermittently until late 1825. For example, as the anniversary of the destruction of the temple approached, a rumour circulated that her house was to be demolished. This led the owner to request protection from the Governor. This official had already been made aware of the displeasure of the Colonial Office over the treatment of dissenting missionaries in the West Indies. In particular, the Colonial Secretary, Lord Bathurst, had asked Governor Warde to enjoin on all justices the protection of all classes in "the peaceful exercise of every religious right and privilege which the law of the colony may appear to have secured to them." [29] Bathurst was at this time reacting to the developments of October 1823. Warde could not take refuge in evasion, as he had done earlier, and he issued instructions to the magistrates to protect the intended victim. The magistrates for their part yielded grudging compliance.

A later investigation traced the source of the rumour to one Edward Jordan Jones, who based his allegations on his own perception of "public aversion" to Mrs. Gill. [30] There is no indication as to the basis of Jones' suspicion, nor did the magistrates seek to discover one. It is possible that the rumour was started by Jones as a scare tactic, and that others joined in because of the effect it was likely to have. On the other hand, there is a possibility that the rumour might have become a reality had not the Governor instructed the magistrates to intervene. Some of them had felt no inclination to intervene when the chapel was being destroyed.

As if in retaliation for her approach to the Governor, the magistrates of the town wrote to Mrs. Gill concerning an allegation that she had concealed arms and ammunition in her house. Subsequently, they all visited her, accompanied by constables, to investigate the charge. Suspicion of the offence originated with a constable whose name the magistrates did not reveal. They declined her invitation to them to search her house. Instead they warned her against using her house for such large meetings, contrary to the law, especially since the majority of persons gathered there were slaves. [31] In effect, the magistrates had concluded that her house was being used as a conventicle; and there was a seventeenth century law against this which would later become the basis for objections to the re-establishment of their mission. But they were also objecting to the presence of slaves at such meetings. In this case there were also two seventeenth century laws they could invoke, though these had been directed against the Quakers. In the event they prohibited Mrs. Gill from having such persons at future meetings. [32] This was an area of some doubt among members, some believing that only the free coloureds could assemble, while Mrs. Gill was unwilling to exclude the slaves. In the light of the prohibition of the magistrates, she was left with no choice but to comply.

The magistrates' refusal of the invitation to search Mrs. Gill's house strongly suggests that they knew the allegations to be false. What the incident demonstrates is the propensity of the magistrates for the kind of intimidation which one would associate with persons who were not in judicial office. And this element of the situation was a major cause of the fears of the Methodists: that where they had a right to expect relief, there harassment seemed to originate. The Council, which contained the principal law officers of the Crown, was no more to be relied on than the magistrates. After investigating the action of the magistrates, in response to a directive from Bathurst, the Council concluded that

Mrs. Gill's conduct was liable to infuriate the public, and also that the suspicion concerning the arms and ammunition could have arisen from veiled threats contained in a letter she had written seeking protection from the Governor. But the alleged threats are not evident.

The Process of Amelioration

In 1824 the Methodist District Meeting took two important decisions which had a bearing on their intention to restore the mission. One of these was the appointment of Samuel Woolley and William Goy to be the new missionaries in Barbados. This decision followed a resolution of the Missionary Committee that the missionaries were to commence the rebuilding of the chapel without delay. The other decision was the acceptance from Mrs. Gill of the offer of her house and land for the mission, at a price of £ 1700 Barbados currency. Regarding the old site as unsuitable, and anxious to take advantage of the new offer, the District Meeting granted the missionaries wide discretion, provided they adhered to the Committee's resolutions. [33] These, however, were not minuted; and no action was taken during that year. The following year, the Committee appointed Moses Rayner to Barbados. The District Meeting confirmed the appointment with the provision that Thomas Murray should take Rayner's place, if the latter went to England as he had sought permission to do. At all events a missionary was to be sent to Barbados.

The decision to send a missionary to Barbados was destined to be affected by other developments. The amelioration programme of 1823 was based on the premise that the religious instruction of the slaves was indispensable for its success. Such was the initial response of the colonies that the Colonial Office sought other means to promote religious instruction. The government position was summed up by Wilmot Horton in this way: "The first, and unquestionably the only basis on which you can proceed is – moral and religious instruction, practically enforced and secured." [34] With a view to assist the colonies in providing this instruction, two dioceses were created in 1824 in the West Indies. One was the Diocese of Jamaica, which included the Bahamas and the Central American colony of British Honduras. The other was the Diocese of Barbados, which included the islands of the Eastern Caribbean and the mainland colony of British Guiana.

In addition, an Act of the British Parliament in 1825 provided funds for the two bishops appointed, two archdeacons, and for a number of other ministers. The rationale for this arrangement was to ensure a more active role for the clergy in the amelioration programme, and to ensure that the clergy were financially independent of the colonial legislatures. The bishops were to supervise and co-ordinate the work of the clergy. These had been anything but energetic for many years, while missionary bodies arriving in the 18th century had shown how much could be done despite the hardships they experienced. But the efforts of the missionary agencies were limited by financial and manpower constraints. Neither finance nor manpower affected the Established Church to the same extent, and therefore that body was well situated to carry out the tasks required.

The very nature of this arrangement placed the missionary agencies at a disadvantage. By virtue of the constraints referred to, they could not carry out any programme on the scale likely to be effected by the Established Church. On the other hand, the provision of an increased and improved staff of clergy was likely to create in the minds of the colonists the impression that that church was adequately staffed for the tasks demanded of them, and that therefore the missionaries were not needed. As we shall see later, this argument was used in an effort to exclude the Methodists. The Bishop of Barbados proved to be very energetic, unlike his counterpart in Jamaica, in establishing schools for the religious instruction of the slaves.

The small Methodist group in Barbados had looked forward to the early return of a missionary. The two appointed in 1824 did not assume duties, probably because of the lingering hostility in the island. By 1825, when another was appointed, the first bishop – William Hart Coleridge – had already arrived in the island. However, he would hardly have entered into his tasks when Moses Rayner arrived in the harbour as the new Methodist missionary in April 1825. Animosity towards the Methodists still ran high in the island, so that the return of a missionary was viewed as an affront to the inhabitants. The editor of *The Barbadian* denounced the "insulting attempt" to force missionaries on the people in defiance of their avowed dislike. [35] *The Barbadian* was a pro-planter, pro-church paper, and its correspondents on this subject were not favourably disposed towards the re-commencement of Methodist activity. A few days later, it published an open letter to the Bishop of Barbados under the pseudonym "Philo Ecclesiae". The sentiments of the letter are probably representative of a much larger body than might be assumed from its apparent individual authorship.

Appealing ostensibly to friends of the Church of England, the writer made every effort to exploit local prejudice both against Methodism and against Mrs. Gill. He was not apparently in favour of the threats to destroy her home, but did not conceal his aversion to the efforts made to protect that "hot brained enthusiast of the Methodist persuasion". Repeating the widely held view that the *Toleration Act* did not extend to Barbados, he stressed the public aversion to Methodists

> who are incessantly dinning our ears, and insulting the clergy of our church, by the senseless, puritanical, bigohed, intolerant, and ignorant cry, that they heard no *gospel preaching* until they went to a Methodist chapel. [36]

The letter then suggested that the Secretary of State for the Colonies had insulted the Bishop of Barbados by authorising Methodists to function, after so recently setting up an ecclesiastical establishment in Barbados. It called upon the Bishop to protect the island from those who sought to undermine the Established Church. [37] Who these were, and how the Bishop was to effect this protection, the writer did not go on to say.

This letter appeared on the same day on which the House of Assembly met and sent to the Governor a memorial on the subject. The argument about the disrespect to the Bishop of Barbados was also repeated in the memorial. While it is true that the newspaper might have been available before the Assembly met, it would not be surprising if it was the paper which reflected the views of the Assembly rather than the other way around. Despite its hostility and its own brand of bigotry, the letter had drawn attention to one feature which undoubtedly aggravated the tendency towards intolerance which was already evident in the island. It is a feature which could not fail to annoy, even though the records give no indication of attempts to rebut it on the part of the clergy. The accusation that the clergy did not preach the Gospel was as insensitive as it was false. While it might have been true that the clergy of the Established Church lacked the vibrance of the Methodists, and the latter's emphasis on a "personal religion" such differences did not justify the charge. That "Philo Ecclesiae" should write as he did indicates that the allegation rankled. And it might well suggest that there was great aversion to the Methodists on the part of members of the Established Church.

The House of Assembly was unwilling to have a Methodist missionary readmitted to the island. During the course of deliberations on this matter, the Assembly examined one of the magistrates who impressed on the members the likelihood of violence should another missionary be allowed to land. The Assembly therefore cautioned the Governor against so impolitic an act as the readmission of Methodist missionaries whom they regarded as "obnoxious" persons. The Assembly's memorial came to a climax by drawing his attention to a law of the mid-seventeenth century which prohibited the holding of conventicles. [38] This was the first occasion that this law was being invoked against the Methodists. And it is strange that it should have been done at this stage, when the Methodists had been functioning in the island for many years previously. But the Assembly had determined to keep the missionaries out, even if it meant invoking a defunct law as the means of achieving that end. It never occurred to the members of that body that justice required the law to apply to all groups of the dissenting tradition. Neither did it appear important to them that the Moravians were not being brought within the ambit of the law in question. They seem to have settled on a policy of obstruction which took paramountcy over the reality or otherwise of any threat from the Methodists.

The Barbados Privy Council, for their part, argued that prejudice against Methodists was being intermingled with "alarm and indignation" at that time. The members exploited to the full alleged rumours to the effect that the Governor was embodying the militia in order to enforce subjection to and acceptance of the missionaries' views. They attributed to public agitation the Governor's decision to call out the militia, and alleged that sympathisers with the Methodists had begun to change sides as a result of this. They also exploited the view that the Methodists, regarded as "incendiaries" by some people, were returning to the island for revenge. Hence they questioned the wisdom of the Governor in employing force, if that was his intention, to support such vengeful purposes. Finally, they warned that the Governor incurred a heavy responsibility by resorting to military force. "Time and conciliation", they urged, "would perhaps have been found more powerful than Arms, as engines of conviction." [39] The Governor assured the legislature that he had made preparations for any missionary wishing to land, and asked for the assistance of the Assembly in preserving the public peace. He also assured the Council that he was inviting any missionary who arrived to land, and also that he was enclosing to them the papers from the Assembly and Council. [40] Those papers were not likely to convey to the missionary an assurance of safe conduct, and the Governor himself hoped the missionary would not disembark.

By this time the Methodist missionary, Moses Rayner, had arrived in the harbour. His decision to return to St. Vincent cannot be held against him given the circumstances which prevailed at the time. [41] Admittedly he was somewhat timid, but his correspondence with individuals on shore, and the discouraging reports he received from the Governor, did not hold out much hope for the re-establishment of the mission. In addition, Warde had already shown himself to be indecisive at the time that the chapel was destroyed. He could not be expected to be more resolute in the face of the clearly stated objections of the Assembly and the Privy Council. He was under an obligation to ensure the right of everyone to freedom of religious expression, but the atmosphere in the island threatened his ability to do so. *The Barbadian* newspaper was quick to note the withdrawal of Rayner to St. Vincent, urging him to stay away since the remaining Methodists had been attending the Cathedral. On the ground that the Bishop had started schools for the religious instruction of the slaves, the paper asserted that there was no need for sectarian preachers. [42] However, there was a considerable degree of exaggeration in this assertion, given the fact that the Bishop had only been in the island for three months.

The animosity toward the Methodist missionaries seems to have abated slightly by the end of that year. This might have been due to the unpleasant publicity which the island had attracted as a result of a debate at Westminster on the treatment of Shrewsbury. In June 1825, Sir Thomas Buxton moved a resolution expressing Parliament's "utmost amazement and detestation" at the "scandalous and daring violation of law", and seeking to secure the rebuilding of the chapel at the expense of the colony of Barbados, while pledging Parliament's assistance to the King in preventing such outrages in the future. [43] The language was characteristically forceful, and put the Government on the defensive. There were some inaccuracies in his presentation of the facts, but the general run of events was acknowledged by speakers on both sides. [44] At the end of the debate, the original resolution was withdrawn in favour of one substituted by Canning. This latter reprobated the events surrounding the demolition of the chapel in Barbados, approved the course followed by Bathurst, and expressed Parliament's support for any measure aimed at securing religious toleration to all.

As was usual in the West Indies, reaction in Barbados to the debate was sharp. The vehement protest of Renn Hamden, a member of the Council and the principal speaker at a public meeting against the adverse reflection on the respectable inhabitants of the island, suggests that Buxton's censure had hit the mark. His dismissal of the destruction of the chapel as the delusion of young men, comparable to the "breaking of glass windows, or joining in any other thoughtless freak" [45] too easily minimised the seriousness of the offence. He would appear not to have regarded the act as an offence at all. But far from convincing the reader that the act was trivial, Hamden raised the question as to whether he was trying to cover up the actions of culprits known to himself. The fact that the perpetrators had gone undetected for so long would appear to contradict his contention that the respectable inhabitants did not condone the atrocity. The tenor of his own speech suggests that he himself was not firmly against it. His claim that he was not a friend of the Methodists was sufficiently clear not to have needed further expression. His call for the vindication of the respectable inhabitants elicited no response, with the solitary exception of the editor of *The Barbadian*. The latter disclaimed any desire to give any encouragement to the missionaries, [46] and stopped short of condemning the destruction of the chapel. The editor, Abel Clinckett, was the brother of a clergyman of the Established Church, and showed a decided bias against Methodists. It would hardly be an exaggeration to say that he was bent on keeping alive public hostility towards the return of a missionary. But he would already have been aware of the insistence by the Colonial Office that missionary activity among the slaves should be uninhibited. From that perspective, his efforts were not likely to gain much support among the population.

The year 1826 was to witness the formal re-establishment of the mission in Barbados. The Conference appointed Thomas Murray, who had been the District Meeting's alternate for Rayner in 1825. On this occasion the meeting decided that Rayner should go instead, because Grenada had petitioned for the return of Murray. And so it was that Rayner returned to Barbados. Rayner's explanation of his decision to return is somewhat muddled and shows only his continued unwillingness:

> I had hesitated from an idea of the expediency of waiting the arrival of an English Governor, but as there was no vacancy for me to fill in St. Vincent, as I thought my going during the administration of a President, a Barbadian, might argue confidence in him and the people also, and as I feared an English Governor might be too forward rather than too re-

luctant, owing to orders some time past received from the British Government, to call out the military force, and thereby irritate rather than appease the party who might be disposed violently to oppose landing, I decided in favour of proceeding immediately. [47]

Rayner therefore arrived in Barbados a not very enthusiastic emissary of the Missionary Committee. The Governor was still Sir Henry Warde who was then on leave in England. Officiating for him, the President of the Council, John Brathwaite Skeete, was to prove a formidable barrier to Methodist efforts to continue missionary activity in the island.

In an effort to avoid public notice, Rayner landed shortly after dawn and proceeded to the house of Mrs. Ann Gill. [48] Very surprisingly, his arrival attracted no attention in Bridgetown. Apart from a brief altercation between the customs officers and the captain of the vessel which had brought him and his family to the islands, there was only one brief reference to his having landed. Under "Marine Intelligence", *The Barbadian* of March 14, 1826, merely noted the arrival of Rayner and his family in the brig Diamond from St. Vincent. [49] Given the opposition to their landing a year or so earlier, the apparent indifference is a little surprising. It may be that their opponents had decided that attempts at obstruction were futile. The fact that they were allowed to land without let or hindrance did not mean that they were going to find it easy to resume their activity. On the contrary, official obstruction was going to prove a major cause of frustration.

Two tasks faced Moses Rayner when he began his second stint as a missionary in Barbados. One was to collect the scattered congregation and to restore the mission, complete with a chapel. The other was to undertake an expansion of Methodist work, by taking advantage of the offer of William Reece, shortly after Rayner's arrival, to provide the mission with a chapel and lands from his estate in Christ Church. The attempt to revive the Methodist mission was fraught with difficulty for the missionary. Rayner was concerned to have a clear determination of the status of the mission, and to obtain that, he was obliged to approach the officer administering the Government. That officer was John Brathwaite Skeete, President of the Council. In response to Rayner's application for recognition of his right to function in the island, Skeete drew the missionary's attention to the impediment posed by the old Act against the holding of religious conventicles. However, he promised Rayner the protection due to him as a British citizen as long as he conducted himself in accordance with existing law. Later on the same day, Skeete informed Rayner that no encouragement would be given to the Methodists as the Bishop had already made provision for the religious instruction of the slaves. [50] In essence, therefore, Skeete was using the same arguments advanced by the Assembly and by a correspondent in the press the previous year.

The distinction so clearly drawn in Skeete's replies was not lost on Rayner. He would have preferred recognition as a missionary; [51] but on this occasion, he did not press the point. What is surprising is that the Council disapproved of the course followed by the President. Sitting on this occasion in their legislative capacity, members regarded the President's peremptory refusal as running counter to the "Liberal spirit of the times" on matters of religion. They regretted the influence on the President of an act passed during the "infancy of the Colony's legislation", pleaded for a review, and offered in their legislative capacity to remove all unnecessary restrictions if the local law was too rigid. [52]

This was not the only surprising course to be taken by this body, which had tried to dissuade the Governor from permitting a resumption of the mission. The explanation for their present course was in part the "liberal spirit of the times". In part, it was also the clear position taken by the Colonial Office, influenced as that was by the Parliamentary debates of 1824 and 1825 on the Smith and Shrewsbury cases. Skeete therefore had little or no support when he pleaded, as the basis for his refusal, his desire to avoid confusion. He remained of the view that, as long as the statute forbidding conventicles remained unrepealed, he could not accede to Rayner's request. His position did not receive the support of Bathurst, [53] thus leaving the President somewhat isolated.

While not accepting Skeete's decision about the mission, Rayner remained patient and considerate. He sought to allay any fears about vengeance on the part of the Methodists, or about any desire to score anything against their opponents. When his renewed application to have Mrs. Gill's house registered as a place of worship was turned down, he informed the President of his decision to pursue his vocation as a missionary and to re-establish the Methodist mission as he had been appointed to do. [54] The prospects were not flattering; but the Methodists seem to have had their hopes set on the support of the Governor whom they believed to be under orders from the Colonial Office to facilitate them. What they certainly did not reckon with was the ease with which local officials were able to circumvent instructions from that office. And, given the fact that the British Parliament was unwilling to legislate for the older colonies, their struggle promised to be long drawn out.

The period from March 1826 until his departure in 1830 was one of considerable difficulty for Rayner. The whole issue resolved around the question as to whether the English *Toleration Act* extended to the island. A similar question had arisen in Jamaica when missionaries were faced with renewed harassment in the wake of news about the Demerara rebellion. At that time, in mid-1824, the Attorney General declared the English Act of 1689 to be in force; but the 1812 Act had not yet been introduced into that island. In Barbados the attention of the missionaries was focused on the *Places of Religious Worship Act,* 1812. [55]

The second clause of this Act provided that there should not be any congregation or assembly for Protestant worship unless that place of worship had been registered in the court of either the Bishop or the Archdeacon. The big question was whether or not the Act applied to Barbados. The general feeling in the island was that it did not apply, and the stance taken by the President and the Assembly indicates this. The old statute to which the latter referred was one which demanded uniformity of worship according to the "government and discipline of the Church of England". [56] Another question was whether the newer Act superseded the local Act. The Barbadians would have answered firmly in the negative. A related question, which had not been raised at that time either, was whether the local statute could still have been considered to be in force. It had not been invoked for many years, despite being on the statute books. And the Methodist Society had been allowed to function without let or hindrance during the period from 1788 to 1823.

On his part Moses Rayner was firmly convinced that the British law applied to the West Indies, a conviction that seems to have been based purely on the notion of Britain's supreme authority over the Empire.[57] Also, he seemed determined to ensure that Colonial Office policy on the toleration of missionaries be adhered to. It was this conviction which was responsible for his persistence in challenging the decisions of the President and successive Governors. His failure to have Mrs. Gill's house registered as a place of worship led to a number of actions. First of all, he reluctantly agreed not to preach until he had received further instructions from the Missionary Committee. [58] This in effect meant confining himself to class meetings and house-to-house visiting. His second course was to renew his approach to the President, but this time without any reference to the English *Toleration Acts.* On this occasion, he based his demand on instructions he believed to have been sent out by the Colonial Office for the protection of the missionaries. His contention now was that, as there had not been any case to determine whether the local law was still in force, and in consideration of their thirty years' work on the island, they might be granted temporary permission to function. When the President prohibited him from functioning without a licence, and told him none was forthcoming, Rayner refused to submit. [59]

Thirdly, Rayner considered appealing to the Colonial Office. He was still of the view that the British Government could compel the local authorities to accord religious freedom to the missionaries. Quite obviously, he was ignorant of Colonial Office policy not to impose legislative measures on the old West Indian colonies. Under the circumstances, he would have felt justified in recommending that the Missionary Committee seek the support of the Colonial Office in confirming that the Act of 1812 applied to the West Indies. [60]

Rayner's final course was to act publicly in defiance of the President's prohibition. In May 1826, he began to administer the sacrament in Mrs. Gill's house. [61] The following month he began to hold regular public morning services, which included singing. [62] The inclusion of singing was one way of serving notice that they were no longer prepared to meet in privacy. Under the circumstances, it was not surprising to learn that threats were made against them. Despite this, by August of that year the Methodists had begun to hold regular evening services, both on Sundays and during the week. [63] In other words, despite the prohibitions of the President, Rayner had fully restored the operations of the mission. For two reasons it can be said that in doing so he had run a calculated risk. On the one hand, the magistrates in Bridgetown had shown a proneness to invoke the law against the missionaries or against Methodist work generally. This can be demonstrated by reference to their attitude to Ann Gill. Their prohibition of meetings in her house indicated that they, too, believed the local Act against conventicles to have the force of law. But that belief may well have been undergirded by prejudice against the Methodists. On the other hand, it is evident that Methodism had not increased in popularity since Shrewsbury's departure.

The situation, when Governor Warde returned to the island, in August 1826, was one of great uncertainty. It was clear that Rayner had been acting without the requisite legal authority; but the fact that there had not been any prosecution would suggest a stalemate. To all intents and purposes, he had successfully bearded the lion. And with the confidence born of this limited success, he approached Warde in the hope of attaining a final settlement. Warde's reply to Rayner showed nothing so much as his capacity for evasion. In the first of two letters to the missionary, Warde declined to reverse the decision of President Skeete, but offered to the missionary "the same tolerating indulgences which other religious persons enjoy on the island." [64] Quite rightly, Rayner was not satisfied with this decision, and pressed for a more explicit statement from the Governor. Rayner was of the view that

> the proper line of conduct for His Majesty's representative is to give his sanction and protection to the mission... Tolerating indulgences, as they are called, are not sufficient for the protection of our cause here. [65]

On this occasion the Barbados Privy Council, which discussed the correspondence, took the line that as long as the Act against Conventicles remained on the statute books the Governor could not give a licence to the missionary. The Privy Council then added the ominous rider that no licence could deter a mob such as that which destroyed the chapel. [66] The Council, consisting of the same persons who months before had not supported the President, had changed face and was using the very argument advanced by that individual. The reason for this remarkable *volte face* is not clear from the records. It is quite likely that Rayner's acts of defiance had upset the councillors, who might have expected of him a less forceful approach. Alternatively, they might have accepted the line of argument, which surfaced earlier, that the Bishop of Barbados had made adequate provision for the slave population.

Given the lack of support from either branch of the legislature, Governor Warde emphasised to the missionary that his earlier response was final. He only added that he would accord Rayner "every legal protection" at his disposal. Although differently phrased, the offer of legal protection did not confer greater benefits than the "tolerating indulgences", especially since the Governor had regarded the President's ruling as final. Warde would seem to have denied the legal sanction sought by Rayner. Warde had also left unanswered the question as to who was entitled to the legal protection – whether Rayner the British citizen or Rayner the missionary. It was as a British citizen that President Skeete had promised Rayner protection, and Warde upheld that decision. Apart from being extremely vague, Warde's decision was a personal concession which in no way bound his successor. So that the Methodist Society was at best an institution functioning on sufferance, and not one with a right to function in the colony. The key to their continuance was the goodwill of the person who was Governor for the time being, and that of public officials in the island. Surprisingly, Bathurst expressed his approval of Warde's communications with Rayner. [67]

Rayner's persistence in seeking clarification of his status was matched by his determination to keep the mission going. "Every attempt to intimidate and move us", he wrote, "has but more fully rooted and fixed us." He therefore set himself to accomplish his next task – the construction of a new chapel. This was a calculated risk since he was not yet in a position to gauge the kind of response such action was likely to evoke. He was sufficiently aware of a measure of hostility with respect to the re-establishment of a mission in the island. However, he hoped that "by a patient and steady perseverance" he would have been able to build without exciting undue violence. [68]

The first pre-requisite for the reconstruction of the chapel was the acquisition of a suitable site. For several reasons the Methodists were unwilling to build on the site of the former chapel. These were first, that the old site was better suited to the activities of their persecutors, in that the street was narrow and a nearby alley allowed easy escape; secondly, they argued that the site was too small for the size of the chapel they contemplated, and left no room for a missionary's house; thirdly, that it was folly to erect a chapel in Bridgetown so close to the street; and finally, that the site had never been considered suitable, and had only been used out of sheer necessity. The idea that the site had never been considered suitable was not strictly accurate. It was only at the District Meeting of 1824 that the suitability of the site for rebuilding was raised. On that occasion, with Mrs. Gill's offer in front of them, the meeting concluded that the old site was unsuitable and that Mrs. Gill's was more eligible.

The alternative site, which had the strong support of the local body, was a piece of property in James Street belonging to Ann Gill. Its attractiveness was based on its large size, allowing space between the chapel and the road as well as space behind the chapel; and also on the fact that it could accommodate both a chapel and a dwelling house for the missionary. To Rayner and his advisers these advantages far outweighed the disadvantages of having the establishments of two copper-smiths in the neighbourhood, or even of having on the site some old buildings which needed to be demolished. The prospect of having adequate space for the mission, especially to render the chapel less vulnerable from a hostile mob, enhanced the eligibility of the property. Hence Rayner pressed the Missionary Committee to acquire it.

Mrs. Gill's offer was a generous one. Her proposal to sell the property for £ 1700 local currency or £ 1135 sterling was essentially the same price as she had asked in 1824. The terms of the transaction were that there should be a downpayment of £ 500 sterling, a further £ 250 six months later, and the balance in twelve months. The trustees, willing to accept the offer, sought authorisation from the Missionary Committee to commence building a dwelling house for the missionary. [69] The chapel was to be built at a later date. They estimated their project - purchase of the existing property and erection of the new building – to cost £ 3000 sterling. [70] It must be pointed out that they did not have the two-thirds of the cost which the rules of the Committee required them to have.

Any hopes which Rayner might have cherished of getting on with the task were dashed as a result of the dilatoriness of the Committee. In a special case, decisions should have been made quickly. However, several months elapsed before the first response was received from that body. Nothing more clearly illustrates the difficulty of functioning under a highly centralised system, the vortex of which was located so remotely. In vain did Rayner watch each incoming packet and plead for a reply. When at last that decision arrived, the Committee had limited the total cost of purchasing the site and erecting the chapel to £ 2000 sterling. They recommended to the local body a square chapel, fifty feet by fifty, whereas the local body had in mind one seventy feet or seventy-five feet by fifty feet, and high enough to accommodate galleries at some future date. [71] The request for reconsideration was unsuccessful.

While the decision of the Committee settled the matter of cost, by confirming the ceiling of £ 2000, it left outstanding the matter of the site. As the missionaries were unwilling to build on the old site, they decided to purchase Mrs. Gill's property and do what they could about the rest of the funds for the project. The final settlement was not to Mrs. Gill's advantage, however, in that she was forced to accept £ 1000 sterling instead of the £ 1135 sterling she had originally asked. This was an unfortunate turn of events for one who had done so much for the mission. Not only had she allowed the use of her house for services free of charge, but she had also provided free accommodation for Rayner and his family. [73] It is small wonder, then, that she only very reluctantly agreed to accept the price of £ 1000.

The progress of the work was dogged by delays, in part through the length of time it took to obtain title to the land, and later through a delay in the arrival of material. Work on the new chapel did not begin until mid-March, 1824, [74] by which time Rayner had still not received the approval of the Governor for them to function. The financial constraints imposed by the reduced grants from the Committee severely hampered their progress, and even led Rayner to undertake personal supervision of the work. [75] Despite the threats which he reported receiving the previous September, no hostility seems to have attended the construction of the building. Once the task of building had commenced, initial progress was so rapid that by July of that year, the roofing of the structure had been completed. Progress on the building slowed down after the roof was completed, as a result of delay in the arrival of certain materials required for finishing, and from the shortage of funds. The process eventually came to an end with the dedication of the chapel on May 24, 1829. [76]

The completion of the chapel brought again to the fore the question of the status of Methodism in the island. By this time there was a new Governor in the person of Sir James Lyon, who had arrived in the island some three months previously. Application to him was followed by certain developments which showed the deviousness of some public officers, and the extent to which efforts were being made to frustrate the missionaries. In the first place, the Governor referred Rayner to his Secretary, having actually passed the application to the President of the Council. The Governor was then on the point of leaving the island temporarily. In the second place, Rayner communicated to the President their intention of opening the chapel for public worship, only to be instructed by the latter to await the Governor's return to the island. It can only have been annoyance at the tactics of these officials which led Rayner, in defiance, to dedicate the chapel without official sanction. In fact, his letter reporting these events also carried his request to be removed from the island, which by then had thoroughly sickened him. [77]

By the time the chapel in James Street had been completed in 1829, the erection of another had started in Christ Church. This project was entirely the work of William Reece, the owner of two estates in the parish. Shortly after Rayner's arrival in 1826, Reece had approached him with the request that he visit the estates and catechise the slaves there. Rayner, however, hesitated to accept the offer on the ground that he lacked the legal sanction to function as a missionary. [78] His explanations were somewhat different two months later. They were that he lacked a horse, and that he was already fully occupied in town on Sundays. [79] It would not have been impossible for Rayner to visit the estates during the week, and thus capitalise on the offer. He did send a young man, [80] presumably one who had the necessary transportation. What seems to have happened is that Rayner opted for caution, since he was not sure of the attitude of the government.

We cannot say for certain what impression his hesitation made on Reece. What we do know is that Reece undertook the construction of the chapel himself. The building, fifty feet long and twenty feet wide, was intended to be permanent since it was constructed of stone. This chapel was designated "Union Chapel", partly because it stood midway between Reece's two estates, and partly because he had hoped that it would become a focus of unity for the black population on the neighbouring estates. [81]

In the light of his concern to see missionary labour undertaken on a wide scale in the area, Reece's appeal for the provision of a resident missionary was not surprising. The terms he offered for such an appointment were: first, that he himself would provide an acre of land or more for a cemetery, with a mission house and chapel to be perpetually located on it; second, that he himself would furnish the stones and lime for the erection of the mission house; third, that he would make an annual contribution to the support of a resident missionary; and finally, that he would obtain on his own account the material necessary for finishing the house, while the mission was to pay him rent until the debt for the material had been liquidated. His offer was readily accepted by local missionaries – a second had arrived by this time – one of whom optimistically foresaw enormous crowds being attracted to the mission. [82]

In the intolerant atmosphere which pervaded Barbados, Reece's activities were not viewed with favour. Other planters, such as Harding of Buttals, had supported Methodist missions; but none had gone to the extent of building a chapel and dwelling house. Reece himself was a convert to Methodism, and from that perspective his action was not unexpected. A Bridgetown merchant had rendered ready assistance to them in 1788 when they first arrived. Reece, however, was a member of a prominent Anglican family which produced at least one clergyman in that Church. So from this perspective his course of action was unusual. His action made him the only planter patron of missionary work in Barbados, though he differed from patrons such as Stephen Drew in Jamaica. Drew, like Reece, also built a Methodist chapel on his estate. [83] The Methodist correspondence does not indicate that Reece controlled the mission, but there was a tendency on their part to defer to his wishes.

The active support which Reece gave to the Methodists led to threats against them as a body, and against their benefactor. The missionaries again became targets, and were cited before the court for failing to enrol in the militia. By the local *Militia Act,* exemption from such service had been granted to ordained ministers. To those enforcing the Act – the magistrates – that exemption applied only to clergy of the Established Church. This exclusion of themselves, however, was the very issue which the Methodists were determined to challenge. And hence they appealed to the Governor, claiming exemption by virtue of their being ministers and by reason of the *Toleration Acts* of England. They made the further claim, that orders sent out from Britain had clarified the point that British toleration extended to Barbados. [84] This appeal was never decided. While the President delayed, the case against them was abruptly dropped. What this shows, as happened with the law against conventicles, is that at any time any law could have been invoked against them notwithstanding the fact that the law had fallen into desuetude. In effect, up to that time they enjoyed no protection, and that lack of protection was an all-pervasive threat.

The completion of the chapels, followed shortly afterwards by the disastrous hurricane of 1831, set the stage for the final act in the Methodists' struggle for legal recognition. Both chapels had suffered damage; in the case of Christ Church, damage was done to a chapel under construction to replace one that was considered too small. It was the end of the restoration process which brought to the fore the need for a licence to function. By this time Rayner and Stephenson had gone and the new missionaries were John Edmondson and James Rathbone. Their application to have the James Street chapel registered was unexpectedly assisted by Henry Sharpe, [85] who later became Attorney General. In an opinion to the Bishop of Barbados, Sharpe asserted that the Act of 1812 did require the Bishop to register the chapel. Sharpe contended that the English Acts could not simply be said not to apply. To support his contention, Sharpe noted that the *Navigation Acts* were generally held to apply to the colonies, although they were "modern" and did not specifically refer to these colonies. Finally, he argued that while the local law, which had been enthusiastically invoked, would have operated against the Methodists, that law had already fallen into desuetude. [86] The long drawn out dispute was finally brought to a quiet end in 1832 with the registration of the two chapels.

Amelioration

The struggle of the Methodists in their efforts to re-establish the mission coincided with the efforts of the Colonial Office to have an acceptable slave code framed by the old colonies. Jamaica proved to be particularly opposed to the efforts emanating from London. This colony in 1826 produced a slave code, several clauses of which would have affected the missionaries adversely. These restricted the use of slaves as preachers or teachers, prohibited the demand for or receipt of money by missionaries from the slaves, and declared illegal the holding of night meetings. Because of the offending religious clauses, the Act was disallowed, much to the displeasure of the Jamaican legislature and to the joy of the missionaries. [87]

A similar attitude to that of the Jamaican legislature was demonstrated by that in Barbados. Like its counterparts in the other islands, the Barbadian Assembly had become adept at circumventing the demands of the Colonial Office. In this regard, there were two courses open to the Barbadian Assembly. One was to do nothing, the other was to do very little. Insofar as the Assembly did anything, its production was not acceptable in England. The usual practice was for laws passed in the colonies to be sent to London for royal approval. But the logistics of approval or otherwise, and any necessary revision to the satisfaction of the Colonial Office, meant that the *status quo* could remain exactly as the planters wanted for a considerable length of time.

The first effort of the Barbadian Assembly was so unsatisfactory that, apart from recommending its disallowance, the Colonial Officer supplied Barbados with explanatory notes on the Trinidad Order of 1824 to guide the Assembly in framing a substitute. The best efforts of Bathurst notwithstanding, the Barbados Assembly proved to be recalcitrant. It passed an Act consolidating the slave laws which, in the eyes of the Legislative Council, fell short of the demands of the Colonial Office. However, even the Bill proposed by the Council prohibiting the use of the whip in the field, or the flogging of females over fourteen years of age was rejected by the Assembly. Two other Acts were passed by both houses in October 1826. One of these sought to remove the financial impediments to manumission; the other facilitated the baptism and marriage of slaves. This latter provided that owners should have their slaves instructed in the Christian religion and baptised by a minister of the Church of England. With the owners' consent, these same slaves were to be married by any minister of the Established Church; and there were not to be any shops or markets on Sundays, Christmas Day, Good Friday, except for a very limited time on certain days. [88] Even so, all the Acts together did not meet the requirements of the Colonial Office with respect to the amelioration of slavery.

As was the case in Jamaica, the *Consolidated Slave Act* had a bearing on religious functions in the island. For example, it allowed slave evidence to be accepted in civil and criminal causes with two provisions. One was that the slave needed to present a certificate of baptism from the minister of the parish in which he was baptised; the other was that the slave needed to present a certificate from a clergyman of the Established Church to the effect that he was sufficiently instructed in the Christian religion to understand the nature of an oath. The scope of the *Act Encouraging Baptism and Marriage* has been briefly indicated earlier. These Acts were passed by both houses of the Legislature and had received the Governor's assent. In effect, therefore, both Acts failed to recognise the presence or the function of either the Moravians or the Methodists. That discrimination did not only relate to ministers of those denominations; it extended to their slave members, in that those who were baptised or instructed by them were barred from giving evidence in court. To all intents and purposes, therefore, a policy of religious discrimination with all its attendant evils was maintained through the law.

It is these Act to which Huskisson as Colonial Secretary addressed his attention in 1828. In a despatch criticising Barbados' response to the demands for amelioration, Huskisson stressed the pivotal role of religious instruction as a means of advancing civilization safely. To this end he believed that provision should be made for it by law, and that Sundays should be altogether free, "devoted to religious duties and to moral instruction." As he spelt out his perceptions of the task one suspects that there was more below the surface than he appeared to be stating. Huskisson wrote:

> I am aware, however, that whilst provision is made for securing to the slave sufficient time and opportunity for religious instruction, and every latitude is allowed with respect to the mode of his instruction which the spirit of toleration demands, it is very fit, notwithstanding, that certain local regulations should be established to guard against those abuses and that misapplication to which the best institutions are liable, and to obviate those disorders which might be occasioned, or the apprehen-

sion of which might at best be reasonably entertained, if an unrestric-
ted liberty were permitted, to assemble considerable bodies of the slave
population at unseasonable hours, or without the previous sanction of
their owners. [89]

Huskisson's despatch would suggest that he himself was not altogether unaffec-
ted by the prejudices of the Barbados planters. The "abuses" and "disorders"
from too great freedom of assembly at "unseasonable hours" reflect some of the
stock charges against missionary activity in the region. The Colonial Secretary
was actuated by the fear of servile conspiracy, and was therefore concerned
about the security of the island. Whether it was through his eagerness to appease the planters or for some other reason, Huskisson recommended confirmation of the *Consolidated Slave Act.* In this regard, he had followed a course different from that he had pursued in Jamaica. It may be said that the Barbadian
Act did not contain the same kind of discriminatory clauses against the missionaries as were to be found in the Jamaican Act. As a result, Huskisson did not feel
called upon to recommend the extreme course of disallowance. But the Barbados Act did have certain defects which related to other aspects of amelioration. Huskisson's hopes that the Barbadian legislature would have corrected those
defects which he had indicated, were never realized. That body had made its
token response to amelioration, and was as recalcitrant as ever. *The Consolidated Slave Act* therefore remained in force until slavery was abolished in 1834. [90]

    While the legislative machinery had stalled over the provision of a suit-
able slave code, there was a commendable sign of energy on the part of the churches in their work among slaves. This was particularly so in the case of the Established Church. In 1825, that body was actively engaged in evangelization of not
less than 72 estates. And this figure does not include some 29 estates in St. Lucy
in which the curate was one of a number of persons who visited. By contrast, the
same report showed the Moravians to be active on three estates. Two of these
were in St. James and one in St. John; but none in the parish of St. Thomas,
where the Sharon station was located. The Methodists were active on three
estates in the parish of St. James, but not in the parish of St. Michael. The mission in the town was temporarily closed as there was no missionary at that time.
The work was managed by lay persons. (See Table 1).

    No fewer than 51 of these estates were served by "White Servants",
"Proprietors" or "Overseers". What the religious affiliation of these persons was

it is not possible to say. Disregarding the denominational affiliation of those who attended the slaves, the fact that 158 estates showed evidence of active evangelization shows a remarkable change in attitude on the part of the plantocracy. It might be argued, for example, that a large number of the planters in the island were not really opposed to the evangelization of their slaves. The extent of the planter support might be attributed to the clergy-planter initiative of 1823. Given the assurance of the clergy at that time that their programme would exclude reading and writing, it is very likely that they foresaw no threat as a result of such activity. When this has been said, it must be pointed out that in the nine parishes there were still 163 estates on which no religious instruction was being given. It might also be observed that, only in a limited number of cases, were the Moravians and Methodists active on estates. These were Mt. Standfast and Coxe's for the Moravians, and Rock Dundee, Carlton's and Sion Hill for the Methodists. [91] All of these were in St. James. In the parish of St. George, Charles Harding of Buttall's was instructing his own slaves, using the same subject matter as formed the common basis for Anglican instructors: the Creed, the Lord's Prayer and the Ten Commandments. Basically, the same programme was followed by other white planters or servants. This would suggest that the planters were themselves solid supporters of the Established or Anglican Church.

Table 1

Parochial Returns of Plantations, etc. Presented to the Right Rev. Lord Bishop of Barbados, 1825.

Parish	No. of Plans. Served	Persons Attending	Content of Instruction	No. of Plans. Not Served
St. Michael	11	Rev. R. F. King	Cr., L.P., 10 Comm., Parts of OT	19
St. John	7	Rev. J.H. Pinder	Cr., L.P., 10 Comm., Catechism	13
	1	Moravian Missy	–	
	1	White Servants on estate	–	

Table 1 (Continued)

Parish	No. of Plans. Served	Persons Attending	Content of Instruction	No. of Plans. Not Served
St. Philip	13	Rector	Cr., L.P., 10 Comm.,	21
	11	White Servants on estates	Church Catechism	
Christ Church	14	White Servants	Cr., L.P., 10 Comm.,	20
	1	Prop's family	Catechism	
	2	Female hired		
	2	Manager(s)	Prayers + Catechism	
	2	Rector occasionally		
	1	Proprietor	Prayers + Harte's Lectures	
St. Thomas	15	Catechist	Cr., L.P., 10 Comm.	32
St. Peter	11	White Servants	Cr., L.P., 10 Comm. Ch. Catechism	
	1	Proprietors Coloured man from Bridgetown		19
St. James	2	Moravian Missy		16
	3	Methodist Missy		
	13	Catechist (Under Rector)	Cr., L.P., 10 Comm.	
St. Lucy	29	(Bookkeeper (White Servant (Curate)	Catechism Liturgy, + NT	
St. George	5	Oversees (1)	(Cr., L.P., (10 Comm.,	23
	4	Rev. R. King	(Catechism	
	5	Rev. W. Pinder		

Source: Papers Respecting the Religious Instruction of the Slaves in the West Indies, in Correspondence and Papers Relating to the Slave Trade, 1826-1827, *British Parliamentary Papers,* Slave Trade, 71, Irish Univ. Press, 1971.

(N.B. (1)   There are no returns for St. Joseph and St. Andrew.

     (2)   There was no Methodist missionary in the island at this time.

Cr. = Creed; L.P. = Lord's Prayer; 10 Comm. = 10 Commandments

     The increased activity of the churches was reflected in the attendances of slaves at churches of different denominations. In 1830 the Anglican returns showed that slaves were attending that institution though, on the whole, their numbers were small. The exceptions to this general observation were the parish of St. Michael with three churches, and the parish churches of Christ Church and St. Philip. The numbers in the two last fluctuated. In St. James and St. George, free coloured and slaves were not distinguished; but in any case those numbers were small. The St. James report noted that the attendance of slaves increased considerably for fasts and festivals, and this may have been true of other parishes. There were no figures for the chapel in the parish of St. George. (See Table 2).

     In the case of the Moravians, there were some 250 regular worshipers at Sharon and about 40 to 50 at Mt. Tabor. The aggregate of persons under Moravian influence was 842 at Sharon and 140 at Mt. Tabor: figures which include those for Sunday or Day Schools. There were no white members, and there was no distinction between free coloureds and slaves. However, the Moravian membership was usually composed of slaves with only a sprinkling of free coloureds. Antigua in 1830 returned a membership of 5447, of which 5035 were slaves. [92] The Methodists, for their part, had a large number of slaves attending their Sunday services. The number returned can only be regarded as an approximation, the return showing 360 for each of four years. (See Table 3). One cannot accurately assess the extent to which they attracted the slaves. There was some growth among free coloureds so that the numbers in 1829 were almost double those of 1826. The number of coloureds attending their services tended to be larger in other islands, as for example Antigua. In 1830 there were 50 whites, 900 free coloureds and 2050 slaves in that island. [93] And this growth in the freedmen membership seems to have persisted despite the fact that "depreciative moral and behavioural judgements" might have driven some into the Anglican Church. [94]

Table 2

Attendance at Anglican Churches in Barbados, 1830

Parish	Whites	Free Coloured or Free Blacks	Slaves
St. James	80-120	20-60a	
St. Joseph	125	20	
St. Andrew	76	12	12
St. Lucy	60	14	40
St. George	140	110a	
St. Michael	950	425	650
Christ Church	70-100	20-30	60-80
St. Philip	75-200	30-50	100-400
St. Thomas	30	4 or 5	50-60

Source: Returns from all Slave Colonies Belonging to the British Crown, 1831-1832 (660), Vol. XVII, *British Parliamentary Papers,* Slave Trade, 80. Irish Univ. Press, 1969. (N.B. There are no returns for St. Joseph and St. Peter.

"**a**" applies to both free coloureds and slaves.

Table 3

Methodist Hearers, 1826–1829

Class	1826	1827	1828	1829
Whites	5	12	15	17
Free Coloureds	100	130	130	180
Slaves	360	360	360	360

Source: Returns from all Slave Colonies Belonging to the British Crown, 1831-1832 (660), Vol. XVII. *British Parliamentary Papers,* Slave Trade, 80, Irish Univ. Press, 1969.

Each denomination also administered a number of Sunday and other schools. In 1830, for example, the Methodists had three Sunday schools catering to some 312 students, the Anglicans had some 6 schools with 552 students for those parishes which distinguished such schools. The Moravians did not indicate the number of schools they had, but noted that some 982 persons were receiving religious instructions at their own stations. In addition to their Sunday schools, the Anglicans administered one estate school and several other parochial schools. The moravians also administered elementary schools. Though a large number of the Anglican schools in the parishes were for whites only, a considerable number of them catered for free coloureds and slaves. In most of the schools, the pupils were taught to read and write, and in some of them arithmetic was added. In some like the Central schools and the Bishop's Schools in St. Michael and Christ Church, religious instruction formed a separate subject, and needlework was taught to the girls. [95]

The missionary organisations in Barbados were not involved in the aggressive fight for emancipation which characterised their counterparts in Jamaica. In that island, they were transformed from "reformers allied with planter patrons...to reformers...who opposed the slave owners." [96] Those in Barbados were not subjected to imprisonment or arrests, but they were denied the space to become nuisances to the planters. Colonial Office policy required that they be allowed the freedom to evangelise. However, slave owners, by having their own evangelization programme based on the formularies of the Church of England, ensured that they themselves retained control of the situation.

Chapter 3

GROWTH AND DEVELOPMENT AFTER EMANCIPATION

The abolition of slavery in 1834 set the stage for Britain's last experiment involving those who had been enslaved. This was the system of apprenticeship, which was to apply to those ex-slaves who were over six years of age when the Act abolishing slavery came into effect. The apprenticeship was intended to last for four years in the case of non-praedial workers, and six years in the case of praedial workers. Enshrined in the Act was the idea that the former slave owners were entitled to the services of the apprentices, hence the provision for the further labour of these persons, under the supervision of stipendiary magistrates. At least for a limited period the planters were assured of a supply of labour. However, the Act made them liable for the support of the aged and the infirm. [1]

As was the case with the amelioration programme of the 1820's, so here, religion was to play an important part. The twenty-first clause prohibited employers from compelling apprentices to work on Sundays, except in cases of necessity or for domestic services. It also prohibited any employer from impeding their attendance at religious services of their choice. Stanley, the Colonial Secretary, drew the attention of the West Indian Governors to the provision in the 61st clause whereby Parliament sought to remove all obstacles to religious toleration. To effect this the Act declared to be in force the "Places of Religious Worship Act" of 1812, the recognition of which the Barbadian officials were unwilling to concede the Methodists in 1826. Stanley stressed Parliament's desire to ensure "the fullest opportunity of free intercourse" between religious teachers and their followers. Stanley further emphasised that religious freedom was indispensable. He was not wholly accurate, however, in suggesting that religious freedom was widespread and that dissenting ministers enjoyed "the utmost possible freedom in the discharge of the duty which they have undertaken". [2] This error notwithstanding, the Colonial Office was insisting on religious instruction coupled with religious freedom as a principle of emancipation. And this meant that the door was open for dissenting missions to participate in the instruction of the apprentices.

Planter opposition to the abolition of slavery was to be expected, given their reaction to the amelioration programme of the 1820's. They did not approve of Britain's "interference" in the internal affairs of the colonies, nor were many of them mollified by the method by which compensation was paid to the former slave owners. The average price of slaves in newly acquired territories such as Trinidad and British Guiana was higher than in the older established slave colonies. As a result, the rate of compensation was higher in those two colonies than elsewhere in the West Indies. [3] The "inadequate compensation" for loss of property was not well received in the older colonies.

Accustomed as they were to rely on force, the planters and attorneys had great difficulty adjusting to the changed circumstances. For them it meant the loss of that higher rank and authority which the structure of plantation society accorded them. The approach which characterised the planters during apprenticeship may be summed up in the words of a respondent to the Committee which was appointed to investigate conditions in the West Indies in 1842. Replying to a question about the attitudes of managers, he observed:

> I should say that the conduct generally, on the part of managers of estates towards the negroes had not been conciliatory: on the contrary, they have brought with them into the state of freedom the habits and associations of slavery and a degree of harshness has characterised their general conduct towards the negroes, both as to the manner in which they have conducted themselves towards them in the time of work and...out of the time of labour; they have treated them with great hauteur and distance, and exhibited much of pride and sometimes of violence towards them. [4]

In Jamaica planters charged the freedmen exorbitant rents for their houses and provision grounds, and sought to compel them to work on the estates by making such labour a condition of land tenure. Some even tried to force them to accept low wages. A similar coercion was characteristic of the Windward Islands, where different rates were established for resident and non-resident labourers, and where labour contracts were used to enforce labour and occupancy arrangements. [5] Similar coercive measures were resorted to in Barbados where efforts were made to force the ex-slaves to work longer hours, and where they were denied rations and other allowances. A tenantry system was developed in which some persons were charged a labour rent rather than a money rent, and in which they were forced to accept a low wage. The level of wages varied between 10% and 25% lower than that paid to non-resident workers, and extended to the family of the tenant. Monetary penalties were imposed on the tenants for failing in their obligations, and their crops were confiscated on eviction. [6] The planters went even further and refused to give to the 14,000 free children their customary allowances. This attempt to force the apprenticeship of free children was firmly rejected by the ex-slaves. In much the same way, planter pressure in Jamaica and the Windward Islands was forcefully rejected. [7]

The system of apprenticeship was no more acceptable to the slaves than it was to the planters. The view that they were "thankful for any change for the better", and that they "hailed the partial boon with every demonstration of exultant joy", [8] is not one supported by missionary reports around the region. One Methodist missionary writing from Tortola described the apprenticeship as obnoxious to the slaves; but he hoped that they could be persuaded to accept it, since the slaves were not impervious to reason or persuasion. Another Methodist missionary writing from Abaco in the Bahamas, gave an impression of sullenness rather than exultation. He had joined a magistrate in explaining the apprenticeship system to them, and had addressed them on "the advantages of submission, sobriety". He had also "recommended to them a spirit of gratitude for the great benefit conferred upon them by a wise and humane legislature, to which *they listened with great seriousness,* and retired in the most peaceable manner *apparently* well pleased and satisfied with what they had heard." [9] This appearance of satisfaction was probably misleading, as was the emotion with which August 1, 1834 was greeted. Yet it does not mean that they were truly happy.

To those who had endured slavery all their lives, apprenticeship was an unwelcome burden; but they adjusted to it because the boon of freedom would still be theirs in a specified time. That the slaves were desirous of obtaining their freedom cannot be doubted. However, when that freedom came, the ex-slaves did not simply escape from the estates – the "symbol of enslavement." As Prof. Hall has shown, the ex-slaves were often prepared to remain on the estates and to continue to occupy the houses and grounds they once enjoyed. Their flight, he argued, was not "from the horrors of slavery", [10] but was "a protest against the inequities of early 'freedom'." As one respondent informed the Parliamentary Committee in 1842, the ex-slave had a "natural love of independence...not wishing to be tied down to give so many days' labour continuously and contin-

ually; wishing to be at liberty to do anything else he might want for himself." [11]
This conception of freedom meant to some ex-slaves the right to determine how
their leisure moments should be spent, and the right to have whom they wished
on their properties. Essentially, therefore, freedom also meant having the same
control over their own activities as the white population had over theirs.

The difference in perception between planters and slaves suggests that
some changes in attitude were necessary if the new situation was to work satis-
factorily. As was said earlier, the planters were not disposed to give in easily to
a system which they perceived as ruinous to themselves. The British government for its part had intended the churches to play an important role in this exercise, by providing religious instruction for the apprentices. This will be discussed in another chapter, and hence will not be developed here. Suffice it to
say that, as in the case of amelioration, the churches were to be an important
part of the process of training for freedom. Hence the Abolition Act ensured
that religious toleration was recognised as integral to the development that was
to take place.

With the advent of abolition and the promise of religious freedom, the
churches responded with enthusiasm to the opportunities they faced. In the
words of William Knibb, the Baptist missionary in Jamaica, they had come to
"the tomb of colonial slavery" and could bury the monster in the confidence that
there was no hope of a resurrection. [12] Some churches either requested
more missionaries, or praised their missionary authorities in London for decid-
ing to send them. There was a genuine belief that the churches and chapels would
lack the necessary accommodation for the anticipated increase. The belief may
be summarised in the Barbados Report of the Methodists for 1833:

> Religion, we are happy to say, has a greater ascendancy now than at any
> former period, not only amongst us, but also in the church. A brighter
> day has begun to dawn on our western hemisphere, and we trust that,
> with the enjoyment of civil freedom, multitudes will be delivered from
> the thraldom of sin and satan, and be brought into the glorious liberty
> of the sons of God. [13]

Taken altogether these show considerable confidence on the part of the missionaries, a confidence founded on the belief that the existence of slavery was a barrier to the attendance of the slaves at worship and that, with the removal of slav-

ery, there would be unimpeded success. This belief would not be borne out by their experience.

In October of 1834 the Colonial Secretary, T. Spring Rice, sent a circular to West Indian Governors with a view to obtaining information which could enlighten British Government policy. In response to that request, the Governor – Sir Lionel Smith – sent a lengthy questionnaire to the three religious groups in the island at that time. These were the Established Church, the Moravians, and the Methodists. What the Governor sought to determine were: first, whether there were sufficient means for the moral and religious education of those about to be emancipated; and second, if the means were insufficient, exactly what were the deficiencies and the estimated cost of their improvement. Answers to his queries were submitted by each rector of the Established Church, while the other two religious groups each sent in a single comprehensive report.

The responses of the Methodists showed, first of all, that they had two chapels - one in Bridgetown and the other in Christ Church. Apart from these, there were four other stations – one at Bath in Christ Church, a second in the vicinity of the Garrison, a third in Black Rock, and a fourth at Scotland in St. Andrew. In these four localities, they assembled in the homes of adherents, or of persons who were sympathetic to their Society. They reported to the Governor a membership of 1,370 – a figure which was very unlikely at that time. Their actual membership, as returned to the District Meeting in 1835, was 587 for the year 1834. [14] This discrepancy can be easily explained as resulting from a failure to distinguish members from adherents or hearers. The latter attended their services, but had not been admitted to full membership. Their circuit reports listed only the full members and those on trial, the latter of whom were usually small.

In the second place, the Methodist missionaries contemplated the erection of four new places of worship, one at each of the stations which currently had none. This would have entailed the outlay of a considerable sum of money, the amount quoted being £ 2,950 sterling. Even as they wrote, they needed a further sum of £ 165 sterling for projected extensions or to build schools. Apart from lacking the financial resources locally for such a building programme, they did not expect any assistance from the Missionary Committee. That body had previously rejected requests for help from the Society in Barbados.

Thirdly, with an eye to their future successes, they declared themselves to be in need of three additional missionaries. One of these was intended for work in St. Andrew, if they were able to erect a chapel there; the destinations of the other two were not given. In view of the fact that they contemplated the erection of two new chapels in the vicinity of the city, one of the missionaries might have been intended for that destination. The motivating factor seems to have been the view expressed at a later date by one of the missionaries that the whole world was open to them. [15] This enthusiasm on their part was the result of a concern to engage fully in the evangelization of the ex-slaves, a process that they believed had been hampered by the restrictions of slavery.

Fourthly, the missionaries explained their lack of day schools on the ground that they lacked the funds to provide them. There was no question, one might add here, of their being unmindful of the need for such schools, because they had always regarded education as a vital part of their mission. On the contrary, it was their intention to build two schools. The only obstacle in the way of their realizing that objective was the lack of resources. It is this absence of funds which explains one feature of their report – that they alone of the three denominations reported having no salaried teachers. Such teachers as they did have functioned in the Sunday School, where teachers were always voluntary personnel.

The responses of the Anglican clergy showed that the Anglicans had approximately 20 places of worship in the island and some 8,610 regular attendants. These responses were incomplete since three parishes did not indicate the number of persons who attended regularly. Nearly every rector indicated that there was need for a greater number of clergy, and that there could be an increase in the number of places of worship. There were forty-five schools altogether, some parishes having two or more. Again nearly all rectors were agreed on the need for more schools, and consequently for more teachers. [16]

The responses of the Moravians show that they were the only ones who were not anxious to expand their operations. The average attendance at their two chapels was in the region of 900. They would have been prepared to extend both chapels to accommodate 800 persons in each, but they lacked the financial resources to do either. They had already embarked on the erection of a stone chapel in Bridgetown, and contemplated disposing of 4 acres of land at Sharon to help defray the cost. But with most of their members being apprentices, they were not very hopeful of raising the funds. In fact, merely to complete or extend existing buildings they would have needed to find 2,350. To their already existing schools at Sharon and Mt. Tabor, they recognised the need for a school for the Bridgetown station. The help of a planter, Edmund Haynes, was promised for the building of a larger school at Mt. Tabor. It was a staggering task that faced them and they opted for consolidation rather than expansion at this time. [17]

All of the respondents agreed that there was a great need to expand the religious and educational opportunities in the island. Governor Smith, who was sympathetic to the cause of the newly emancipated population, forwarded the responses to the Colonial Office with the observation that the needs identified by the churches far outweighed the resources of the colony. Not only that; but expressing pessimism about the co-operation of the legislature, he concluded that the plan would fail without aid from Britain. The Methodist Society was one of three denominations competing for public support. Competition with the Established Church was unequal because of the relationship of that institution to the state. The only hope for the Methodists seemed to lie in gaining the respect and support of the populace in order to ensure the means to carry out their programmes. Methodism had not been popular with the planters and professionals; and while some planters saw religious instruction of the ex-slaves as ultimately making them better servants, [18] the prejudices of the pre-emancipation era were not likely to be easily overcome. On the whole the Barbadian planters could not be said to have seen the missionaries as "allies of convenience", as Green stated generally of the West Indies.

Addressing the Problem

Between 1834 and 1845, the Methodists embarked on a programme of expansion aimed at meeting what they perceived to be the needs of the newly emancipated population. At the former date, the Society had reported having six stations; by the latter year, however, the number of stations had increased to ten, each with a chapel or chapel/school. In 1835, for example, they expressed the desire to erect chapels at Scotland in St. Andrew and at Speightstown in St. Peter, which were also to serve as schools. Even before these projects had been carried out, they were planning the erection of a chapel at Heddings in St. Philip. Construction of the chapel/schools at Speightstown and Scotland was approved by the District Meeting of 1836. In both cases the Meeting noted that the amounts granted by the Missionary Committee in London were insufficient for the tasks contemplated. In the case of the Speightstown project, the Meeting considered an additional sum of £ 150 to £ 200 necessary; but they were of the opinion that pew rents and collections would have enabled them to liquidate that debt. In the case of Scotland, no suggestion was made as to how the additional funds were to be obtained. It is a safe guess that the Superintendent in Barbados would have been expected to devise means of meeting the deficit.

Later in the year 1836, other congregations were started at Welchtown in St. Peter and at Holetown in St. James. By 1837, they had started missionary work at Cluff's Bay in St. Lucy, and contemplated similar work at Paynes Bay in St. James. In nearly all of these efforts they were building chapels, for they did not always find it convenient to conduct services in the homes of planters. Two such were offered to them in the parish of St. Lucy where several white inhabitants were said to attend. Because of the need to build, their expansion entailed a great deal of real estate as well as maintenance costs. By 1845, most of their surviving stations contained substantial chapels. These included the Garrison Chapel (later called Dalkeith), Bethel Chapel on Bay Street in Bridgetown, and Ebenezer Chapel in St. Philip. In all these efforts they received little or no support from planters at this time, a notable exception being Benjamin Gaskin, a member of the House of Assembly. He attended the chapel in Bridgetown, and offered them land on his estate at Oxnard in St. James for a chapel. [19] For some unexplained reason, this offer either was not taken up or fell through. It was not until the 1850's and 1860's that we find evidence of further offers, which enabled them to build chapels at Beulah and Rices in St. Philip.

In the period 1834 – 1845 the Established Church had erected eleven new chapels of ease and rebuilt one other. Three of the new ones were in the parish of Christ Church, two in the parish of St. Michael, and one each in the parishes of St. Lucy, St. Andrew, St. Thomas, St. James, St. George and St. Philip. The restored chapel was that of All Saints in the parish of St. Peter. With the already existing eleven parish churches and eight other chapels of ease, the Established Church was well represented across the island. The Moravians in the same period had completed their chapel in Bridgetown in 1834 and built a new one in 1840. [20]

The rationale for the building programme undertaken by Methodists is provided by comments from two sources. The first of these originates with the District Meeting of 1835, and has reference to the construction of schools or chapel/schools. From the minutes of that meeting, we get a strong impression that the establishment of schools was vital to the prosperity of Methodism. This can be taken to mean that schools constituted, for that body, an integral part of their missionary enterprise. It is not to be thought, however, that they saw themselves as offering what we might today call a general education. Such a notion had not yet become current in England where popular education was still in its initial stage. But religion and education were closely linked in England, where the latter subserved the purpose of the former. [21]

The other expression which helps to indicate a rationale for the building programme comes from the pen of William Fidler, the Superintendent at that time. With respect to the chapels he explained that missionary effort was lost where a chapel was not erected. [22] This would suggest that, while an anticipated increase in numbers played no small part in their undertaking, the desire for permanence was equally influential. The letters of the missionaries betray no dissatisfaction with the use of the homes of members or sympathisers. On the contrary, they reflect the positive value of such homes as new stations were opened. It is a fairly safe assumption that such an arrangement was tentative at best, depending on their ability to retain their members. On the other hand, increasing membership rendered the limited space of private homes inconvenient. A building of their own was therefore an asset, quite apart from its adding respectability to their cause in the eyes of both freedmen and the upper class. This concern was never far from their minds at any stage of their history.

The membership figures for the first decade after the abolition of slavery show steady growth on the whole. Whereas in 1833 there were 480 full members, of whom 358 were free persons and 122 slaves, by the end of 1834 the returns showed a membership of 587. [23] This number increased rapidly up to 1838, by which time the membership had grown to 1,331. Thereafter the rate of growth was smaller, so that the number of full members rose only slightly to 1,350 in 1839, remained almost stationery in 1840, decreased in 1841, then increased in 1842 and 1843. There are no figures for 1844 and 1845; and the aggregate of those who benefitted from Methodist activity [24] are given as 4,550 in 1842 and 4,695 in 1843. This shows limited growth from the 1,370 reported in 1834, given the fact that it represents pupils of their schools as well.

At the time of emancipation in 1834, Barbados formed part of the St. Vincent District which then included the two islands named as well as Grenada, Tobago, Trinidad and Demerara. The number of full members in this District declined from 1828 to 1833, in which latter year there were 5,857. That number rose to 6,312 in 1834 and 7,184 in 1835. In 1836 the island was removed from the St. Vincent District and placed, somewhat illogically, with Demerara. The growth in the number of full members for this District seems to have been commensurate with the rate of growth in Barbados. In fact, Barbados was responsible for a large proportion of the aggregate, varying between just under one-third to almost a half.

The pattern of growth noticed in the Methodist church was characteristic of both the Moravians and the Anglicans. In the case of the Moravians, the number of communicants in 1834 was 362, while the number of those who attended services was 1,972. If, following the Methodists, we add the number of persons attending Day and Sunday Schools, the number of those who benefitted from their ministry would be higher than the 1,972 returned. Though such schools existed, there is no record of their membership. By 1843 these had risen to 3,757 communicants and others who attended their ministry. In the case of the Anglican Church, no communicant figures are recorded. The number of those who attended on Sunday mornings in 1834 was 7,540 and 19,975 in 1843. Using the formula of the Methodists, the number of those benefiting from Anglican ministry was 9,334 in 1834 and about 23,000 in 1843.

The evidence reveals that the ex-slaves were attending the various churches in large numbers, but not so large as to justify the conclusion that there were few of them who were not Christians. This exaggerated opinion was given by William Sharpe of Barbados to a committee investigating conditions in the West Indies in 1842. Another witness, G. Carrington of Barbados, supports the pattern of improved attendance. However, he goes further and attributes the improved attendance at church – he seems to have meant the Established Church – to the number of parochial schools provided. No parish, he asserted, was without a school and they were usually well attended. [25] What he might have added was that the establishment of schools was often a means of proselytising, in that pupils were expected to attend the church which established the schools.

As we have seen above, the overall growth of Methodism was in contrast with their general expectation that, with the advent of emancipation, there would have been a swell in the tide of membership. There are a number of factors which help to explain this slow growth. First of all, the Methodists seemed to have experienced considerable difficulty in establishing themselves in certain parts of the island. For instance, in spite of the support given them by William Reece, the progress of the Methodist Society at Providence was very slow. Before the abolition of slavery, Reece had made it possible for his slaves to attend the Providence Chapel. However, the freedmen were not enthusiastic about attending the chapel after emancipation. We find, for example, that on the very eve of emancipation, the resident missionary was complaining about the lack of response of the slaves. And despite the improvement shortly after August 1834, the old pattern returned and the missionary began to complain of the station as a barren spot. [26] This general view of the area was supported by William Moister, under whose ministry there was an increase in 1836, [27] and by Francis Whitehead who in 1844 described Providence as being constantly "unfruitful" and the people there as mostly old and irregular in their attendance. [28]

TABLE 4

Comparison of Barbados and Its District(s), 1834-1843

Year	Barbados Full Mem.	District Full Mem.
1834	587	6312
1835	698	7184
1836	905	2794
1837	1056	2895
1838	1331	3129
1839	1350	3150
1840	1352	3175
1841	1323	3208
1842	1470	3242
1843	1564	3396

Sources: (a) 1834–1835. Minutes of the St. Vincent District for 1835 and 1836 respectively. The St. Vincent District then included Demerara.

(b) 1836–1843. Minutes of the Demerara District for 1837 to 1844.

Note: District Meetings were held in January, and the minutes recorded information for the previous year. In the early years, the minutes did not record the number of hearers or attendants.

TABLE 5

Moravian and Anglican Membership 1834-1843

Year	Moravian Attendants	Anglican Attendants
1834	1972	7540
1835	2827	–
1836	2827	–
1837	3192	–
1838	3728	–
1839	3881	–
1840	3757	13890
1841	3157	19795
1842	2801	13320
1843	–	19975

Sources: For the data on the Moravian Church, K. Lewis, *The Moravian Missions in Barbados,* 1816–1886, Frankfurt, Verlag Peter Lang, 1985, p. 227. For the data on the Anglican Church, see *Barbados Blue Book,* 1834, pp. 122-123; 1839, pp. 170-171; 1840, vol. unpaged; 1841, pp. 140-141; 1842, pp. 140-141; 1843, pp. 136-137. No data available for other years.

The programme of expansion on which the Methodists embarked was beyond their capacity to provide for pastorally. For most of the period 1834 – 1845 there were only three missionaries in Barbados, and occasionally they were reduced to two. Given the emphasis which the Missionary Committee placed on pastoral oversight and preaching, the work was beyond their existing manpower. This conclusion can be supported by reference to the nature of the information demanded of each missionary to determine whether he had exerted himself in the cause. Some of the questions to be answered at the annual District Meeting were:

1.   Are earnest attempts made in every place where the brethren preach, to form classes?

2.   Are the Societies regularly met after the Public Services?

3.   Is sufficient time allotted, in the arrangement of the Quarterly Visita-
        tion of the classes, for the preacher to acquaint himself with the state of
        each member and to give suitable advice to each?

4.   Do the brethren pay sufficient attention to pastoral visitation calling
        regularly upon every family within their reach, in order to pray with
        them and give them advice?

        The answers to these questions formed part of the minutes of the District
Meeting, and afford considerable insight into the diligence or lack of it on the
part of the missionaries. With respect to the first question, one District Meeting
responded that the missionaries had done as much as was practicable. On one
occasion, the reply to the question was simply that too many commitments on
Sundays rendered the fulfilling of this duty well nigh impossible. In other words,
the missionaries were already heavily pressed as things were. The answers to the
second question are as imprecise as those to the first. And the reason was similar – that such minute examination was impossible in the light of existing commitments.
        The answers to the third and fourth questions also indicate how hard-
pressed were the missionaries. On average, besides leaders' meetings and
prayer meetings, missionaries preached four or five times per week in Barbados.
The same is true of missionaries on other stations in the District, only a few
preaching two or three times a week. With respect to the last question, the answer
was generally the same. However, there were two exceptions to this. In 1837,
the District Meeting acknowledged that this duty was not performed as well as
it should have been. The other exception was in 1843, when the District Meeting, in answer to the question, simply reported that Mr. Mansie was unable to
make many visits. The missionaries were constantly hard-pressed, and it was impossible for them to perform to the best of their ability, or as others expected
them to do under the circumstances. This conclusion is borne out by one other
question in the light of which the answers above might be taken. It was: How often in the week do each of the Brethren preach; and by what other engagements
is their time filled up? The three missionaries in Demerara each reported preaching twice on Sundays and twice during the week. The Barbados missionary, by

contrast, preached five times on Sundays and on three other occasions during the week. He was therefore carrying a very heavy load, given all the other things expected of him.

Given the work load just indicated and the paucity of their staff, the extent of the expansion they undertook showed considerable courage on their part. In addition to this, the considerable emphasis placed on pastoral oversight by the missionaries would suggest that stability at the level of staffing was highly desirable. And yet it is precisely at this level that instability manifested itself due to the fact that the Methodists clung tenaciously to the principle of itinerancy. The magnitude of the problem may be demonstrated by considering the number of missionaries who served the island. The evidence indicates that no fewer than sixteen missionaries had served here in the years 1835 to 1845. Of this number, four served more than one tour of duty – Phelp, Fidler, Hudson and Branston. Phelp's two tours of duty amounted to four years, Fidler's to six and a half, Hudson's to three, and Branston's to five years. In three of these cases – those of Phelp, Branston, and Hudson – the missionary spent one year at first, returning after a year or two elsewhere. Except for Joseph Biggs, who served three consecutive years, all the others served two years or less.

This frequent change in stations did not pass without protest on the part of the missionaries, Fidler being perhaps the most outspoken critic of the policy. Arriving in Barbados in 1835, he not only questioned being transferred to Demerara the following year, but also the fact that Barbados would thereby have suffered a change in Superintendents twice within a single year.[29] Eventually, no change took place in 1836, but two of the three missionaries were moved in 1837. In February 1838, Fidler wrote to the Committee offering to remain in Barbados until the end of that year, [30] even though his appointment to Demerara meant that he should have moved to his new Circuit in March. Nevertheless, he was gone in just about a month and the island was left with only two missionaries. There were only two missionaries in 1839 and 1840, with the result that the Speightstown – Scotland – St. Lucy mission had to be closed. [31] Like Fidler before him, William Hudson in 1841 protested his removal to Demerara after only one year in Barbados. Having gone to Speightstown, where there had not been a missionary for three years, he represented to the Committee the lack of confidence which such frequent change inspired in the members, and the deleterious effect which this would have had on the Methodist cause. [32] His efforts were to no avail. Fidler, who had returned to the island in 1843, fared no better in 1845. While he did give way to the new missionary, he noted that all three missionaries were due to leave the island during that year. [33]

Protests against the lack of continuity which itinerancy entailed were obviously not taken seriously. All three missionaries were gone by the beginning of 1846. What tended to highlight the instability further was that there were occasional differences in missionary approach between personnel recently arrived from England and those with longer experience in the West Indies. The former, imbued with firm convictions as to what was proper according to the norms of English Methodism, had great difficulty in adapting themselves to practices which had evolved in the West Indies. It is true that it was only towards the end of the century that these differences resulted in open conflict. At that time the plans for the establishment of a West Indian Conference also called for a liberalisation of the church's structure, and clearly suggested the likelihood of West Indian leadership. But even in the 1840's, the germ of the problem was there, though only an occasional comment indicated its existence.

The protests of Fidler and his colleagues indicate a far more serious problem than that dealt with above, and that is the logistics of successful administration of the West Indian missions from such a remote centre of control. As Methodism operated in the West Indies, the final decision concerning expansion and the deployment of personnel rested with the Missionary Committee. Lacking personnel with first-hand knowledge and experience of conditions in the mission field, the Committee were sometimes unwilling to accede to proposals submitted by the missionaries. In addition to this, the Committee had no desire to permit too great devolution of authority because of their interest in retaining control over the funds from their missions. The result was that matters which could have been dealt with locally suffered delays on the part of the Committee.

This administrative handicap prevented the construction of galleries at James Street for quite a while. It also delayed the acquisition of property in Speightstown; and it took an enterprising Superintendent like Fidler to proceed without the necessary authorisation. Similar enterprise marked his action in 1843, when he acquired the site of what is now the Bethel Methodist Church. Others had shown interest in the site, and Fidler thought it worth his while to steal a march on his competitors. [34]

The Difficult Years 1846–1863

In the post emancipation period up to 1845, the West Indian colonies received assistance from Britain in funding education for the ex-slaves. This funding was reduced over a five year period, eventually coming to an end in 1845. Almost on the heels of this came another change which was to have serious effects on economic conditions in the islands. This change involved the passage of the *Sugar Duties Act* in 1846. By this Act the British Government gradually equalised the duties on sugar imported into Britain. The measure was by no means popular either with the abolitionists, who feared the expansion of the slave trade, or with the West Indians who saw in it the ruin of the plantations. [35] The reality was that, even though the production of sugar increased, the decline in prices meant that the planters were not doing well. Comparative impoverishment meant that the labourers suffered reduced wages. Since the bulk of the Methodist membership came from this class, financial embarrassment would result in an inability to provide for themselves or to be regular in their attendance at church.

During the period 1846 – 1863 there was irregular growth in the number of those who attended the various churches. The exception in this case was the Moravian church, in which there was decline between 1853 and 1855 with only a marginal rise in 1863. Anglican figures are somewhat irregular, because each year a number of parishes failed to submit returns. Such figures as we have indicate a pattern of uneven growth. The Methodists showed a rapid increase between 1846 and 1852 with a more gradual rise to 1857. There were fluctuations after this year, however, showing a slight increase by 1863. [36] The year 1854 seems to have been one of great general increase. In that year there was an outbreak of cholera in the island, where sanitary conditions were not as good as they should have been. Some 20,000 persons perished in that outbreak. It was in this year that the Methodists recorded their highest number of full members, 4,046. In the following year the numbers began to decline, and the number of full members never again picked up. Commenting on this, the 1855 Report for Barbados stated: "every society was reinforced through the universal dismay, and now every society feels a fatal reaction". Surprisingly, however, the number of persons attending Methodist institutions remained fairly stable for a few years.

There was great encouragement in the parish of St. Philip where first Ebenezer, followed by the chapels at Beulah and Supers, showed signs of increase and so gave considerable encouragement to the missionaries. The work in this parish had begun after emancipation, and had grown to such an extent that by 1857 the District Meeting decided to create a separate Circuit of the stations in that parish. In addition to the three already mentioned, there was one other station called Shrewsbury. Providence in Christ Church was made a part of this second Circuit, even though that station continued to have its own resident missionary. In the same year the District Meeting agreed to the appointment of a missionary for the new Circuit, its first Superintendent being the Rev. Henry Bleby. Bleby had served for a number of years in Jamaica and later Antigua, before he joined the missionary staff in Barbados.

While the numbers in the Ebenezer Circuit did not always grow, the membership in the Circuit consistently represented a very high proportion of Methodist membership in Barbados. Thus the Ebenezer Circuit in 1857 had a membership of 1,617 out of the Barbados membership of 3,445. In 1859 its membership was 1,526 out of 3,404, and in 1862 it was 1,374 out of 3,089. Some of the decline at Ebenezer can be attributed to the expulsion of some persons from full membership. [37] The rest merely reflects the fluctuations which the Methodists experienced between 1846 and 1863.

The comparative success of the Ebenezer Circuit was due to its having good lay leadership for the most part. Such leadership compensated for the fact that the missionaries had been unable to give constant attention to the development of the station before 1857. This lack of direct pastoral oversight was not confined to the St. Philip area. Speightstown, once thought to be an important station because of the large number of residents, was intermittently left without a missionary. This was because whenever Barbados was short of a missionary, the station was left vacant so as to keep the city provided for. The decline in the missions at Scotland, and at Hope in St. Lucy, must be attributed to the failure to maintain a regular missionary at Speightstown. Hope station in St. Lucy had shown signs of promise in 1853, but had not maintained this early promise. Only in 1859 did it again give signs of encouragement. Apart from brief glimmers of hope at Paynes Bay in St. James in 1859 and later in 1862, all the causes for rejoicing seem to have come from the parish of St. Philip.

If generally speaking there was little sign of numerical growth, there were often uncomfortable indications that all was not well. For instance, it sometimes became necessary to remove from office persons who held responsible positions. In one case, at Scotland in St. Andrew, the day school teacher who was also local preacher was removed for an act of dishonesty. He seems to have been guilty of some defalcation in his school returns which led the Education Committee to remove his school from the list of those which received grants from that body. But his dismissal, far from resulting in his "retiring into penitent obscurity" as the minister had expected, led to his opening a school in the same district. His preaching on Sundays had the effect of drawing away several of the local children from Methodism. Reporting on this the minister commented with obvious sarcasm: "such was the consistency and taste of some of the people of Scotland". [38] And yet there was more to the issue than that. The very fact that the lay preacher could deplete the congregation in this way would seem to suggest a considerable degree of loyalty to the man rather than to Methodism. From this period onwards, the decline of Methodism in Scotland was fairly steady.

Shrewsbury in St. Philip, like Scotland, was a rural area; and for a long time after the station started, it was without the direct oversight of a missionary. The example of lay persons in positions of responsibility in this situation counted for much more than it did in those stations where a missionary was resident. If therefore the principal lay members proved to be unsatisfactory, the effect on the local congregation was likely to be devastating. This was the case in 1859 when the individual serving as school teacher, leader, and local preacher was found wanting. Exactly what his fault was the minister's report did not specify, except to describe it as a "disgraceful fall" – almost certainly a euphemism for sexual immorality. Discipline was swift, however, as the minister sought to uphold what he considered the standard of "christian morality". The effect of this development, according to him, was that the detractors of Methodism in that area used the opportunity to ridicule them. [39]

Disciplinary problems were becoming an issue for the missionaries at this time. Previous reports on the island did not indicate the expulsions of members, even though such action must have played a part in the reduction of their numbers. There was a high number of expulsions in the three years for which we have records. In 1859 the first Circuit expelled 60 and the second Circuit 102. In 1862 there were 86 expulsions in the second Circuit, while the Hope Station in St. Lucy merely reported expulsions due to neglect on the part of members. In 1863 there were 27 expulsions in the Second Circuit. [40] These expulsions had their origin, as one of the missionaries explained at one time, in the rapid expansion after emancipation. And that expansion made it difficult to maintain the discipline of the church.

Quite apart from problems such as these, the missionaries often complained about the apathy of members and attendants, and one can reasonably surmise that there might have been more complaints had all the missionaries been inclined to repeat the same things. Of those stations concerning which apathy had been reported, three stood out prominently - Providence, Scotland and Bethel. Providence tended to be unreliable even when other stations were showing signs of growth. The extent of the apathy at Providence was such that by 1851 the missionaries had begun to despair of the station. In that year, the annual Circuit Report compared it to a young and beautiful person who had become "pale and wan, under the influence of a wasting consumption and sinking into an untimely grave". The antidote for that situation was "continuous and uninterrupted Christian ministry, including a sleepless pastoral care..." [41] The need at that station was primarily for a minister; and the inconsistency in the pastoral provision there must be regarded as one of the causes of their difficulties. Lack of interest on the part of the residents of the area was certainly another. In 1859, for instance, lack of interest seemed to have been the reason why the members of the congregation were allegedly unwilling to walk to church. As was very much the case with Ebenezer, the members had long distances to walk. It is open to question whether the Providence members had longer distances to walk to chapel than the members of the parish church. However, we do not get the impression that the parish church experienced a similar problem. On the contrary, figures returned in the Blue Books show attendances there to be regularly over 1000 persons. And even today the parish church is some distance away from the surrounding settlements.

The case was somewhat different with respect to the Scotland station. One missionary attributed the neglect of worship to the former slaves' having bought plots and built houses, with the result that they were no longer grateful to God for their prosperity. [42] This assessment seems to be harsh and lacking in a real understanding of the peculiar situation of the freedmen. While it may be conceded that attention to their homes may have made some of them neglectful of their obligations to public worship, it is very unlikely that their absence necessarily constituted a lack of gratitude to God. The fact is that the missionary was impatient at their failure to respond in a manner which he considered suitable.

It is also at Scotland that the note of hopelessness was sounded like a never-ending refrain. Almost every year between 1851 and 1859, there was a depressing report on the Scotland station. The idea of abandoning it was first mooted in 1851 when the report on the station described the people as "heart-less". The Circuit Report for 1853 spoke of the demolition of the chapel because it had been endangered by landslides. Yet, despite an increase of twelve members, it was suggested that the requiem for Methodism in that district had been sung. [43] The returns for 1854 also showed an increase in membership – though not in piety, it lamented. Lack of progress was evident in 1855 also; and when the foundations of the temporary chapel collapsed in 1857, further decline was a foregone conclusion. By 1859 there was still no chapel, the area was reportedly difficult to reach, and its abandonment recommended to the Committee. In this case there was quite clearly more than apathy at issue.

The third station – Bethel – was probably the most difficult of the three, and a source of great anxiety to the missionaries. The Bethel chapel was situated on Bay Street, which at that time was regarded as a depressed area of the town. The station was originally named "Nelson Street", indicating that it might have been located there at first. The people who made up the congregation were for the most part poor and underprivileged. So great was their poverty that those who did attend the chapel preferred to do so at night, when their threadbare clothing was less likely to attract attention. The peasantry prided themselves in their appearance in public, so that this must have been a burden to those who were regular members. Since they were unable to provide themselves with proper clothing, it is reasonable to assume that they were also unable to pay their dues with any degree of regularity. The result was that their membership lapsed. In 1848, the station was reportedly at a standstill because of persistent strife. Five years later no progress could be reported in its development because the people had been showing a preference for more profane activities. Here, as was reported of Dalkeith in 1853, a liquor shop nearby served to provide a forceful counter-attraction to the activities of the chapel. [44] And in more cases than they would have liked, the "spirituous" seemed to have been winning over the "spiritual". In 1857, Bethel was noticed as among those stations which occasionally discouraged their ministers; and in 1862, it was said of Bethel as well as of James Street that there was nothing interesting to report. By the latter date, the state of these station reflected the general atmosphere of stagnation or staleness in Methodism.

Another factor which affected the character of Methodism at this time was internal dissension. This tended to show itself in the form of petty squabbles in different congregations. It was exhibited in its most sustained and virulent form at the James Street chapel. The disunity there arose from a conflict in the mid-1840's over the matter of church discipline. It was never quite resolved, and became a regular feature in that congregation between 1845 and 1862. For more than a year, from early 1846 to mid-1847, the state of the Methodist Societies could have been accurately described as depressing. In a letter to his superiors in March 1846, one missionary detailed the existing situation as follows:

> Distrust, hatred and agitation, with all their concomitant evils have effected a lodging in each separate society, and in every department of each society...They say Methodism has been set at nought by those who ought to have been its guardians. [45]

By the end of the same year, the two resident missionaries were even more depressing in their report on the city. Both reported the persistence of division, one being apprehensive of some sort of secession. Some six months later, there was a different and more accurate explanation of the division. This was to the effect that the "politics, secularities and legislation of Methodism have been discussed too freely in this place". [46] The truth is that the dispute about the participation of some Methodists in such organisations as the Oddfellows Society had given impetus to the discussion of broader issues such as the nature, teaching, and polity of Methodism. The Oddfellows Society was one of those fraternal groups like the Freemasons, which was frowned upon by many churches. Discussion on the character of Methodism would be further extended by the end of the century to include greater participation of the laity in the government of that body.

Another source of disquiet in the James Street station was what one report described as the tendency to alter the practices of Methodism. Although the report did not specify the exact practices which had been threatened, what was developing at this time was a keen contest between practices in England and those which had evolved through experience in the West Indies. Among the practices to be noticed later would be that of permitting female leaders to vote on disciplinary matters. The steady influx of English recruits to the ministry in Barbados was beginning to create problems for the local body; but there were no reflections on this in the District Meetings or generally in the correspondence. Methodism, even in its earliest manifestations, had made no pretence at liberalism; both missionaries and laymen had been required to abide by the letter of the law. That might have been necessary at first, given the unfavour-able atmosphere in which Methodism had erupted onto the English ecclesias-tical stage. However, missionaries functioning in the West Indies had found modifications of their pristine rigidity to be necessary. Each new missionary at this time, especially if he had experience in an English Circuit, had found the modifications in the West Indies to be a betrayal of Methodism. The result was that, in the late 1860's and the 1870's, nostalgia for early Methodism became a marked feature of these missionaries. It was not surprising, therefore, that they did not approve the local trends.

The extent to which missionaries might have been involved in the per-sistence of divisions at James Street cannot be gauged from available evidence. We do know, however, that there was not much agreement among successive missionaries over the handling of the Oddfellows affair.

There was one report which suggests that the entire development was susceptible of some further examination. The simple circumstance was the re-ported attempt of those who opposed William Fidler to get his colleague Phelp appointed to James Street. [47] This can mean one of two things: either Phelp was known to be an opponent of Fidler, or he had shown sufficient signs of in-decision to indicate that he was likely to be won over. Phelp's letters do not in-dicate his own stance on Fidler's handling of the James Street crisis in 1845. The question still needs to be asked whether he maintained sufficient of that pro-fessional detachment which would have precluded his being used. No firm answer is possible, given the limitation of the evidence. Such, however, was the deleterious effect of the divisiveness on their progress that the Superintendent believed that growth had been jeopardised. [48]

Another aspect of the disunity was the existence of social distinctions between the two city congregations. The root cause of this cleavage was the dif-ference in social status between the classes of persons who attended each of the chapels. Henry Bleby made a passing reference to this when reporting on the difficulties associated with the reconstruction of the James Street chapel, thus giving us the first real hint of the problem. In doing so, he drew attention to "the strong party feeling yet dividing the two societies and congregations in the city" which, in his view, aggravated existing difficulties. [49] What was the displeas-ure to which he referred? We know from another source that there was a decline in the James Street congregation because the members of that chapel had to share the Bethel chapel for worship. The reason given was that the Bethel chapel was far from the residences of the James Street congregation. [50] This explanation appears to be superficial, given the distance between James Street and Bethel, and the fact that some of the James Street worshippers were likely to have their own means of transportation. In addition, it would have been known to them that the inconvenience was only of a temporary nature. The extent of the division showed itself in the fact that each congregation continued its own morning and evening services independently of the other. As a result, there were four services in the Bethel chapel every Sunday. This separation suggests a greater degree of prejudice and disunity than any of the missionaries would have been prepared to admit. And this explains Bleby's vagueness about what took place. In any case, we may have to recognise that Bleby's own conservatism did not make him averse to the maintenance of social distinctions. And the missionaries regarded themselves as part of the upper and respectable classes. Thus the Barbados Report for 1854 noted that, among the higher classes of society touched by the cholera epidemic, was their Chairman of the District, William Bannister. Distinctions based on class and colour were not uncommon in the seating arrangement in the churches, with the exception of the Moravians. Such distinctions were often not the result of policy, but rather of custom. So that even where a clergyman or missionary was not himself prejudiced, it was difficult to correct a habit that was ingrained in the society. The holding of four services suggests that there was pressure to prevent too great intermingling of the two sets of members.

What Bleby's letter did not explain was that class as well as colour separated the two congregations. At a very early stage of Methodist work in Barbados, the new chapel in Bridgetown attracted those members of the mercantile and professional groups who wished to associate themselves with Methodism. These would have included some of the English and creole whites, as well as the more prosperous members of the free coloured community. On the other hand, the Bethel chapel attracted persons of a meaner social and economic status. As a result, membership of the Bethel chapel consisted of a class of persons who did not blend well with the members of the James Street congregation. The inability of the two congregations to enjoy harmonious relations, even during a period of temporary inconvenience, points to a fundamental weakness as much within the Methodist organisation as within the rest of the community and other churches. Thus the two congregations mirrored the kind of division which there was in the wider society. In a way, the Methodists as a body were not able to break free of this kind of prejudice. The 1870 Report for the First Circuit noted that the congregation at Bethel Chapel was "much inferior both in intelligence and social status to that at James Street ... The Chapel is built in the most disreputable part of the City..." [51] The persistence of the sharp distinction only shows that it was deeply rooted and not something limited to the period of inconvenience.

During this period concern was shown for improvement in the size of the missionary staff. What the Methodists were concerned with was the provision of an efficient ministry to their current and future members. In this regard it was important to ensure that there was a sufficiently large staff to enable them to serve their various stations with reasonable efficiency. The Missionary Committee in London were never able to meet the demand of the local missionaries, especially as the Committee felt increasingly impelled towards the needs of other parts of the world. This, however, did not cause a reduction in the demands. Thus in 1848, the Superintendent, John Corlett, requested an Assistant Missionary for Barbados, offering, as an alternative, to employ two or three good local preachers. With an outlay of £ 50 per year he believed that as much could be achieved by them as by any Assistant Missionary. In addition, and perhaps more significantly, the Society would not be plagued by constant demands for salary increases. [52] As yet there was no great consideration for raising up an indigenous ministry to meet current or future demands.

Further requests were made in 1849. One of these was occasioned by the illness of the James Street missionary, Henry Padgham. Padgham's disability considerably increased the burden of his colleague, Corlett, who found it beyond his capacity to function with reasonable efficiency. [53] Another request originated in the break-up of the fledgling Cluff's Bay congregation in St. Lucy. [54] The need for closer supervision has already been discussed while considering the subject of itinerancy. The issue in this case was the failure of the Missionary Committee to fill vacancies promptly. It may be that the Committee did not have at their disposal as many missionaries as they would have wished to deploy in the West Indies. They were, after all, considering other avenues for their resources. On the local scene, however, such failures gave rise to speculation and even harsh criticism. The persistence of a vacancy at Speightstown reportedly caused such dissatisfaction in the north of the island that the residents had begun to complain that their money was being used on others. Their annoyance can easily be understood since the station had then been vacant for approximately three years.

Another dimension in the issue of adequate staffing was the connection made between such staffing and the stability of the mission. One missionary, writing in 1849, suggested that the Barbados Mission was regarded as awfully mismanaged. This view seems to have arisen from the fact that some stations tended to remain vacant for years. Their inability to fill these stations was a source of concern for them. This was especially the case at the Providence station where the Methodist benefactor, William Reece, had made ample provision for their work in Christ Church by providing them with a chapel, a mission house, and revenue from his estates. Nevertheless, the station was not always supplied with a missionary. It was to guard against its being vacant for any extended period that the Reece family made a new offer to the Methodists. Isaac Reece, nephew of the benefactor, proposed first, that he would pay £ 50 to them if they were prepared to allow the missionary to continue there the following year. If his wish were accommodated, he then promised to continue to support the Society annually. Finally, he offered to appear before the District Meeting as his own advocate to persuade that body to rearrange the Circuits in such a way as to enable a missionary to be regularly resident in Christ Church. In commending the plan to the Missionary Committee, Henry Bleby warned them against treating Reece's offer lightly. He argued that the income generated by the parish justified their having a missionary. And, as if to strengthen his case, he informed the Committee of Reece's willingness to assist their appeal to the legislature for financial support. [55] The generosity of the offer reflected Reece's desire to see developed the work in which so much of his family's fortunes had already been invested.

Normally, as was the case with Mrs. Gill, such an offer would have been presented to the District Meeting by the Superintendent. Up to 1863, when the proposal from Reece was put before them, the District Meeting consisted of the ministers only. No lay person had ever attended or been invited to a Meeting. It was therefore an unprecedented step for Reece to be present and to function as his own advocate. [56] Reece owed this privilege partly to the circumstances of the District Meeting being held in Barbados, and partly to his being a relative of the benefactor. One cannot overlook, however, the fact of his being one of the representatives for Christ Church in the House of Assembly, and a respectable person whose assistance the Methodists were already courting. As was to be expected, the District Meeting accepted Reece's offer. Their reasons repeated some of those already noted in Bleby's letter; but they stressed the fact of Reece's influence and the service he could render with the rebuilding of the chapel in Christ Church. They further argued that the Reece family had wanted a missionary exclusively for Christ Church, and that had been the testator's wish. Finally, they observed that the good conduct of Methodists had earned them the support of the landholders, hence it was necessary to keep a man at Providence. [57] Henry Soper was therefore re-appointed to Providence and another missionary was appointed to the Ebenezer Circuit to assist Henry Bleby. [58] All those reasons stated above must have been the result of discussion at the District Meeting; certainly, no previous mention was ever made of this exclusive wish of William Reece.

Given the emphasis which the missionaries placed on the spiritual development of their members, lack of improvement in this area was a constant source of anxious concern. As early as 1852, one missionary began to complain of the need to break up the spiritually "fallow" ground. [59] His comment is significant since it immediately follows a report of prosperity in their work. Clearly he was not interested solely in numbers, although his hopes for a revival as a result of the yellow fewer of 1852 might have given that impression. By 1855 the stagnation in their development had led to a clear call for a spiritual revival by one of the younger missionaries. [60] Two years later, the Report for the First Circuit acknowledged that there had been no progress in any area of their work. "We looked for great things ... we have sown much and bring in little", the Report complained. With respect to the Bethel station, it noted that "signs following" were not as "numerous as in other places". The missionaries believed that, in their desire for prosperity, they had "sought it not by faith", concluding that they had forgotten that success came from the Lord. And so, for the future, they pledged themselves to greater self-abnegation and dependence on the Lord. [61]

The truth is that the missionaries could not accurately determine the cause of the decline, and, in their bafflement, were becoming desperate. In mid-1863, one of them described the church as filled with dry bones, [62] and consequently, morally offensive. Watson, the writer in question, was a newcomer to Barbados who had decided that the general tone of Methodism was other than it should have been. Indeed, even the bold responses of the congregation to the prayers were considered by him improper; for he expected the responses to be more subdued, [63] indicating a spirit of reverence. It is reasonable to assume that the new missionaries voiced their displeasure to the members of the congregations, even if they did so in pastoral admonitions; in which case, repeated criticisms might well have been one of the causes of decline. But the nature of the evidence is such that one is limited to conjecture at this point.

From the late 1850's onwards, "revival" became a watchword of the missionaries. In order to effect this, various special services were attempted. In some chapels, there were increased prayer meetings during the week, the meetings being held immediately after the regular services. The early morning attendances were not particularly good, nor were the responses satisfying to the missionaries. On other occasions, there might be a whole week of such special services; or prayer meetings on the estate might be revived. By far the commonest forms of such special activity were open-air meetings, directed chiefly at those who were neither members or attendants. These open-air meetings seem to have started in Christ Church, but they soon spread to other parishes in the island. [64] The efforts were not only intended to attract persons towards Methodism, they were also intended to counteract the influence of the Established Church. Just as the Tractarian [65] clergy were inclined to denounce the Methodists, so they, in their turn, were concerned to denounce the "evil" influence of those "papists". This raises the question whether the competitive efforts of both sides might have helped to drive would-be adherents from both bodies. The question is not one for which the present writer can find an answer, but it is not unlikely that such hostility bred indifference.

The Closing Years

By the beginning of 1864, Methodism in Barbados was at a fairly low ebb. This state of affairs was represented by the Report of the First Circuit as follows:

> Spiritual dearth and death, and desolation have largely prevailed. The spirit of discord has extended among our people, and has occasioned a wide spread havoc. [66]

The ministers of both Circuits complained of poorly attended services, and of the neglect of class meetings. But the decline was not only in Barbados, it affected the St. Vincent District as a whole. In taking cognizance of this, the District Meeting of 1864 acknowledged that decline had been taking place for fifteen years previously. The causes of this decline, members asserted, were two in number. First, that only twenty-six years had elapsed since emancipation, and that "society" in the islands was still in the process of formation. The second cause was that the "superstitions and traditions peculiar to a semi-educated state of society" still prevailed. Therefore a higher morality and a "more advanced state of civilisation" could not be attained. A more succinct way of stating the case would have been that their exaggerated expectations had been disappointed. They had anticipated a wave of members after emancipation, but a quarter of a century had not yielded the results.

Though the number of those who attended the Methodist ministry remained fairly constant, the number of those who became full members showed an overall decline. The reasons for this will be discussed more fully later. But it needs to be said here that expulsions constituted one of the reasons for that decline. Such expulsions were most frequent in the Ebenezer Circuit, which on two separate occasions expelled more than one hundred members in a single year. Every Circuit had to effect such expulsions as members failed to meet the demands of the missionaries. The same pattern of membership was characteristic of the other churches, though the Moravians showed a distinct tendency to increase. Anglican records continued to be piecemeal.

Even where the numbers were maintained, concern was expressed about the quality of persons admitted to full membership. The 1869 Report for the Bethel Circuit referred to the low spiritual state of those who neglected the class meetings, adding, with characteristic severity, that they were "utterly destitute of spiritual life". [67] Lack of "vital godliness", coldness, or luke-warmness, were reported the following year of Providence and Supers in the Third Circuit. The overview to the Report of the First Circuit generalised that the population was becoming "more than ever immoral, ungodly, and utterly negligent of the public worship of God". [68] What the ministers were faced with, as the century neared its end, was a growing apathy towards religion and a converse growth in secularism. This can be deduced from the complaint of one Report in 1869 of the "unseemly conformity to the world". The attitude was not confined to the Barbadian population, for English Methodists settling in the colony were themselves accused of "setting the bad example of negligence". [69]

Sometimes the problem was compounded by a lack of proper leaders. The problem in this case was twofold. In the first place, the missionaries had difficulty replacing persons who were old, or who were being removed by death. The need was therefore expressed for "youthful, active, intelligent, and pious leaders" to take the place of the tiring stalwarts. In the James Street and Bethel chapels, there was the further problem of a decrease in male leadership. For instance, Bethel in 1870 reported four male leaders as against sixteen females, while at James Street there were four males and twenty eight females. [70] And since only males functioned as local preachers, this deficiency threatened the missionaries with an inability to provide for all the chapel services. In 1875 and 1878 the problems were still with the Methodists, probably going hand in hand with a decline noticed earlier in male membership. [71]

Table 6
Comparison of Persons Attending Churches

	Anglican	Moravian	Methodist
1864	21200	2471	–
1870	22371	2399	10830
1871	23121	2352	11630
1876	–	2706	11100
1882	–	3199	10175

Sources: Moravians: Kingsley Lewis, *The Moravian Missions in Barbados, 1816-1886, p. 227;* Anglicans: *Blue Books,* 1864, pp. 228-229; 1871, pp. T1 - T2; 1871, pp. T1 - T2. Methodists: 1870 - MMS Box 161: Minutes of the St. Vincent District, 1871; 1871 - Box 162: Minutes of the St. Vincent District, 1872; 1876 - Box 164: Minutes of the St. Vincent District, 1877; 1883 - Box 166: Minutes of the St. Vincent District, 1884.

The second aspect of the problem related to the suitability of some of the leaders for such office. In a noteworthy letter written towards the end of 1872, one missionary's analysis was such as to raise questions about the selection process for leaders. He noted first of all that where the leaders were not such as to gain the respect of the members, the work was likely to be stagnant. Next, he observed that there was a need for men and women of influence, piety, and diligence for the work of God. Finally, he made the telling observation that in no other denomination was the spiritual care of the members entrusted to the *lay leaders.* And in this case, there were many examples of the blind leading the blind. [72] It may well have been a case of the rapid depletion in the ranks of the leaders causing missionaries to appoint persons who were not really suitable. The compromise now created a problem in that current office holders appeared to be retarding the progress of the body. It may on the other hand be that, as they settled down, they were anxious to be considered something more than a peasant organisation, hence the need to attract persons of influence to their leadership. The missionary's letter would appear to disguise very thinly the persistent desire for respectability so as to gain the support of the upper classes.

One of the most serious problems as regards maintaining their membership was the decline of interest in the class meeting. The class meeting performed a pivotal role in early Methodism. Those who showed an interest in membership were immediately formed into a class, and other members were expected to meet regularly in class. It is in the class that their spiritual growth was nurtured. As early as 1864, signs were beginning to appear that the members were losing their interest in the class meeting. Thereafter, from 1869 to 1881, neglect of class meetings became a perennial complaint in almost every Circuit. [73] The only exception was the Speightstown Circuit, from which no such complaint has been recorded. In the case of Ebenezer, there were no such complaints after 1874. Despite the complaint that the class meetings seemed no longer to have the value they previously had, only on two occasions were any explanations attempted. The first was given in 1870 by the James Street missionary who explained that the meeting was regarded as a "disagreeable infliction". [74] But he did not say why or in what way it appeared so. The second explanation was given by the Providence missionary in 1877 to the effect that the members did not wish to have fellowship with each other. [75] This latter explanation is of course judgmental, and too general. Taken together, however, they would suggest that members either did not see the class meetings as vital to membership, or that they wanted a change in the system. The latter might be the more likely explanation, emphasising the continuing failure to readjust to new circumstances practices which had always been adhered to.

The pattern which emerges from this study is that of irregular growth in membership. The pattern of rapid growth during the first years of emancipation was not dissimilar to that in other parts of the West Indies. Thereafter, as was noticeable in Jamaica, the membership of the church began to decline. But that decline was not as great as in Jamaica; in fact, Findlay and Holdsworth suggest that the Eastern Caribbean, including Barbados, was the bright spot for the Methodists as far as membership was concerned. [76] Methodists in Barbados always constituted a high percentage both of membership and hearers within the District to which the island was attached. Especially after 1863, they always constituted twenty-five per cent or more of those in the District. But the numbers were falling, and did so steadily.

One also notes the fact that full membership was not keeping pace with the number of those who were hearers. The missionaries might well have been correct in alleging apathy to some extent. Whether because af the rigid discipline they imposed or not, many who attended seem to have regarded being present as sufficient. They either did not, or could not, maintain the level of enthusiasm expected of them by the missionaries. Even so, it is worthy of note that over 12,000 persons claimed Methodist allegiance in the 1881 census.

The missionaries' correspondence reflected a great degree of despondency. That despondency was prominent from the late 1850's. It did not emanate merely from the decline in membership, though that in itself would have been disturbing to the missionaries. Rather, the despondency they showed emanated from the fact that their membership seemed not to compensate for the efforts of the missionaries. People were unwilling to become full members, class meetings were not as highly regarded as before, strife and disunity were common in some congregations, and some of the leaders were of poor quality. It is small wonder that the missionaries undertook the process of pruning which saw numbers reduced in several stations. These "removals" were also for moral lapses. Notwithstanding the depression of the missionaries on occasions, their performance was not bad overall. Compared with Methodist efforts elsewhere in the West Indies, they had managed to keep Methodism alive and well established.

Chapter 4

EDUCATING THE FORMER SLAVES

In June 1833 the British Parliament passed a series of resolutions dealing with the abolition of slavery. The fifth of these resolutions pledged Parliament's support for the West Indian legislatures in providing education on "liberal and comprehensive principles". [1] As has been clearly demonstrated by Carl Campbell, the education to be provided was neither comprehensive nor liberal. [2] It was primarily Christian education which the government sought to promote, and hence instruction in the doctrines and precepts of Christianity were intended to form the "basis" and the "inseparable attendant" of that system. A detailed plan had been drawn up by the then Secretary of State for the Colonies, E.G. Stanley, in 1833. This plan underwent revision after submissions by the Missionary Societies which operated in the West Indies, and review by Stanley's successor at the Colonial Office, T. Spring Rice. Eventually, the plan was refined and adopted during the early administration of Lord Glenelg. This process of consultation and review took approximately two years, so that the scheme was not ready for implementation until 1835. [3]

In order to implement this programme, the British government thought it best to make use of those Missionary Societies which had already been engaged in the West Indies. These were the Society for the Propagation of the Gospel, the Methodist, London, Baptist, Scottish and Moravian Missionary Societies. The reason for giving preference to the protestant groups was not necessarily the desire to disseminate protestant christian values so as to combat heathenism, as Olwyn Blouet suggests. [4] Part of the strategy was to restrict the spread and influence of Roman Catholicism. There was a strong body of anti-Catholic feeling in the Parliament and in the nation in the 1820s. As a result, while Catholic emancipation was achieved, it was not without considerable opposition in the House of Commons and temporizing on the part of Prime Ministers Canning and Wellington. While the dissenters opposed the Catholics on doctrinal grounds, others regarded the Catholic church in England as a state within a state having allegiance to a foreign monarch. [5] Concern for the loyalty of the Catholic population had been part of the political development in early nineteenth century Trinidad. That same concern led to the eventual detachment of Catholic Trinidad from the Venezuelan Diocese of Angostura, and to the appointment of an Englishman as Catholic Bishop for Trinidad and the neighbouring islands. [6] There was therefore an anti-Catholic approach in place at the time of emancipation.

To deal with Trinidad and the other islands in which the Catholic church preponderated, the British government decided to promote a non-denominational system of education similar to that being followed in Ireland. The idea for such a system was given expression by the Rev. John Sterling. It was to him that the replies from the West Indies in response to a circular from T. Spring Rice, were sent early in 1835. In his report, Sterling offered a series of observations on the superiority of the Protestant bodies for advancing the cause the government had in mind. In his view, the Protestants demanded the acceptance "of certain moral and religious principles", which were capable of producing right action as well as the qualities most needed in the community. He further asserted that to "encourage the religion of Protestants is to advance the objects for which society itself exists." According to him, Protestants did not consider this position true of the tenets of the Roman Catholics. Nevertheless he favoured government support for Roman Catholics on the Irish pattern. Sterling's proposal did not originate the idea, but rather served to support what had already been contemplated by the British government. [7]

The agency employed in the task of implementing the non-denominational process was the Lady Mico Charity. First established in the seventeenth century, the intention of the Charity was to rescue "English slaves from the Barbary States." For nearly two hundred years the funds, which were invested in 1686, were unused. By 1833, the Charity had accumulated some £ 115,519. Following a ruling of the Court of Chancery, the money was used for the education of the newly emancipated slaves in the West Indies. [8]

The aims of the Mico Charity were not incompatible with the aims of the government. The schools operated by the Charity were to promote religious education in particular, and to this end all teachers were to be religious; but the Charity was not to encourage sectarian teaching. [9] It was thus possible for persons of different denominations to head the Mico Committee in the West Indies or to serve as teachers. [10] This non-denominational characteristic made the Charity a useful adjunct to the missionary societies. But insofar as the agents of the Charity were all Protestant, as a matter of policy, the Charity could be re-garded as anti-Catholic. It served to facilitate the denial to Catholics of any share in the parliamentary grants.

The Negro Education Grant, as the Parliamentary fund came to be called, consisted at first of £ 25,000 sterling. Of this amount £ 20,000 was to facili-tate the construction of schools, the other £ 5,000 to erect Normal Schools for the training of teachers. In 1837 the amount was increased to £ 30,000, decreasing from 1841 until its termination in 1845. [11] The government was to provide two-thirds of the cost of the buildings and the other agencies one-third. The very nature of the funding formula suggests that those organisations with better resources could have received a greater proportion of the Parliamentary grant. The Methodist Missionary Society in December 1835 communicated to its missionaries its in-tention to seek £ 5,000, its own share being £ 2,500.[12] The Societies of the Estab-lished Church were not likely to be so restricted and therefore would have re-ceived more. For example, the Society for the Propagation of the Gospel alone received from the Parliamentary fund a total of £ 62,385. It expended altogether the sum of £ 171,777. In fact in 1835 and 1836 the S.P.G. and the Church Mission-ary Society together received £ 19,854 of the £ 50,000 allocated to education of the ex-slaves in those two years. By contrast the Methodists received only £ 5,000 for the same period. [13]

In addition to this grant some legislatures and vestries made limited fi-nancial provision for education. The legislature of British Guiana, for example, voted £ 2,500 per year in 1836 and 1837 for education. Jamaican vestries and the legislature had made school grants to the Established Church in the years fol-lowing emancipation, although no general provision was made for education un-til 1844. Similarly, Barbados had made no general provision for education until 1846, even though that island's legislature and vestries enabled the Established Church to spend £ 4,285 on education in 1840. [14] Considering the amount avail-able through the Negro Education Grant, and the support of its Missionary so-cieties, the Established Church was well placed to carry out extensive building projects.

The level of funding made available by the Negro Education Grant re-sulted in a proliferation of schools of different denominations and of the Mico Charity. The Charity alone had 138 schools in operation in 1840, though the bulk of these were not in those islands where Roman Catholicism was strong. For example, Trinidad and the Windward Islands accounted for only 52 of the Mico schools. The Charity would appear to have established schools in those islands where there was a need for schools and not where it was intended to counteract Roman Catholic prejudices. In fact it is to be noted that the Charity began its operations in Jamaica [15] and not in any of the Catholic islands. In the island of Barbados there were 155 schools of the Established Church in 1834, out of a total of 405 in the Diocese. A large proportion of those schools would have been Sunday Schools, and other evening schools operating in the same buildings as the day schools. Latrobe found 213 schools in the island in 1837, of which 33 were Sunday Schools. The Moravians then had three schools and the Methodists two. The S.P.G. had built 15 new schools in the two years ending in 1837. In Jamaica, in 1835, the Anglican Church reportedly had 142 schools, some of them obviously Sunday Schools; the Methodists about 28 and the Moravians and Baptists 26 and 42 respectively by 1839. [16]

The proliferation of schools on the part of the Missionary Societies quite naturally involved some duplication of effort in the anxiety to promote denominational growth. The danger which could result in establishing more schools than a community needed were noted by Sterling in 1835. He recommended therefore that for a school to be assisted by the Parliamentary grant the community had to require it. [17] It goes without saying that any such school could have been established without drawing on the grant. In any case denominational rivalry was more the norm than the exception. There was rivalry between Anglicans and Dissenters in Jamaica, friction between the Bishop and the agents of the C.M.S., and between the various bodies and the Mico Charity. There were differences of opinion between the Bishop of Barbados and the directors of the C.M.S.; and friction between the Bishop and the agents of the C.M.S. was averted in the island by channelling the latter into other parts of the Diocese. [18]

In Barbados the rivalry between those who provided education was intense, and this can be seen in their perception of the purpose of the schools. The Bishop of Barbados, W.H. Coleridge, had displayed great energy in the establishment of schools. However, he seems to have formed the opinion that planters might employ free children on the estates at a fair wage, once such children were guaranteed education "for at least two full hours in every week." He was also concerned that those in the town be enabled to engage in practical trades so as to equip them for the roles they were to play in the society. [19] As Rudolph Goodridge indicates, Coleridge's perception of the needs of the society was realistic. It is not accurate to conclude, as he does, that Anglican schools were therefore limited in the scope of their curriculum. As will be shown later, other denominations were no less limited even though they did not explicitly express the need for the social arrangement Coleridge espoused.

Coleridge, who was the embodiment of the High Churchman, had little tolerance for non-conformists or for the Mico Charity. A major concern of his was to have the catechism of the Established Church form part of daily instruction, because he conceived of the schools as nurseries for the church. In this regard Coleridge shared the perception of the Bishop of London that education should have been left to the Established Church. [20] If the Bishop of London was "spitting into the winds of change", the Bishop of Barbados as a member of the Council nevertheless was in a position to exert influence in educational decisions.

The Methodists on their part had fixed notions about the purpose of their schools. Each school was an extension of the mission, and those being educated were also being prepared for membership in the Methodist church. The District Meeting for 1835 took note of the energy displayed in Barbados by clergy of the Anglican and Roman Catholic churches. Charging that these clergy demanded that the children being educated join their churches, the meeting asserted the absolute necessity of schools for Methodist prosperity. The Barbados mission made subsequent references to energetic proselytising by the Established or Anglican Church. [21]

This connection between the church and the school remained a constant element in the Methodist understanding of the church's function. For example, the Circuit Report for the year 1843 exulted that fruits of their efforts were beginning to appear at the Scotland School, because many were being converted. [22] Similarly, the Report of 1852 noted that nearly all the students of the Paynes Bay School had become members. [23] It was not until 1859 that we have the first clear statement as to how a Methodist school was to be regarded. Speaking of the Day School at Rice's in St. Philip, the Report of the second Circuit stated:

> it is no exception to our other day-schools, which are what Mission Schools should be – places in which due prominence is given to the Bible and to Religion, and where young immortals are taught and trained for the life that now is, and for that which is to come.[24]

The Superintendent of this Circuit was Henry Bleby, who seems to have caused offence to members of the legislature. But Bleby was not alone in his perception of Methodist schools. Another Report in 1865 emphasised that Methodist schools were an integral part of their mission, and that their chief concern with the youths was their salvation. [25] In that same year the school connected to James St. Chapel was closed. The master, Teague, had been at the school for three years before the closure. He might have been bitter over the loss of office; but his re-flection on the closure is not inconsistent with the assertions of missionaries. Henry Hurd had closed the school because neither the children nor their par-ents had become members of the Methodist Church. The same Barbados Re-port for 1865 noted that missionary work depended on having pious teachers on the spot to serve as examples and to counsel members, as well as to educate their children. [26] From this perspective, it seems to be suggesting that Teague had not been a success in building up the congregation.

Like the Methodists, the Moravians also maintained a close link between education and the wider function of the Church. Maynard expressed the Mora-vian position succinctly when he wrote:

> The importance and necessity of Christian Education as a means of ensuring the prosperity, permanence and extension of the missionary work has made it at all times a matter of vital concern to the directors of Moravian Missions. [27]

For this reason it became a major concern for the missionaries in Barbados who began establishing schools in the early years of slave amelioration. The perspec-tive of their education programme is revealed by the Superintendent of the Bar-bados Mission, John Ellis, who reported that some 700 to 1100 children were taught to read their Bibles, and that "many of them also receive instruction in Writing, Arithmetic, and Sewing..." Another missionary reported the realization of a cherished goal of himself and his predecessors in that there was an improve-ment in the singing of the hymns.

Ellis' interest was not limited to hymn singing or purely sectarian con-cerns, though that was obvious enough. He was also interested in seeing the youth trained in habits of industry in "the use of Agricultural implements". As a result he sought to encourage their cultivation of a plot of land on a nearby plantation. This effort was frustrated by the owner who had other ideas. [28] At Sharon they tried to encourage field work for the children until 10.00 a.m. daily, but the ex-periment never got going.

The partisan interests of the various denominations suggested the possibility of conflict such as rivalry could generate. There was little likelihood of Moravian involvement in any conflict since that body followed a policy of co-existence with other denominations. Any conflict therefore was likely to involve the Anglicans and the Methodists. The first signs of such conflicts appeared in 1842. In that year there was a decline in numbers in the Methodist school in Speightstown. The decline was attributed to the "establishment of schools in this town and neighbourhood and the influence which had been used to remove our scholars." [29] One can only assume that the report was concerned with the activities of the Established Church. An earlier letter by the missionary in Speightstown alleged that the Established Church had set up several schools in the area, and had been advocating an increase in schools. The writer further alleged that the Established Church had been claiming such work as exclusively theirs. [30]

There is no question that an increase in the number of schools in that district would have had the effect of reducing numbers in already existing schools. And the assertiveness alleged of the Established Church seems to correspond with the outlook of Bishop Coleridge. Some of the more extreme adherents of the Oxford Movement in England used to insist that pupils attend the parish church on Sundays. [31] Bishop Coleridge was an adherent of the movement, and some of the clergy might also have been. They might well have insisted on a similar attendance. But that in itself could not have removed Methodist pupils from their own schools. The impression given by the Barbados Report for 1840 was that the Methodist teacher at Speightstown was forced to improve his performance so as to attract pupils who would have gone to other schools where the tuition was free. [32] The competition in Barbados was such that the Demerara District meeting, held in the island in 1843, expressed the need for intensified efforts in Bridgetown. The immediate cause was the presence of "a *Romish Priest* disseminating error and superstition among a Protestant population."[33]

This broad outlook of the various denominations coincided with the limited perspectives of the British Government. This limitation was based on the belief that a people so recently emancipated needed such a preparation for eventual freedom. The London Missionary Society expressed the perspective of the British Government when it described the education proposed as "the best and only foundation of social order, industry and happiness." [34] It was an English model of education, [35] which did not seek to address the needs of the societies in the West Indies. And since the agents were primarily English personnel, or monitors trained by the English, and all using English text books, the education imparted was intrinsically English. While the ministers of the church assisted this process, we must not lose sight of the fact that they were also pursuing denominational interests. Membership in the schools was never quite detached from membership in the particular church.

One of the problems which adversely affected the proper functioning of the schools was the lack of persons suitably qualified to conduct them. [36] The provision of qualified teachers was recognised as a primary requirement by the British Government, but England could not supply the deficiency which there was in the West Indies. [37] As early as 1835 the weakness had been observed by Rev. John Sterling in his report to the British Government. The weakness was apparently attributable to two causes: one was that the teachers had been selected locally, and had not been sent out from England; the other was that the clergy and missionaries were easily satisfied with the personnel available to them. [38] As Olwyn Blouet has noted, schools were built before teachers were trained to staff them. [39] In the rush to have the schools in operation and to advance the cause of particular denominations, it was inevitable that poorly qualified persons would be selected. For example, the replies to Coleridge's queries in 1835 suggest that the teachers were good church members rather than persons with pedagogical skills. [40] The problem of the Moravians in this regard have been briefly portrayed by Kingsley Lewis, and were similar to those of the Established Church. In summary their difficulties lay

> in having teachers whose interests lay elsewhere; in having teachers of the desired religious and moral deportment, but with little knowledge of teaching; in having teachers who though perhaps qualified in other respects did not share the missionaries' views on other important matters; and in having teachers whose personal lives were not beyond reproach. [41]

The same general malaise affected Methodist work in Barbados in the field of education. More often than not, the person selected was pious rather than competent, and his selection was made with an eye to his usefulness in missionary work rather than in teaching. For example, the first teacher recommended for appointment in Barbados was Edward Grogan, who had to close his own school because he could not get enough students through whose fees to obtain a salary. He was described as converted, and as having a good prospect of becoming an Assistant Missionary;[42] but nothing was mentioned about his skill as a teacher. Grogan was actually recommended to the Demerara District Meeting of 1836 for appointment as an Assistant Missionary; but the Meeting not only rejected him as incompetent, it expressed regret that his pretensions had been encouraged. However, Grogan continued at the school for a few years longer until his death in 1840, when the school on Nelson Street had to be closed. [43]

Better material was found for some of the other schools. For example, Francis Church, a zealous and apparently competent master, served at the Speightstown Methodist School for a number of years. Under his management, this school made good progress, reaching its maximum enrolment in 1840, and being regarded by some as the most efficient in the Barbados Circuit. The records do not reflect whether he had any training, but they do show his school maintaining its numbers even in the face of competition from the Established Church. The Methodists also found a zealous and able master in Stretton Maddison, who served as head of the school at Scotland in St. Andrew from 1840 to 1847. Some difficulty was experienced at Byde Mill, where a former apprentice was once head of the school. He was reported as a zealous teacher and preacher, who almost joined the ranks of those emigrating to Demerara.[44] Why he did not continue in office is not stated in existing records, but it may well have been due to inadequate remuneration. His place was filled by Miss Jane Waldron, who was said to be giving great satisfaction.[45] For some years she remained the only female teacher in any of the Methodist schools; perhaps the only female teacher in any school. Not all the teachers were persons recruited in the various islands. The missionary societies were able to recruit in England persons who came out as missionaries, thus reinforcing the connection between religion and education. The teachers were assisted by a number of pupil teachers or monitors, the drafting of whom into the system was intended to serve the cause of economy.[46] These youthful persons were not equipped to teach, but rather to pass on what little they had learnt to junior students.

The existence of the three groups helped to establish a hierarchy within the ranks of the teachers. Quite a large number of the teachers were white – European and local – and some were coloured. The European teachers were apparently more highly esteemed than the "native" teachers. Not only were they considered better educated, they were also regarded as better suited to perform the role of acculturating the ex-slaves in European patterns of behavior. In 1837 in Jamaica 40% of salaried teachers were non-white, in Barbados the proportion was 30%.[47]

It is difficult to say how many coloured teachers the Methodists had at this time. Only one of them – a young woman at the Byde Mill School, St. George – has been so designated in the records. It is possible that another teacher – James Brewster at the James Street School in Bridgetown – was also coloured. Two of the prominent teachers – Francis Church and Stretton Maddison – might have been Englishmen. The disparity in remuneration between them and the other teachers lends support to the view that European teachers were more highly regarded than the others. For example, Francis Church and Stretton Maddison were consistently paid at the rate of £ 100 per year, while Jane Waldron – a coloured woman – and Joseph Brewster were paid £ 30 in 1842. In the following year Brewster, Waldron and another teacher were paid only what they collected by way of fees. In 1846 the successor of Francis Church at Speightstown was paid £ 54. 3. 4. The other teachers were paid a variety of rates, no doubt based on the fees they had collected. The change of rates at Speightstown would suggest that the incumbent was no longer an Englishman. Similar disparities were evident in British Guiana where, of three teachers in 1842 and 1843, two were paid £ 150 a year and the third £ 87. 10. No reason has been given for the differentiation. It is more than likely, however, that the causes are the same as in Jamaica and Barbados.

The factor which had the greatest effect on the delivery of education was cost. Unlike the Established Church, the Methodists and the Moravians lacked the resources to pay their teachers adequately. In all three denominations parents were asked to pay fees, but for the most part the poverty of their conditions militated against their ability to pay. In the early years this lack of adequate remuneration was the main cause of depletion in the teaching service. Those who were able to do so quickly left to pursue other careers. [48]

Lacking financial support from the legislature and the vestries, the Methodists in Barbados were left to depend on the fees paid by parents. The amount charged by each school seems to have been left to the person who administered the school. Records of the fees collected exist only for the year 1843, and even then only for two schools. These show that the school at Scotland collected fees of £ 61.16.3, while at Speightstown the fees collected amounted to £ 41.5.8 1/2. [49] Since the salaries for teachers at these schools amounted to £ 100 each, the teachers were being subsidized at the rate of some £ 40 and £ 60 respectively. This reinforces the view that they were considered highly valuable and that they were probably Englishmen; for other teachers received only what the fees provided.

The collection of fees had not been devoid of a measure of difficulties. The Moravians experienced this problem early, but obviated it with a variety of concessions which eased the burden of the parents. In the case of the Established Church, there were several cases in 1837 of inability to pay. This was especially so in Speightstown where Latrobe reported only about 20 children capable of paying the fees of 3 1/2d. per week. Only in the case of St. Matthias was anyone successfully collecting the fees. [50] Very early in this period Methodist reports show that some parents were finding the exaction beyond their means. This was the case in the northern town of Speightstown. Writing in 1837, the missionary, Phelp, complained of the unwillingness of parents to contribute to their children's education. He also stated that the fee system had failed the Established Church. [51] In another letter some fourteen months afterwards, the same missionary alleged that the people of Speightstown were not interested in the education of their children. In support of this contention, he cited his having called a meeting of parents to discuss the plight of the school. Only a third of them attended, the others absenting themselves on the grounds of illness. By his own account his meeting served no practical purpose. Few of those present offered any objection to his proposal of weekly subscriptions; but none of those who agreed to his proposal paid. [52]

Phelp's report is somewhat exaggerated, and betrays a lack of understanding of, or sympathy for, the people of the Speightstown area. At that time, Speightstown might have been described as a depressed area. There was much poverty and unemployment as well as a fairly high degree of petty crimes. [53] The people, therefore, were in no position to pay the fees demanded of them. A fairer conclusion would have been that, whatever their interest, they lacked the means to keep their children in school. The same missionary, writing some years previously in Providence, had expressed strong opinions about schools. Country schools were a headache with which he persevered because he deemed the education of slave children important. [54] In another letter he stated, with respect to the former slaves, that British notions about their aptitude had been mistaken. Phelp is therefore not a good guide to the attitudes of the freed population towards education.

There are other good reasons for questioning Phelp's assessment of the issue of fees. One of them can be found in the Latrobe Report which was contemporaneous with Phelp's letter. Reporting on the Moravian school at Sharon, Latrobe noted that the fees there were above average and yet were usually paid. The missionary, he continued, used his discretion to exempt orphans, children of "really poor" people, and the second or third children of the same family from the whole or part of the fees. [55] In other words, the missionary provided a measure of relief for those who would have found the fees burdensome. This incentive had not been provided by the Methodists.

Another reason for challenging Phelp's opinion comes from a later Methodist Report. Writing in 1843 the superintendent, Fidler, noted that, in addition to paying the fees, pupils had to furnish themselves with pencils, pens, ink and paper. This report noted significantly that some pupils had gone to places where these had been provided. [56] What Fidler recorded about Scotland does not appear to have been new, nor had it been confined to Scotland. A third reason probably lay in the administrative arrangement for the island. Campbell noted that the General Superintendent of the Methodist Church in Jamaica insisted on the payment of fees as a condition for keeping schools open.[57] There was no similar policy in Barbados, and hence schools which were unable to maintain themselves remained open. On the other hand, the Moravians at Sharon seemed to have experienced no difficulty in collecting their fees for 1837. Their facility in doing so was in no way affected by the fact that their fees were higher than average.

Early in the year 1841, the missionary societies operating in the West Indies were advised of the British government's intention of reducing, and finally terminating, the Negro Education Grant. The basis for this course of action was the conviction of the Colonial Office that the West Indian legislatures had a responsibility to provide education for the entire population, and the perception that the labourers could pay for their children's education.[58] Placing the responsibility for education on the legislature was a novel idea since, even in England, education was regarded more as the work of benevolent organizations than of the state.[59] In the West Indies it was not the policy of legislatures to provide for popular education, though provision was sometimes made for particular schools or for one denomination. The vestries involved themselves in education to the extent of funding parochial schools; but these, linked to the Established Church, did not provide general public education.

The new policy of the Colonial Office raises certain questions: first, did the local legislators see the need to do so? Having unwillingly acquiesced in the abolition of slavery, they were not likely to be more willing participants in the education of persons whom they considered destined only for agricultural labour. They had been firm opponents of the education of the slaves; and their recalcitrance with respect to the amelioration programme was such as to discourage any hope of greater enthusiasm.

The second question concerns the question of providing the education. The termination of the Negro Education Grant came at the very time when the British free trade policy threatened West Indian sugar with loss of revenue. Many of the Barbadian planters saw ruin in the *Sugar Duties Act* of 1846, which equalised the duties on all sugars entering Britain. This did not make them amenable to taking on additional responsibilities for the newly emancipated. Thirdly, the Secretary of State urged that the labourers be encouraged to show gratitude for their freedom by making sacrifices for their own and their children's education. [60] But given the small wages of the labourers, and the demands on their earnings, such sacrifices were virtually impossible. The difficulty was that sugar was labour intensive only during the harvest season, so that regular employment was limited and the chances of affording all they needed slim.

The immediate effect of the change of policy was retrenchment. The S.P.G. communicated to the two Bishops its intention of reducing its contribution to the same extent that the Parliamentary Grant was being reduced. In Jamaica the Assembly and the vestries reduced their grants to the Established Church, thus giving rise to some retrenchment in that body's operations. The curtailment of funds in Jamaica was not of long duration because by 1844 the Assembly had initiated funding for all schools.[61] Ironically, it was the Mico Charity which was hardest hit. The Charity had received large grants from the Parliamentary Fund, exceeding fifty per cent between 1838 and 1841. Nearly all their schools were closed, some being taken over by the Established Church, others passing to other denominations. [62] In particular, this group ceased active work in Barbados; thereafter it was the Established Church, the Moravians and the Methodists who carried on schools in the island. Neither of the missionary groups had the resources of the Established Church, and it is to their credit that they continued to maintain schools and to build more.

Introducing Popular Education

In the year following the cessation of the Negro Education Grant, the Barbados legislature made a small provision of £ 750 per year towards general education, paying £ 375 for the half year following the passage of the Act in question. [63] Thereafter funds were provided annually at this level until 1850. Concurrently with this small allocation, the legislature also granted £ 512.16.4 to the two Central Schools in Bridgetown. This latter allocation continued for several years until it was formally terminated in 1876. [64] Vestry grants were also made towards the stipends and allowances of teachers, for the provision of furniture and equipment, or for general repairs. In a few parishes, notably in the parish of St. Michael, education and poor relief were returned jointly in the Blue Books. This renders it difficult to determine how much was actually allocated to education in such cases. Not all the parishes made provision for education on a regular basis; the parish of Christ Church was notorious for doing so only twice in some eighteen years. [65]

The *Education Act* of 1846 had made provision for the payment of teachers; but it had not made the level of provision which would have enabled the dissenting churches to benefit from it. The Methodists complained about their inability to respond to the needs of the island in that very year. [66] They themselves had been making valiant efforts to maintain their various schools. In 1846, for example, they managed some six schools with an aggregate of 415 pupils, while in 1848 they were managing eight schools with a decrease to 322 pupils. [67] In 1846 the Anglicans were managing some 59 schools, and their school population at the end of 1845 was 3,383. In 1844 the Moravians had four schools with 359 pupils.

The 1850's mark a turning point in Barbadian education as it was from this period that general education really began. Two acts passed the legislature, one in 1850 and the other in 1858. The *Education Act* of 1850 aimed at making provision for a "more extensive and general education of the people." In order to achieve this, the Act provided for the appointment of an Education Committee whose major responsibility was to promote education by making grants to recognised institutions. The Committee was to be assisted by an Inspector of Schools, whom it was authorised to appoint. This officer was to advise the Committee on the award of grants; but the Committee itself was free to visit schools, and was not completely dependent on the Inspector.

A second Act was passed in December 1858 to amend the Act of 1850. The new act was the outcome of a report of a joint committee of both houses of the legislature. Among other things, that Report drew attention to the need for greater provision for moral and religious instruction, as well as provision for the training of both male and female teachers. The Report was to a large extent inspired by the Principal of Codrington College, Richard Rawle, and showed a restricted outlook as regards the utility of the education process. The Committee was of the view that "For the State to educate a man beyond his station is not only unnecessary, but prejudicial..." The Committee determined that the subjects of instruction were to be reading, writing, arithmetic, grammar and geography. The bulk of the children, they declared, had neither the time nor the means for anything else. The Committee therefore had in view a kind of education which would prepare the rising generation for their "unavoidable duties." [68] A similar attitude was abroad in other parts of the West Indies. For example, in Trinidad a planter expressed the view that to educate the labouring population was to risk labour shortage on the estates. And in Jamaica a Stipendiary Magistrate suggested that education in the island had the effect of incapacitating the ex-slaves "for any employment save that which is above him", that is, for manual labour. [69]

Even though members of the legislature felt that the labouring population were destined for the estates, there was no serious attempt in that body to discuss "industrial education". Jamaica had for years sought to promote this kind of education in order to ensure a constant supply of labour. The Jamaican legislature had gone so far as to offer monetary awards to institutions which provided training in agriculture or other industrial skills. [70] Compulsory industrial education had in fact been recommended by the Stipendiary Magistrates and some planters, but their effort had not been successful with the British Government. [71] In Barbados not much attention seems to have been given to it because the legislators knew that the labourers had no alternative to the estates and the limited avenues for trade.

The *Education Act* of 1858 provided for a full-time Inspector of Schools, who was to visit all grant-aided schools and to report semi-annually to the Governor, as well as to the Bishop in the case of schools of the Established Church. The fourth section of the Act provided for the supervision of every school by a Committee comprising the Minister concerned, " and two laymen to be appointed annually by the Education Committee on the recommendation of the respective ministers..." This Committee was to be chaired by the minister concerned. The Act authorised the appointment of pupil-teachers. It also required the Education Committee to provide instruction for teachers, and to hold annual examinations for teachers and pupil-teachers. These were all to be certified, classified, and remunerated according to their performances. [72] The subjects of instruction at the schools were to be reading, writing, arithmetic, geography, history and music, in addition to religious instruction.

The very fact that the Inspector was required to report to the Bishop on schools of the Established Church, and was not required to report to the superintendents of the other churches, implies some discrimination on the part of the legislators. But neither the Moravians nor the Methodists seem to have made an issue of it. The Moravians are said to have opposed the public examination of teachers, and also to have found the rules of the Committee inconsistent with the 1858 Act. But there is no support for that in the minutes of the Education Committee or in the press, or for Kingsley Lewis' assertion that the Rev. James Edghill forced the suspension of the Education Committee's rules. [73]

Barbados at the time was not faced with a large Roman Catholic population, nor with a multi-religious situation such as Trinidad had then. But with rival dissenting and established churches, and with strong local prejudices, it had its own share of serious problems. Even so it did not approximate the situation which developed in the Bahamas, in which the Established Church sought to impose its perspectives on the rest of the population. In those islands the National School system followed by the Church of England was imposed as against the British and Foreign School Society system which the Dissenters favoured. All schools were required to use the liturgy and catechism of the Established Church, the catechism being required to be taught daily. Teachers were also to attend a weekly service at Christ Church, Nassau. Among the opponents of the Dissenters was the Rev. J.M. Trew, one of the C.M.S. missionaries and a leader of the Mico institution in Jamaica, who would have encountered Bishop Lipscombe's hostility to the organisations he represented. The atmosphere in the Bahamas seems to have been more hostile than in Barbados. Denominational hostility was so great in those islands that the Board of Public Instruction, in which the churches were represented, was dissolved in 1847. [74]

The Education Committee established under the Act of 1850 consisted of the President and two members of the Council, the Speaker and three members of the House of Assembly. The Committee, which was chaired by President

John S. Gaskin, included Francis Goding, Grant E. Thomas, Nathaniel Fodering-ham, Nathaniel Forte, Speaker John Thomas, and Attorney General John Sealy. Effectively a Committee of the legislature, the Education Committee could be expected to reflect the thinking of the Houses from which the membership was drawn. In Trinidad in 1851 a similar Board was appointed with the Governor as President and containing members of the Legislative Council. In that island, the intention was to set up a purely secular system of education, [75] whereas in Bar-bados the concern still was to have a basically moral and religious form of edu-cation. It must have been for purposes of control that the system was adopted of having the Board or Committee of Education composed of legislators.

When the Barbados Education Committee held its first meeting on November 18, 1850, the members appointed as Inspector of Schools Robert P. Elliot, the master of the Boys' Central School. The Committee noted that the appointment needed the approval of the Governor and of the Bishop of Barba-dos. [76] Since the Central Schools were managed by a Committee appointed by the Established Church, it is more than likely that Elliot was a member of that body. His headship of the Boys' school would suggest that he was highly regarded by the authorities of that church. His appointment as Inspector was not likely to encounter objection from the Established Church. The post of In-spector was fraught with difficulties, since it suggested someone who could be viewed as interfering. Elliot served as Inspector until 1883, when this study ends, and his relationship with the Methodists was not very good. That and his obvi-ous connection with the Established Church created a very fertile atmosphere for conflict.

In its early meetings the Education Committee concentrated on fram-ing rules for granting financial aid to schools. Because so much of what follows hinged on those rules, a summary of them is given at this point. Those who ap-plied for aid on behalf of their schools were required to state the location and denominational affiliation of the school, the daily average attendance, the rev-enue received by the master and its source. Each school was to keep a register showing the daily attendance. When an application was received the duty of the Inspector was to visit the school and verify the information given in the applica-tion. As soon as the Committee was satisfied as to the merits of the claims, a grant was made to the school. Where an application was made for grants for fit-tings, the school was required to pay to the Committee whatever money was raised, and the Committee undertook to pay the tradesmen and other workers.

Two-thirds of any grant made for this purpose was to be applied to furniture, blackboards, and other such items, while one-third was to be applied to the purchase of books. In every case, however, the Committee's grant was a matching grant, and was not to exceed £ 10. [77]

Where schools administered by the Established Church and the Moravians were concerned, no problems arose over recognition. However, the Education Committee raised questions about two Methodist schools, both in the parish of St. Philip. One of these was the Beulah Methodist School, concerning which the Committee wanted to be informed as to whether the master, Renn Shepherd, was a minister and whether the school was truly Methodist. The other was the Shrewsbury School, where the same queries were raised about the master called Kirton. [78] It is quite possible that these were innocent questions arising from a lack of information in the applications. It was the custom among the Methodists to employ as "local preachers" the same persons who served as teachers. So that it is quite possible that the duality of functions created uncertainty for the Committee. However, as we shall see later, a series of conflicts took place between the Inspector and Methodist teachers, and these would suggest that this officer was not altogether unbiased where they were concerned.

One of the planks of the system was the requirement that each school should maintain an average of fifty students before it could receive a grant for any quarter. This policy was rigidly adhered to until 1878. Each of the three denominations concerned in education managed schools which from time to time did not attain the required daily average. In the case of the Methodists, there were often schools with thirty or forty students on roll. In 1854 the enrolment of five of the eleven Methodist schools fell below the average attendance demanded; four out of ten, and four out of eleven did so in 1856 and 1857 respectively. In 1862 and 1863 the proportions were four out of fourteen and four out of seventeen respectively, while in 1869 and 1870 they were four out of fourteen and five out of seventeen respectively. In other years there were variations on the pattern. Only in 1871, 1874 and 1875 did the records show attendances uniformly above the average. Therefore, a portion of the schools were at various times ineligible for grants. [79]

The returns submitted each quarter by any school were to demonstrate that the school in question had maintained the daily average, and were also to disclose the revenue received by the master. These reports were scrutinised by a Sub-Committee of the Education Committee, which determined whether or not the grant was to be paid, or whether further information was necessary. Where there was any doubt, the Sub-Committee was guided by the Inspector of Schools. It was usually a report by him to the effect that the figures for attendance had been inflated or were inaccurate which led to the withholding of grants. At no time do the records show the Committee making independent visits to schools as provided by the Act of 1850. Instead they relied exclusively on his informa-tion to guide them.

There was no voluntarist attitude in Barbados such as the Independents, some Presbyterians and others displayed in Jamaica. In that island the Baptists in particular strenuously fought against the Established Church to the jeopardy of their own cause. [80] The Methodists in Barbados took an opposite view to the Jamaican Baptists, insisting on their right to share the public purse. The three denominations administering schools in the island all participated in the process, and as a rule routinely received grants from the Education Committee.

The pattern which evolved was fairly uniform for all denominations. There was a small number of schools which met the requirements in the first few years, but this number grew in the 1860s and reached its zenith about 1867 or 1868. For example, between 1851 and 1857 the average number of Methodist schools which received grants was four or five; that number increased to eight or nine between 1858 and 1860; it further increased to between ten and twelve from 1861 to 1867; and finally it remained constant at thirteen or fourteen from 1868 to 1875. In the case of the Moravians, the average from 1851 to 1855 was four, jumped to eleven in 1856, rose further to thirteen or fourteen from 1857 to 1866, and steadied at fifteen or sixteen from 1867 to 1875. The Estab-lished Church had an average of 51 in 1851 and 1852; but the number of schools receiving grants fell to 38 in 1854 and rose slightly to 46 in 1857. Subsequently the number rose to 62 in 1858 and 96 in 1865, increasing further to 107 in 1866 and 120 in 1875. [81]

All the denominations had a high proportion of their schools qualify as the process developed. However, applications for grants were sometimes re-jected by the Education Committee. The number of schools of the Established Church whose returns were questioned were few in number. One notes, for example, St. Mary's Boys' School in 1853, which was refused a grant, and the St. Joseph School in 1854. In this latter case the Committee warned the rector that fraud had been suspected, but no action was taken against the school. [82] There were no complaints against Moravian schools.

The bulk of the complaints involved Methodist schools. In 1852 the Methodists applied for grants for four schools, only to be awarded a grant for one school. [83] No explanation of this action has been provided in the Committee's minutes. In 1853 a grant was refused to the Speightstown Methodist School, while in 1866 and 1871 James Street and Dalkeith Methodist schools were also refused grants. In the case of the James Street School in 1866, the master admitted having altered the register to record as present latecomers who had arrived shortly after the roll had been taken. [84] In the case of Dalkeith in 1871, the discrepancy was not disputable, and the master lost a day's pay. In one unusual case in 1856, the master of Shrewsbury School had allowed a student to make the entries, which he signed without checking. On that occasion, the Board allowed the grant.

Some of the cases before the Committee create an impression of prejudice against individuals or against the Methodists. For example, a grant was refused to the Shrewsbury School in 1863 on the ground of inflated returns. In refuting the allegations, the Superintendent, the Rev. Henry Bleby, alleged "certain evil surmisings on the part of the Inspector, without one solitary proof of actual wrong doing", and the subjection of the master to a "dishonourable system of espionage." Letters of protest from himself and the schoolmaster, Mr. Roy, failed to achieve a review of the decision. The Committee emphasised that the Inspector's visits to the school had been made "by the express orders of this board", and assured the minister that the Inspector had only been motivated "by a just and honourable zeal for the Public Service." [85] Bleby, who previously had complained about the conduct of the Inspector, [86] now saw his action as spiteful harassment. But the Committee dismissed his complaints.

On two other occasions, in 1857 and 1864, the Committee ruled against allegations of fraud with respect to Methodist schools. These were made in respect of the Shrewsbury and Belmont Methodist schools. The Inspector's allegation with respect to Shrewsbury was that its numbers during the rainy season were inflated. His basis for that allegation was that the Holy Trinity Anglican School about a mile away showed smaller numbers during the same period. The Committee accepted the explanation of the Superintendent, Bleby, that the Shrewsbury students lived sufficiently close to the school not to be overly affected by the rain. They also accepted his explanation that the minister who visited and recorded attendances had neither been regular nor diligent. In any case he argued that the difference in numbers was not so great as to indicate an intention to commit fraud. [87]

The other case concerned the deprivation of the master at Belmont of his grants for approximately nine months. This case raises serious questions about the methods employed by the Inspector. This officer had alleged gross and consistent inflation of numbers at Belmont, to the extent that the school regularly showed attendances of eighty and over. The Inspector seems to have built his case on the evidence of the master's deputy, who had assured him that the numbers never exceeded seventy. What is surprising is that the Inspector had been aware of the estrangement of the deputy from the master. Yet he did not see fit to question the former's accuracy. The Committee, on the other hand, was obviously impressed by the emphatic support of the minister, Henry Padgham, because Belmont continued to be listed among the schools receiving a grant in 1864. These cases would tend to support the contention that the Inspector often demonstrated "jealousy and dislike of Wesleyan Schools."[88] This charge could not be laid at the door of the Committee, but it would be hard to acquit the Inspector of it.

Quite apart from the capitation grants dealt with above, there were grants for furniture and fittings for the schools. The Committee's rules had made it clear that no grants were to be made for construction or repairs, and that only matching grants would be made for furniture and fittings. It was a point which some ministers missed during the early stages, and the Methodist ministers fairly regularly. As a result applications were made which were not strictly in keeping with the Committee's guidelines. For example, the Committee received an application from the Moravians for a grant for a new school. They had no choice but to reject it. In October 1857 the Committee referred Henry Hurd to their rules concerning grants for fittings, and advised him to raise a sum which the Committee was prepared to match. [89] In May 1858 the Committee turned down an application for the Paynes Bay chapel-school in St. James on the ground that the building was a chapel and not a school. [90] In February 1858 the Committee rejected Bleby's application for a grant for fittings though he was later successful when he had demonstrated that he had raised something towards the cost. [91] This was precisely where the Methodists had their greatest difficulty; so many of their members were so poor that they were unable to raise the funds for their work.

This point can be illustrated by reference to the Ebenezer Circuit in the parish of St. Philip. Early in 1858, the Superintendent, Rev. Henry Bleby, informed Methodist General Secretary Hoole of the need for five schools in his

Circuit. Between his arrival in 1857 and December 1858, he had built three schools and started two others. His expenses in this enterprise had exceeded £ 1000, but he had no prospects of assistance from the legislature. [92] By the time Bleby had left Barbados at the end of 1863, a great deal of debt on the schools still remained unpaid and he had no way of raising the funds for them in a poor agricultural parish. With this kind of debt it is not surprising that Bleby sought help wherever he could, and especially from the Education Committee, but he was not acting strictly within the rules.

There was more involved than occasional slips on the part of the applicants; there was also deep-rooted suspicion of the Methodists, which only emerged occasionally. On one occasion Henry Bleby applied for grants to provide fittings for three schools: Beulah and Rices in St. Philip, and Providence in Christ Church. The Inspector was required to visit all of them and to inform the Committee whether the money was needed to complete fittings, or whether it was needed "to re-imburse the Wesleyan fund from which it had been borrowed." [93] On another occasion, Henry Hurd had applied for a grant to offset the "Considerable expense" of furnishing a new school at Bethel. On this occasion the Committee requested the Inspector to visit and determine whether the grant would be used to defray the expenses of fittings. [94] The fact that grants were made to all except the Beulah school serves to indicate that the Committee were satisfied about the use of the money. Beulah was only refused because the Committee had recently awarded it a grant for fittings.

The nature of the investigations which the Inspector was asked to undertake reeks with suspicion. As far as one can determine, there was no similar expression of distrust towards any other denomination. However, the suspicions of the Committee were not unreasonable given the past record of the Methodists, for they did not always help their cause. Not only did they fail to follow procedures established by the Committee, but sometimes they demonstrated little efficiency in their operations. Several applications were either too vague or so lacking in information as not to be much help to the Committee. The ministers were forced to submit further material. A significant part of the difficulty was that neither of the ministers had kept separate accounts for fittings when he built the school for which he applied in 1861. [95]

An important aspect of the *Education Act* of 1858 was the provision for the certification of teachers. Towards that end an annual examination of teachers was instituted, and a panel of examiners was appointed to conduct these examinations. The first panel was appointed towards the end of 1859 with the following members : the Revs. Richard Rawle, W.W. Jackson, H.P.C. Melville, and H. Buchner. [96] The latter, a Moravian, declined to serve; unfortunately the minutes do not record his reasons for so doing. There is no record of another Moravian being invited to serve until 1869, and on that occasion the Rev. J.Y. Edghill also declined. [97]

On two occasions Methodist ministers were asked to serve as examiners. One of these was in January 1861, when the Rev. Henry Hurd was asked to serve with the Rev. Henry Bleby as alternate. The other examiners were the Revs. Richard Rawle and P. B. Austin, and the Secretary of the Education Committee, James T. Rogers. [98] The minutes of February 12, 1861, record Bleby's withdrawal, which would suggest that Hurd had previously withdrawn. Again there is no explanation for this. On the second occasion, in 1869, Hurd was nominated to replace Edghill who had declined, but he probably also declined.[99] The Moravians were reluctant to serve on secular bodies, and might have interpreted their responsibility to the Education Committee as a departure from their sacred duties. They certainly never expressed any criticism of other religious groups in the way the Methodists habitually did. The Methodists for their part were suspicious of the bigotry they perceived in the representatives of the Established Church. This withdrawal left the field to the Established Church, which not only provided the examiners but the instructors as well. Both groups therefore denied themselves any opportunity of influencing developments in either of these areas.

Another part of the process of certification was the provision of courses for teachers during the long vacation in the middle of the year. Courses for teachers had been started as early as the late 1840's by the Rev. Richard Rawle, Principal of Codrington College. These had been intended to raise the standard of teaching and school management, both of which Rawle considered to be poor.[100] Not much had been done in this area, however, and schools belonging to the dissenting bodies did not benefit from such instructions as he gave. The Methodists in particular were not likely to participate in the programmes he conducted.

The instruction required under the 1858 Act was open to all teachers. The Methodists at first welcomed it as an opportunity to raise the "intellectual standard" at the public schools. One of their Circuit Reports drew attention to the rule that only persons recommended by their ministers were eligible to par-

ticipate in the programmes. It was regarded as providing a guarantee of the moral qualifications of the teachers, but on what basis this assertion was made is
not clear. The other Circuit Report for 1859 praised the teachers in that they
were "of the right stamp, earnest and devoted, and exercised a beneficial influence on our societies and congregations". This Report then observed that several teachers had been attending the government lectures, and that good effects
were expected of the programmes.[101]

It would seem then that the Methodists as a body did not oppose the
programme, and that they were prepared to cooperate with it. No Moravian or
Methodist minister was appointed to the panel of instructors and, judged by their
responses to the examinations, they were not likely to participate. The system
seems to have worked fairly well, and no dissatisfaction was recorded until 1862.
In October of that year Bleby declared to the Education Committee a virtual
boycott of all the courses for that year, with only one of the teachers from his
Circuit attending, and only for one day. He gave as a reason the strong dissatisfaction they all felt about some of the instructors. "Neither I nor they," he wrote,
" could have confidence in men whose hostility to everything Wesleyan is so well
known." They were not confident, he revealed, that the process of instruction or
of examination was likely to be conducted in an impartial manner. At the same
time he sought to allay any fears that he might have been interested in having a
Methodist minister as examiner. On the contrary, he preferred laymen, believing that they were more likely to be disinterested parties than the ministers who
superintended the schools. It was equally true that Bleby had no confidence in
the Inspector of Schools or in the examination process.[102]

That the Education Committee instructed the Secretary to ignore the
letter is a gross injustice to the author; but by then he was regarded as a tiresome
person, because of his agitation for public funding of the Methodist Church. The
issues which he raised were such as to demand very careful consideration by an
impartial body and that is what the Committee never quite succeeded in being.

Given the problems they had encountered so far with the Inspector, and
in other respects with the clergy of the Established Church, the composition of
the panel was not such as to inspire Methodist confidence. For example, the panel
of 1861 consisted of the Inspector, together with the Revs. T. W. Greenidge
and G. M. D. Frederick, both of whom belonged to the Established Church. In
1862 the panel consisted of the Inspector, and the Revs. E. G. Sinckler, G. M. D.
Frederick, John Drayton, E. Lisle Smith, C. J. Branch, and W. Alleyne All-

der.[103] Wider denominational participation, or lay involvement, could have been of benefit under the circumstances. Regrettably, the Methodist proposal to have lay persons conduct the instructions fell on deaf ears.

Although the teachers in Bleby's Circuit boycotted the courses provided by the Education Committee, several teachers of the other Circuit availed themselves of the courses. This would suggest that the real problem came from one source only – Henry Bleby – and not from the Methodists as a whole. Available evidence shows that very few teachers – those who were in charge of the schools – qualified themselves. For example, only 18 teachers in the entire island received certificates in the year 1859. There is no breakdown of the denominations to which they belonged, but the report on individual schools shows only one trained Methodist teacher – at Bethel. There was no trained Moravian teacher, though some of their schools were well conducted. All the others were Anglican. In the report for the period ending in mid-1861, there were 25 Anglicans, 4 Moravians and 1 Methodist in the 30 certified teachers.[104] By 1866 the number of certified teachers had risen by 20% to 36, of which 32 were Anglicans, and two each were Moravians and Methodists. At that time the Anglicans had 52 primary schools, the Moravians 8, and the Methodists 15.[105]

There was usually a correlation between the qualification of the teachers and the quality of the school. Only in very rare cases did the Inspector mention schools which were well conducted even though the master was untrained. For example, he was very commendatory in 1859 of the St. John's Boys', Girls', Infants' Schools, as well as the Mt. Tabor, Sharon, and Montgomery Moravian Schools, and of the Ebenezer Methodist School.[106] Very frequently, his remarks on the teachers and their schools tended to be unflattering. Perhaps his worst comment was made in respect of a Methodist teacher, whom he described as " noisy, negligent, and illiterate."[107]

Quite apart from providing basic education for the students, the primary schools were expected to function as Normal Schools, providing opportunities for training pupil teachers. In response to the 1858 Act, the Education Committee requested of the Inspector an evaluation of the primary schools with a view to determining which were suitable for training the pupil teachers. In his report to the Committee, the Inspector distinguished two broad categories of schools: those which were "Eligible" and those which were "Promising", with each category sub-divided. In the category of "Eligible Schools" were those whose teachers were capable of managing the large numbers and ensuring the proper training of the pupil-teachers. Six schools were listed as meeting these criteria, and all were Anglican. A second type of "Eligible Schools" comprised those with capable teachers as above, and those which had the advantage of assistance from the minister concerned. Of the six schools listed, two were Moravian and the others Anglican. No Methodist school qualified as "eligible" for the purpose of training pupil-teachers. [108]

In the category of "promising schools," the Inspector identified three types. The first type consisted of those schools "Where the numbers are good, and the attainments of the teachers beyond the average, but not equal... to the foregoing," that is, the "Eligible" ones. In this type of school, Ebenezer and Bethel Methodist Schools were among the eight which qualified. The second type consisted of smaller schools in which the pupil-teachers were expected to derive real benefit. All seven schools listed were Anglican. The third type consisted of schools which enjoyed a reasonable reputation, but where adequate training could not be provided without outside help. Only four schools were distinguished, two of them Anglican and the others Moravian.[109]

The Inspector's Report indicates that, notwithstanding the large number of schools in the island, only a few of them had attained a standard which made them acceptable as schools of training or as holding out a promise of being acceptable. Between 1861 and 1877 some 31 Methodist pupil teachers took part in the annual examinations, though only 13 of them were successful. The number of Moravian teachers who participated was 62, of whom 49 were successful. In the case of the Anglican Church some 469 pupil-teachers participated in the examinations, with 287 successful. [110] With a pass rate of 79 per cent, the Moravians were performing better than either the Anglicans at 61.2 per cent, or the Methodists at 42 per cent. The Methodist schools would eventually perform very well towards the early 1880's, and in some cases out-perform the others.

The Methodist missionaries nevertheless made efforts to ensure that their schools had well prepared teachers, or that they were sent for training. In so doing, they were also distancing themselves from the local training programme. Some of their teachers had an opportunity to receive training at the Mico Institute in Antigua. As early as 1853, the Methodists had recruited one such teacher for their school at Selah in St. Lucy. [111] Another was appointed to their Speightstown school in 1855, while the teacher at Hope in St. Lucy was earmarked for the Institute in Antigua in the same year. [112] In 1856 and 1857 three such teachers were to be found at Speightstown in St. Peter, Ebenezer in

St. Philip, and at Bethel in Bridgetown. [113] In 1859 a partially trained Mico teacher was recruited for Belmont in St. Michael, and a fully trained Mico teacher for Shrewsbury in St. Philip. In 1867 the teacher at Supers in St. Philip was sent to the Mico Institute in Antigua. [114] The gaps in our records do not allow us to follow their careers; but the frequency with which the Methodists were forced to appoint teachers would suggest that they seldom remained in the service. There was considerable mobility on the part of the teachers; and in the case of the Methodists, only John O'Neal at Bethel and William Roy at Shrewsbury stayed for a long period.

Under the *Education Acts* of 1850 and 1858, grants paid to schools were either to provide fittings and furniture for those schools, or were in recognition of a certain level of attendance. As provided by the Act of 1858 a small sum was also paid to those teachers who had been awarded certificates. This system was not satisfactory to the Inspector who, in his Report for the year 1862, lamented the fact that grants were not dependent on the efficiency of the teaching. A further call was made by the clergy of the Established Church in 1864. Recommending that the average attendance of 50 students be de-emphasised when considering remuneration, they asked that pride of place be given to the efficiency of the school. Their proposal called for a combination of the average attendance and the result of an annual examination. [115]

The result of these representations was the introduction in 1866 of the system of payment by results. The same system was adopted in other islands such as Jamaica in 1867 and in a modified form in Trinidad some time in 1869. [116] According to new rules approved at the end of 1865, monetary grants were in future to be made for every child obtaining a pass in each of three grades of an annual examination. In addition, there was a grant for each pass in Religious Knowledge, and for every pass in each of the "higher" subjects. These "higher" subjects were listed as Grammar, Geography, History, Vocal Music, and Higher Arithmetic. This grant was dependent on a premium examination which was to be held annually, and the premiums were to be added to the quarterly grant given each school. The premiums were £ 10, £ 5, and £ 2 respectively for a pass at first, second or third class. [117]

Because of the irregularity of the reports, it is very difficult to get a clear picture of the performance of the Methodist schools. Only two of the three published Reports in this period contain the Order of Merit. This order was obtained by dividing the gross premium by the gross attendance on the days of examination. In 1867, of the sixty-four primary schools examined, twelve were Methodist; and of the twelve, four came in the first half of the order. Five of the eight Moravian schools were in this section, the other twenty-three belonging to the Anglican Church. [118] Of the seventy-five schools reported on in 1872, five of the thirteen Methodist schools were in the first half of the order. Again the Moravians had five, the others belonging to the Anglican Church. Five of the thirteen Methodist schools were in the last third of the order, two being among the ten which the Inspector considered a discredit to the service. [119]

The payment by results system was not a satisfactory approach to education. Overall there was an increase in numbers, but nothing out of the ordinary. Enrolment figures islandwide rose from 11,892 in 1866 to 12,729 in 1867, reaching 17,803 in 1879. [120] The defects of the system were noted by a number of schoolmasters who, in 1872, addressed a petition to the Education Committee. In their petition, they criticised both the capitation and the premium grants; in the case of the latter they complained that examinations were too irregular to serve as a basis for the payments. Among other things, they recommended that more time be given students on examination days, limitation of the scope of History and Geography, and the award of a premium for Copy Book writing. The petition was signed by thirty-six school masters, of whom six were Methodists; it represented the views of less than half of the teaching fraternity. The clergy also presented a petition which endorsed the requests of the teachers. [121]

The Inspector failed to respond to any of the proposals dealing with the premium examinations. On the contrary, his observations tended to be derogatory of the teachers. He noted that only eighteen of the teachers were certified, and thus only their views were worth considering. How the Committee was to deal with the views of the eighteen, he did not say. He further observed that the Committee should not change rules, framed with reference to certified teachers, for the benefit of those who were "notoriously disqualified." He asked the Committee to note the social status of the schoolmasters, the untrained ones having been domestic servants, mechanics, and possibly clerks. He concluded by observing that the salaries of the schoolmasters compared favourably with those of the workers just named, persons whom he stated worked fifty weeks as opposed to the schoolmasters who had between six and eight weeks to themselves. No decision was recorded in the minutes of the meeting. [122] If what the Inspector was saying is taken seriously, it meant that he regarded the teachers as being of the same level as domestic workers and mechanics. It may well be that this devaluation of the teachers by the system's most influential officer was a major cause of the failure of teachers to remain in the service. Ironically, the Inspector applied two months after this for an increase of his own salary, and by the end of the year was complaining of the defects of the system. He found the method of awarding payments based on the premium to be defective, since a master with large numbers could not give as much attention to the students as a master with a few pupils. [123] In essence, he was corroborating the criticisms of the schoolmasters.

Extending the Process

A change in the development of public education in Barbados was brought about as the aftermath of the Report of a Commission set up in 1874 to examine the state of education in the island. Appointed at the request of the legislature, the Commission was headed by Bishop John Mitchinson, and included the Moravian minister, J.Y. Edghill. There was no Methodist minister in the membership, and it is very likely that none was nominated. One reason for this may have been the feeling of uncertainty which Methodist policy seems to have inspired in some sections of the public. In the early years of Methodism, the rapid movement that resulted from the policy of itinerancy had robbed that body of persons who could have won local confidence. But in Henry Hurd, the Methodists had a missionary who had served continuously in Barbados for over a decade. By this time also, the hostile attitude to Methodism was not as obvious as it had been previously. Another reason for the exclusion may have been the unwillingness on their part to take an active part in the examination of teachers. The Moravians, unlike the Methodists, did not complain about the examiners being from the Established Church, or of their being biased. They also declined to serve as examiners, as Edghill did in 1869; but their actions were not viewed with as much suspicion as were those of the Methodists.

The Mitchinson Report made five major observations concerning education and the way it was conducted in the island. Beginning from the position that education – defined as "sound training and discipline" – was desirable for all, the Report lamented the lack of interest by influential laymen in primary and infant schools. Secondly, it stressed the importance of annual examinations to all concerned. This was particularly the case for the state, it said, in order to ensure that payments were actually based on results. Thirdly, the Report noted the inadequate remuneration of teachers, a feature which was not likely to attract to the profession the most gifted persons. Fourthly, the Report considered various explanations of the poor attendance of children, noting poverty and the apathy of the parents as the most prominent. Finally, the Report took note of a fear on the part of some employers that educating the labourers' children might make them unfit for work in the fields, which was "their lot in life". Such habits of obedience and punctuality as they learnt were calculated to make them better labourers. And even if all of them were educated, the limited opportunities in trade and other commercial areas would leave the rest with only field labour as their choice.

To remedy the defects which they identified, the Commission recommended increased bonuses to teachers who had attained various levels of certification; training for masters at the Mission House at Codrington College, and for female teachers at facilities to be established; and provision for secondary and tertiary education. The Commission also recommended the establishment of an Education Board to include members from both houses of the legislature, and representatives from the three major denominations. [124] Up to this point the Roman Catholics did not attract the attention of the legislature, and had little chance of being considered. Judged by the small grant of £ 50 made to that body in 1871, when supporting grants were also made to the Moravians and the Methodists, their priest was being valued at half the rate of the other ministers of the non-established bodies. In this Protestant island, they could not even form an influential lobby.

The Mitchinson Report shows no real change in the attitude to the education of the lower classes. They were still meant to be labourers for those who were to be their masters, though they were not necessarily confined to field labour. In 1878 a new and more comprehensive *Education Act* gave form to the proposals of the Commission. [125] The Act established a Board of Education which was made up of a President, three members of the Legislative Council, and at least four members of the House of Assembly. Except for the President, the Board was again composed of members of the Council and Assembly. In this regard, it was no different from the Education Committee which preceded it under previous acts. For some reason, which it did not explain, the legislature had rejected the proposals of the Mitchinson Commission that the three major denominations should each be given a representative on the Board. The omission of all may have been a device for omitting the Moravians and the Methodists, or it may have expressed the intention of the legislature not to entertain any specifically denominational representation. This does not necessarily mean that there was an absence of prejudice; but at least care was taken not to make prejudice obvious. The Roman Catholics were not included either in the Commission's proposals or in the new act. Perhaps in the long run Barbados was saved from sectarian conflict by not having each denomination represented on the Board. In the Bahamas, the inclusion of each denomination was productive of disputes over the nature of education. [126]

It was not until 1879 that the Bishop of Barbados was made a member and Chairman of the Board, succeeding in that office the Colonial Secretary, W. Hely Hutchinson. This appointment was not greeted with pleasure in some quarters since representatives of the other major churches were not also included. The omission of the Methodists and the Moravians was blamed on Bishop Mitchinson, allegedly for engineering the omission with the assistance of Dr. J.W. Carrington. [127] The bases for this claim were that the bill had been presented to the Assembly by Dr. Carrington, a member of that body, and that the Bishop had displayed bigotry in ecclesiastical affairs. [128] Admittedly, the Bishop had declared his opposition to the Methodist church and his inability to assist it in any way. One correspondent in the press charged him with doing "everything in his power to injure their cause in this island..." [129] The natural conclusion was that, if the President of the Board was a bigot, he was unfit for the office.

The Governor was forced to defend his appointment of the Bishop. He explained that his appointment was based on Mitchinson's experience in education and his knowledge of the local situation as a result of his role on the Education Commission. The editor of the *Barbados Agricultural Reporter* argued rightly that the Governor would have known the Bishop's qualifications before he decided to appoint someone else for the short period in which Hely Hutchinson served as Chairman. He expressed his conviction that the composition of the Board was aimed at the exclusion of Dissenters. [130] Even if the writer cannot be said to have established the charge of deviousness, he had put his hand on the crucial issue: that religious prejudice was influencing decisions of government. Voices were already being raised against the persistence of "establishment" and of privilege. However, Mitchinson remained as President and his successor, Bishop Bree, became President as well. The sentiments which the editor expressed may well represent a point of view which had gained currency among ordinary Methodists, but there was no complaint from that body.

The new Board had as its function the implementation of the recommendations of the Mitchinson Commission, as far as it was possible to do so. The Board was also required to make rules for the administration of education in the island, receive applications for financial assistance, make grants as it saw fit, and ensure that all grants were properly and usefully applied. All plans for the erection of new buildings and alterations to old ones were to be submitted to the Education Board, which then had the power to amend and vary such plans. The new Board now had two important functions not previously given to the former Education Committee. One of these was the policing function of ensuring the proper use of grants awarded to schools. The other was that of supervising the construction of, and alterations to schools. In the absence of any explanations from the legislature, it can only be assumed that these new functions originated from previous abuse or suspected abuse.

An important section of this Act was that concerning the appointment of committees for primary schools. The relevant section reads as follows:

> Every public elementary school shall be under the immediate superintendence of a Committee composed of the minister of the district, or of the congregation with which the school is connected, and two laymen to be appointed annually by the Education Board, and in each case the said Minister shall be the Chairman of such Committee, and the Committee shall exercise all the rights of patronage in such school, including the appointment and dismissal of the master or the mistress or pupil teachers of such school, subject however to approval by and a right of appeal to the Education Board. [131]

This section differed from section 4 of the 1858 Act in two respects. On the one hand, it did not require the two lay members of the Committee to be nominated by the minister responsible for the school, as did the earlier act. On the other hand, it explicitly accorded to the new Committee all the rights of patronage.

Not surprisingly, this section elicited protests from all the denominations which administered schools. The first to react were the Moravians. The

Rev. J.Y. Edghill argued that he had been the victim of a breach of faith, in that he had been assured that the section would not have affected the Moravian schools since, being under a local Conference, their teachers had "full security against individual injustice." On the other hand, he emphasised his inability to hand over the schools to laymen "however appointed without the sanction of the Mission Board, and I am sure I shall never get their sanction to this step." In asking the Board to reconsider the section, Edghill hinted that the Moravians would prefer to lose the grant than to surrender. [132] To some extent this was an over-reaction, since the Moravians were not being asked to hand over their schools. In any case, it was not the function of the Board to reconsider the section, but only to apply it.

In less than a week a Methodist deputation also met with the Board. Like the Moravians they regarded the schools as an integral part of their mission, and were similarly disturbed by the tenor of the twenty-first section of the Act. They also urged that they had no authority to delegate "patronage" to a committee appointed by the Board without the sanction of the Missionary Committee in London. If the Act were to be enforced, they requested the Board to petition the legislature for an amendment of that section. The Board postponed its decision in an effort to allow both the Methodists and the Moravians to consult with their parent bodies. [133] Revs. Garry and Wright, two members of the deputation, wrote strongly-worded letters to the Methodist Missionary Committee in London. Both stressed the denominational interests and the importance of preserving their schools. They emphasised the integral relationship between school and mission, and the need to maintain their denominational character. Garry added that comments made by the Colonial Secretary and the Solicitor General had led them to conclude that there was a determination to gain complete control of the schools. [134]

Somewhat later than the Moravians and the Methodists, a deputation from the Anglican Church also approached the Board on the matter. Like the others they were concerned about patronage, but not because of external control. Nor was their concern in any way inspired by any change in the inter-relationship of church and school. They were inclined to the view that such committees were likely to destroy the influence of the supervising minister who should be the patron of his school. They expressed their appreciation for lay help, provided that the power to appoint and dismiss was vested in the ministers. They suggested, as a safeguard, a right of appeal to the Board on the part of the laity; and like the Methodists, they urged the Board to seek an amendment of the Act. Their presentation was speedily dealt with by the President, who was then the Colonial Secretary. Somewhat high-handedly he urged them to conform on the ground that no difficulty had yet arisen; but he promised that the Board would appoint lay persons acceptable to them. [135] As far as they were concerned, that settled the issue and no further complaint was heard from them.

As it turned out the protests eventually petered out. Nothing further was recorded about the protest of the Moravians. Either they were not supported by their Board in London, or the rules of the Education Board were regarded as a satisfactory safeguard. Published in 1880, these rules provided for the nomination of lay members by the ministers and for the ministers' approval of dismissals from the schools. In the case of the Methodists, the resolution of the matter turned out to be surprisingly simple. The Missionary Committee expressed their willingness to co-operate with the Board. However, they made two requests of that body. The first was that the minister in question should nominate the laymen from his Circuit Quarterly Meeting. The second was that all Methodist teachers be disciplined by the ministers, with appeals to the District Meeting and the Conference. [136] All indications are that the Board approved the recommendations of the Methodists, and that of the Anglican clergy about the right to appeal for the laity. The apparent crisis therefore passed.

Following the passage of the Act, the Education Board published in 1880 its rules for the management of schools – the most comprehensive to date. For those schools applying for grants, the average attendance was fixed at thirty in the case of existing primary schools, and twenty in the case of existing infant schools. New primary schools and new infant schools were required to attain averages of fifty and thirty-five respectively. Thereafter, a school was not eligible for grants if the Inspector's report on it was unsatisfactory, or if there was any immorality or gross impropriety on the part of the teacher. A quarterly report was required of each teacher, and quarterly visits by the supervising minister. The 72nd rule made it clear that the vestries would not be asked to undertake repairs in those schools where the sacrament was administered, or where the internal fittings were not suitable for educational purposes. The 74th rule required each minister, before the end of the year, to submit to the Board the names of prospective lay appointees for his school committee. The 75th rule stated that appointments and dismissals were to be made with the minister's concurrence. [137] The last two rules settled the subject of an earlier dispute; but the 72nd rule adversely affected the Methodists who, in the late 1830's, had built a number of chapel/schools.

Though the records are somewhat deficient, the Board seems to have received nominations from all three denominations for the appointment of lay persons. The practice, however, was neither uniform nor regular. In 1880, the Anglican Church submitted nominations for ten schools, and in 1882 for schools in all of the eleven parishes, [138] but it is not clear whether all schools were dealt with. Both in 1880 and 1882 there were nominations for Moravian schools. In the latter year, the Moravians submitted only four names: two for all schools administered by the Rev. J.Y. Edghill, and two for all those administered by his colleague, Walsh. [139] The Methodists were the only group which submitted nominations with any degree of regularity. For instance in 1879 they submitted nominations for five schools, and in 1880 for two schools. In 1882 there were nominations for nine schools covering the area from Selah in St. Lucy to Dalkeith in St. Michael. [140] None of the nominations submitted included those schools in the parish of St. Philip; and in the latter year, the nominations did not include Providence or Vauxhall in Christ Church. It would appear that the opposition to the Board was not limited to Henry Bleby, but affected the St. Philip Circuit of Ebenezer. Except for the Moravians, no denomination is on record as having submitted nominations for all of their schools.

The main focus of the Board's attention during this period lay in improving the quality of the teachers in its schools. There were two aspects of this undertaking. On the one hand, the Board continued the policy of devoting time and resources to their training programmes. This not only included courses and examinations for pupil-teachers, but similar activities for masters and mistresses of schools. Courses were conducted in areas such as Grammar, Mathematics, History, as well as Latin, Music and some elements of school management. The Board was still working on preparations for the establishment of two training institutions, but these had not started by the year 1883.

In the years following the passage of the 1878 Act, there was an overall growth in the number of certified teachers. In 1879 the Inspector reported that only eight of the Anglican teachers in the schools he visited were not certified. For the Moravians, eight of ten teachers in the same year were certified as against nine out of fifteen Methodist teachers. [141] By 1882, when the last full Report had been submitted, there were only ten uncertified teachers in the

ninety-six primary schools visited. [142] This means that there was an improvement in the response to the Board's programme, as well as to the Board's determination to discourage unqualified teachers. And this qualification included
school management in addition to the other courses.

The greatest problem lay in the infant schools, where considerable difficulty was experienced in obtaining qualified teachers. Infant schools had been
in operation from the 1850's, but did not qualify for the receipt of grants until
after the 1858 Act. Infant schools were usually headed by female teachers, and
at that time there were very few who met the standards required by the Board.
At no time did the number of qualified infant school teachers in the entire system
exceed fifty per cent, and this was the high point in 1882. The Methodists were
doing exceptionally well in that year in having all six of their infant school
teachers certified. [143]

The efforts of the Board had begun to pay off in that more teachers were
becoming qualified. Standards were not always maintained, in that some schools
showed decline after an initially good performance. In 1882, the Inspector suggested that some seven schools – four Anglican, two Methodist, and one Moravian – should no longer receive grants unless they showed great improvement.
The greater effort made by the Methodist teachers to qualify themselves suggests a greater level of cooperation in the end than had hitherto been the case.
Bearing in mind that previously leaders like Henry Bleby and Seth Dixon of the
Ebenezer-Providence Circuit were involved in the boycott of the training programme, it would suggest that the ministers during this period were more inclined to cooperate with the Board.

As far as the other aspects of the Board's efforts was concerned, emphasis was placed either on removing unsuitable teachers, or on refusing grants
to schools where the masters were of suspect morality. The Board's policy may
well have been indicative of the attitude reflected in the Inspector's Report for
1882. The Report noted that the system in force was based on the combination
of moral and religious with intellectual education. As a result, it stated, the legislature declined financial assistance to any school not supervised by a minister.
It pointed to the need for "fitting agents", criticising the tendency either to make
appointments without investigating the applicant's character, or to retain
teachers who were clearly unworthy of the office. Reflecting on the fact that
many teachers were neither truthful, honest, sober, nor chaste, and that the intentions of the legislature were being defeated thereby, the Report recom-

mended that, as the teachers improved, only communicants of the various denominations should be appointed to teach. [144] There is no record of any response to this either on the part of the Board or of the legislature; but it can be said that the Board made a point of ensuring a certain quality of teacher.

The process of ensuring quality sometimes involved the removal from office of some of the teachers. Sometimes teachers were dismissed for insubordination to the Inspector or to the minister. For example, in 1879 the teacher of Providence Methodist School was dismissed for insubordination to the minister. This dismissal originated in an altercation over salary with the minister, which led the teacher to use abusive language and finally to suffer the loss of office. [145] On another occasion in 1880, the master of Selah Methodist School in St. Lucy was dismissed also for insubordination to the minister. [146] These dismissals were supported by the Board, and it is small wonder that the Bishop objected when a dismissal at St. Barnabas was not upheld immediately. In this case the matter was speedily resolved when the School Committee demonstrated that the teacher had failed to respond to certain requirements in time. [147]

One of the dismissals was for fraud – by a master who claimed to have been ill but whose claim had been questioned by the minister. What actually happened was that he had neglected to present himself for the annual examinations. The Board paid to the school the grant for the quarter which had ended, but made it clear to the Methodist authorities that no further grant would be paid as long as that master remained in charge. By its next meeting, the Board learnt that the School Committee had dismissed the teacher in question. His dismissal was approved by the Board, as was the appointment of his successor. [148] The incident serves to show the kind of attitude that sometimes was encountered among teachers at that time.

Dismissals were often made on the ground of "immorality" – presumably sexual – and in this regard there were several. Of these one involved a Moravian teacher, the master at the Roebuck School, whose dismissal was upheld by the Board. [149] One month previously, the Board had upheld the dismissal of the master of St. Mark's Anglican School on a similar charge. [150] A charge of rape against the master of Rice's Infant School was found to be groundless, and he suffered no loss of grant. [151] In 1883, however, the charge of immorality against the assistant teacher at Paynes Bay Methodist School seems to have been established to the satisfaction of the Inspector and the minister, William Parker, and so he was removed. Some time later the Methodists sought to re-appoint the same person to the Whitehall School, but were warned by the Board that no grant would be forthcoming if the appointment was made. Notwithstanding this clear position, the teacher, Bynoe, was appointed assistant teacher at the school. [152] Either Bynoe was not guilty and therefore did not deserve to be removed from Paynes Bay, or the Methodists were in such desperate straits that they had to re-appoint him in spite of his offence. The latter would appear to have been the more likely, given the fact that the charge had been established. At the same meeting at which Bynoe's re-appointment was discussed, the Board was asked to approve the appointment of a master called White to the Whitehall School. The Inspector produced information to the effect that White had been dismissed for immorality by the Moravians, his original employers, and that he was an uncertified teacher who had neglected to take the examinations. In the Inspector's judgment, there was no place for White within the school system. [153] Neither White's nor Bynoe's appointment was approved, and neither seems eventually to have been retained in office. The circumstances could not have increased the credit of the Methodists in the eyes of the Board. A similar case had previously been drawn to the attention of the Board by the Inspector concerning an appointment pending at Dalkeith Methodist School. On that occasion the Board had taken the view that, since they had received no official notification, they could not act against the school. In any case, they noted that no charges had been filed against the teacher in question. [154]

Under the new rules established in 1880, ministers were required to visit each school under their supervision four times in each quarter. For the ministers of the Established Church, this should not have been a particularly difficult task, since it was very unlikely that any of them had more than two schools to manage. For the Moravians and Methodists it was not so easy, since one minister might have been responsible for as many as six schools. This was the case with the Methodist minister in the Ebenezer Circuit, and it would have been just as bad for the Moravians whose two ministers were responsible for their twelve or fourteen schools. In such a circumstance, the requirement would have constituted a considerable hardship for a minority of the ministers.

During the three years that followed the promulgation of these rules, the churches often failed to fulfil the requirements of the Board. In January 1880, the failure of a minister to visit during one quarter was partly responsible for the non-payment of a grant to his school in which the returns were in dispute. [155] In late 1881 the Board felt constrained to write to the ministers concerning infractions of the rule, and to call for a strict compliance. There is no evidence of grants being withheld, and one can only assume that there had been great improvement. The Board's letter followed a discussion one week previously when the Methodist minister, Wright, had been required to explain the infrequency of his visits to the Paynes Bay School. [156] There were others in the same situation. In 1882 the Board was again calling on a Methodist minister to explain his failure to visit schools, rejecting as an argument the change of staff at the station. And the following year the Board had similarly to request explanations from an Anglican minister. [157] This would suggest that there was not much being done by way of compliance with the rules.

A number of things are apparent from this survey. One of them is that the education system depended on the involvement of all the churches. Unlike the sister colony of Trinidad, and like so many other West Indian colonies, the Barbadian legislature did not establish a secular system of education. Not only were moral and religious instruction the foundation of the system, but the administration of the schools was in the hands of the churches. These churches were the agents of the education programme. The persons who framed the system – the legislators – had only a limited objective. The education of the lower classes was only to make them better labourers, because they had no other prospects in the society. The three denominations themselves had a limited perspective on education. Schools were a part, though an important part, of the missionary task of the church. They were the means whereby proselytization took place. This limited perspective, therefore, opened the door to continued religious rivalry.

In the implementation of the system the Methodists had a number of difficulties to overcome. One of these is that behind many of their problems lay the quality of their relationship with clergy of the Established Church. As will be discussed in a later chapter, bigotry often marked the attitudes of Anglican and Methodist functionaries. Two of the Bishops and a number of the clergy showed little consideration for the Methodist ministers, though they were more thoughtful of the Moravian ministers. In their eyes, the Methodists were schismatics, probably having little more than nuisance value. The Methodists saw the Anglican clergy as papists – a derogatory term – and showed little interest in cooperating with them. This unwillingness to cooperate, related to the disparaging attitude and remarks of some clergy, meant that they could not make any real contribution in vital areas of the education process, such as the training and examination of teachers. The Moravians, as one assembly member stated in 1865, were inclined to cooperate with the Established Church. This cooperation seems to have made them acceptable to the Anglican clergy and to the legislators. The latter were generally supportive of the clergy and tended to look after their interests. Apart from being personally related to some of the clergy, one suspects that these officials would have resented any challenge to their importance – whether the challenge was real or imagined. In this regard the Methodists could not help being vulnerable, since they openly expressed their dislike of the process followed by the legislature and their abhorrence of Anglican practices and privileges.

A considerable part of the problem which the Methodists encountered originated in their poverty. As they themselves frequently commented, their members were from the poorest section of the population. The extension of their school building programme coincided with the policy of their Missionary Committee to reduce its grants to the West Indies. They were zealous to build schools so as to enhance their own image in the island. Bleby in particular engaged in a spate of building for which he did not have the means.

And his frustration must in part be attributed to his failure to obtain funds for his projects. But Bleby must not be given all the blame. It was the custom for the District Meeting to approve all building projects, once members had been satisfied with the Superintendent's arrangements for meeting the costs. This they regularly did, and thus were as blameworthy as Bleby himself. Because of their financial difficulties, the Methodists would not have been able to benefit from the matching grants made for the furnishing of schools. Under such circumstances, one must ask whether they were wise to have attempted so many establishments.

It can be said that neither the Education Committee nor the Board which succeeded it was overtly prejudiced. The membership of these bodies consisted predominantly of persons from both houses of the legislature. During the 33 years under review, the legislature had shown no great desire to assist the Methodists in their struggles to survive. Some of these members would have been members of the Established Church, but nothing in their performance showed favouritism towards that body. Both bodies depended heavily on the opinion of one officer. This was the Inspector of Schools, who seems to have been actuated by prejudice which he was barely able to disguise. There is enough evidence to suggest that he was unduly persistent in his criticisms of Methodist schools and teachers. While his reports frequently note the lack of time to do everything he would have wished, he seems to have had enough time to make repeated visits to certain Methodist schools – such as Belmont and Shrewsbury. In the end, the Board itself had to remind him of the need for objectivity. So that one must conclude that the officer, far more than his principals, was the one in whom prejudice manifested itself.

On the whole the Methodist schools were not as well conducted as one would have expected. This was partly due to the poor quality of the teachers they depended on, partly also to the frequent changes of staff, and partly to the boycott of the training programmes, particularly by teachers in the St. Philip Circuit. The Reports of the Inspector, and Sub-Inspector later, can be taken as a fair index of their quality, especially in the premium examinations. At no time were their schools efficiently managed. The ministers were frequently guilty of inefficiency where their own duties were concerned, and sometimes were openly recalcitrant. In this regard, Henry Bleby was an infamous example. He was always inclined to do things as he wanted, and was very anxious to insist on the rights of Methodists to public funding. As a result he tended to promote recalcitrance, rather than to encourage co-operation.

Methodist contribution to the education process was also limited by their failure to grasp opportunities available to them. Thus they did not participate, when asked, in the examination of teachers. Their reason has already been mentioned, but it was not of such importance as to justify refusing to take part in the work. As a result of their aloofness, they were unable to make any contribution to the development of the teacher training process. Part of the problem was their suspicion of the clergy of the Established Church, several of whom were undoubtedly bigoted. But in refusing to treat with any of them in the area of the examination of teachers they lost a valuable opportunity to help in breaking down that persistent prejudice of which they complained.

Chapter 5

FINANCING THE MISSION

We have already noted that, in the euphoria surrounding the abolition of slavery, the Methodists undertook a vigorous expansion of their work on the island. Both in terms of increasing their manpower and of extending their building programme, the great desideratum was money. Hitherto they had depended on their Home Missions to supply a large proportion of their needs. At that time the fires of enthusiasm for the West Indian mission had been fuelled by the fight against slavery, and the interest which that had generated, and can be said to have been burning brightly. But the abolition of slavery was to witness a decline both in funding and in enthusiasm on the part of English supporters of Methodism.

By the middle of the century English Methodism was itself falling on hard times. There had been a decline in membership between 1846 and 1851, with a consequent weakening of the base for support of the Missionary Committee. As a result that Committee could not continue to fund its overseas missions as it formerly did; and, at a meeting in December 1851, the Committee decided to discourage the dependence of the missions on the parent body. As soon as they were sufficiently mature, the Committee decided, they were to provide for their own support. [1] The case could not be more clearly stated than it was by the General Secretaries:

> Our whole staff of Missionaries and Assistant Missionaries for the 150,000,000 of our fellow subjects in India is only thirteen. Is this small band to be reduced in order to maintain double the number for the one island Jamaica?... [2]

It follows that what could not be done for Jamaica could not be done for the rest of the West Indies. The Missionary Committee was itself extending its sphere of interest, and such funds as it had at its disposal had to be applied to the newer areas.

Except for the James Street Chapel, where some English and middle class coloureds worshipped, every other chapel had a membership composed primarily of the labouring classes. Because of this, the ability of members to meet their financial obligations would have been hampered during periods of great unemployment, or drought, or general hard times. Providing for their operations would have been difficult for the local Methodists. In this chapter we will examine the funding problems of the Methodists, first as regards the sources on which they depended after emancipation, and secondly as regards their efforts to secure public funding.

The Methodists operated a voluntary system in which each member was asked to make regular financial contributions to the upkeep of their mission. The principal sources of income were first the "Class Money" which was a subscription required from each member of a class. This subscription was required not only when the member was present, but also when he was absent. Secondly, and clearly associated with the "Class Money", was the "Ticket Money". A membership ticket was given quarterly to each member who was in good standing morally, and as far as his regularity at worship and class meeting was concerned. This ticket was a significant badge of membership, all the more valuable because its short duration required constant effort for its renewal. Each person receiving a ticket was required to pay a certain sum. A third source of income was pew rents. The sittings in each Methodist chapel were rented. Sometimes the sittings in new additions, or in new chapels, were rented even before the new extensions or chapels were completed. [3]

In addition to these, a source of income comprised grants from the Missionary Committee in London. These grants were both direct and indirect. Each Circuit apparently remitted to London all the funds in excess of those required for the normal needs of the Circuit. These needs included stipends and various allowances for the missionary and his family. A regular scale of expenses authorised by the Missionary Committee in London was notified to the Chairman of each District from time to time, and the missionaries were expected to conform to these arrangements. These expenses included board for the missionary and his family, "quarterage" for himself and his wife, allowance for his children as well as for servants, washing and stationery. In 1827, the board and quarterages for a missionary and his wife with one child amounted to £ 154.4.0. sterling. If at the end of any one year the expenditure of any Circuit exceeded the income, the Superintendent could apply to the Committee to "grant his deficiency." In effect this asked the Committee to write off the excess of expenditure - a process which was by no means automatic. [4]

A direct grant would be money given for any special project outside the normal expenditure of the Circuit. Thus if a chapel, mission house or school were to be built or extended, the Circuit indicated the approximate cost, the amount it was able to raise, and the amount it sought from the Committee. Generally speaking, a Circuit was expected to have two-thirds of the cost before it commenced building. This rule was not always adhered to by the missionaries in the Circuits. Methodist policy also required that the project had to be approved first by the District Meeting, whose endorsement did not necessarily guarantee the award of the grant. For instance, the procuring of a second chapel in Bridgetown had first to be approved by the District Meeting, which then forwarded its recommendations to London.

An examination of the chapel and Circuit accounts brings to light some very interesting factors. In the case of the Chapel Account, except for special building grants from London, the revenue was not very large. In 1835, 1837, 1838 and 1845, for example, the revenue was augmented by grants of £ 200, £ 525.6.8., £ 745.11.10 and £ 1048.9.2 1/2 respectively. When these sums are deducted from the total revenue, the real income for Barbados would be £ 221/8.9 1/2, £ 470.9.10 1/4, £ 412.13.2 1/4, and £ 342.15.2 respectively for the four years mentioned. [5]

Table 7
Barbados Chapel Accounts, 1838-1845

Year	Pew Rents (£)	Total Revenue (£)	Pew Rent as % of Total Revenue
1838	140.8.4	412.13.11 1/2	34
1840	164.0.8 1/4	463.17.1/4	35
1840	185.18.9	426.16.9	43
1845	141.16.8 1/2	342.15.2	41

Source: Barbados Chapel Accounts, 1832-1846, in the *Records of the Methodist Church,* Microfilm Bs. 52, at the Barbados Public Library.

What is most noticeable is that pew rents constituted a substantial proportion of this account. In 1835, the first year after emancipation, pew rents amounted to £ 89.19.0 out of a total revenue of £ 221.8.9 1/2. At that time there were four chapels in the island, and 587 full members. By 1845, when there were nine chapels and nearly 1800 full members, pew rents accounted for £ 141.16.8 1/2 out of the revenue of £ 342.15.2. Whenever a chapel was nearing completion, a major concern of the missionaries was to get the pews rented. One of them went so far as to boast in 1856 that, although the chapel was still unfinished, all the sittings had been taken. [6] By 1876, when the poverty of the population had become a topic of discussion during the Confederation disputes, [7] pew rents were becoming a source of embarrassment to the Methodists. At that time the District Minutes drew attention to the decline in finances of the chapels, and to the impact of the increased cost of living on the poorer classes. The Minutes took note of the fact that eleven parish churches and 32 chapels-of-ease of the Established Church yielded pew rents to the value of £ 588.13.1 in 1874, whereas 15 Methodist chapels yielded a revenue of £ 325.9.11. Pew rents from the James Street chapel alone exceeded the £ 135 yielded by the Cathedral and eight chapels. Despite the high rate of pew rents, the revenue from this head was on the decline and the missionaries found themselves unable to meet the expenses of repairs. Only the Moravians did not have a pew rent system. [8]

There was one characteristic common to pew rents both in the Established Church and in the Methodist churches: they were intended as a means of raising revenue. In the case of the Established Church the rates were fixed by the vestry, of which the rector of the parish was a member. In the case of the Methodist church the rates were fixed entirely by the missionary in office. Dr. Kortright Davis argues forcefully that the pew rents system served the purpose of "social ordering and control which was sustained by the Anglican Church in Barbados." He further argues that "the pew rents system was definitely an extension of the class stratification in the society." [9] If that is the case, it is difficult not to apply the same assessment to the Methodists, notwithstanding the fact that class distinctions were not so clearly marked as among the Anglicans. The cost of a pew would have served to separate the more affluent, white or coloured, from the poorer members.

When one looks at the Circuit Account, one is struck by the proportion of "Class Money" and "Ticket Money" in relation to the total revenue. In the year 1835 these items amounted to £ 254.12.1 out of a total revenue of £ 723.2.11. In 1842 the same items amounted to £ 478.4.11 1/2 out of £ 841.4.11; while by 1845 they amounted to £ 701.19.6 1/2 out of £ 992.19.1 1/2. [10] In fact, from 1840 to

1845 inclusively, these two items constituted over fifty percent of the revenue of this account. This pattern seems to have continued to 1883. We do not have available a full record of accounts for the various Barbados chapels, but the records for the Bethel chapel in the last decade of our period provide strong evidence of the persistence of the pattern. [11] Tables 8 and 9 illustrate the development.

What the two accounts indicate is that a substantial amount of their revenue resulted from direct contributions from their members. These members were often reported by the missionaries to come from the poorer classes, and to be in that condition where they could not pay any more. The problem was the same as that faced by the Moravians in the Eastern Caribbean, which made it impossible for that body to gain full independence as a Province. Their people were impoverished and they could not attain to self-support. [12]

Table 8
Bethel Chapel Account, 1874-1883

Year	Pew Rents (£)	Total Revenue of Total Revenue (£)	Pew Rents as %
1874	32.7.5	72.7.7	72
1875	54.15.6	88.16.3	61
1876	53.4.1	159.6.6	33
1877	60.3.10	141.10.2	42
1878	60.13.10	133.2.4	45
1879	48.1.9	87.16.7	55
1880	40.14.4	80.17.2	50
1881	39.7.9	79.0.5	49
1882	45.4.9	99.1.11 1/2	45
1883	36.16.3	85.8.3	42

Source: Bethel Society Reports and Accounts, 1873-1891. Records of the Methodist Church, Microfilm Bs. 54, at the Barbados Public Library.

Table 9
Bethel Circuit Account, 1874-1883

Year	Class & Ticket (£)	Total Revenue (£)	Class & Ticket as % of Total Revenue
1874	153.13.11	454.13.5	34
1875	153.13.5	479.16.10	32
1876	136.15.3	448.17.3	30
1877	130.16.4	480.19.8	27
1878	138.18.5	355.13.8	39
1879	139.14.8	355.9.0	41
1880	134.15.5	346.15.0	39
1881	118.8.9	239.0.2	49
1882	133.5.7	340.12.1	39
1883	142.8.10	476.7.7	30

Source: Bethel Society Reports and Accounts, 1873-1891. Records of the Methodist Church, Microfilm Bs. 54 at the Barbados Public Library.

Because of the poverty of most of their members, the Methodists were unable to cope with the financial difficulties of the middle and late nineteenth century. They had been dependent on their co-religionists in England and on the Negro Education Grant for the construction of chapels and schools. The termination of the grant in 1845 meant the loss of one source of funding. About the same time they were faced with the possibility of the loss of revenue from the estate of their benefactor, William Reece. Reece had died in 1836, leaving as a bequest to the Methodists "the profits of one half of his Estate." According to the missionary, William Fidler, the value to the Methodists was approximately £10,000 [13] at that time. This estimate was probably an exaggeration on his part. The circumstances leading to the possible loss of revenue were set out by

Fidler as follows: Some time following the hurricane of 1831 the legislature had granted to the Reeces a loan of £ 3300 sterling, at 4 per cent per year, to enable them to restore damaged property. This debt was repayable at the rate of £ 200 sterling per year, with interest "accruing on the remainder." Two annual payments of £ 500 sterling had been made, thus reducing the principal to £ 2300. By 1845 the interest due on this amount in 1844 had not been paid, and poor crops had made it impossible to meet current payments. The Methodists could find no support among the wealthy classes, and there was a real chance of the Reece estate being sold to recover the debt to the government. That debt had already been in existence when the will was made. [14]

In an effort to resolve the difficulty, Fidler addressed several queries to the Missionary Committee for their consideration and advice. One of these was whether the Committee was able to advance the money to meet the instalment and interest that were due so that repayment might be completed within a few years. Another was whether the Committee might become guarantors to a third party who might advance the money they needed, or to the Trustees, who might then be able to negotiate a loan. Fidler's insistence that every effort be made to save the property was not only based on his desire to secure to the Methodists their share of the benefits form the estate; he was also of the view that if they were able to acquire their share of it, they could dispose of it to a "company of negroes", or in small allotments to squatters. [15] This is the only reference which the present writer has come across indicating any interest in helping the ex-slaves in Barbados to acquire property. There is no indication that it was ever followed up.

The real problem was more clearly stated by Francis Whitehead, the missionary at Providence. This was to the effect that the government's demand for payment could only be met by borrowing, and that the Trustees of the Reece estate were unwilling to borrow unless the Committee and other interested parties were prepared to take responsibility for the loan. Whitehead then alleged that there were persons trying to frustrate the Methodists in the enjoyment of their trust.

He wrote:

I am afraid there is a desire to prevent the wishes of Mr. Reece in favour of our body being accomplished. There is a more determined hostility to our cause manifested by the church party in this neighbourhood, and all interested in the matter above referred to are perfectly under the influence of the Rector and Curates of the parish. [16]

The accuracy of Whitehead's allegations is far from self-evident. One has not encountered any evidence to support the claim that hostility to Methodism on the part of the Rector and their own financial difficulties were in any way connected. While it is true that some degree of hostility existed to Methodism in the island, it is extremely difficult to see this interfering in such a way as to prevent that Society enjoying the benefits of a bequest that had been in existence for some nine or ten years.

In the absence of any clear evidence it is a reasonable assumption that some of the Methodist difficulties had their roots in family differences with respect to the Reece estates. The Reece family had long been members of the Established Church, and William Reece, the benefactor of the Methodists, had only joined this church shortly before his death. The disposition of his property seems not to have met with the approval of his relatives. Among these was Abraham Reece who served at St. Bartholomew, St. Patrick, St. Lawrence and the parish church itself – all in Christ Church. [17] He was never very far from the property, and was one of the curates whom the missionaries reported to be opposed to Methodism.

This family also included Isaac Reece, who was later to become one of the representatives from the parish of Christ Church. In 1854, a missionary described him as having "become very friendly of late..." [18] Reece would later become one of the supporters of the Methodist cause in the Assembly; but in the early years he appears to have been an opponent. Two years earlier two missionaries had complained of the covert investigation of Methodist affairs by some lawyers; [19] but they gave no indication as to their perception of the cause. What they did observe was the division of the Reece family over the course to be followed. So that one can conclude that there had long been opposition to the Methodist cause in the island, and that this opposition was as evident among the family of the benefactor, William Reece, as it was in the wider population. In a real sense, therefore, the Methodists were swimming against the tide in Barbados.

In the end the financial difficulty was resolved when Isaac Reece, a nephew of the benefactor, decided to purchase the estates. The sale was duly executed for the price of £ 18,000 sterling. After paying various debts amounting to £ 4500.9.5, the balance was divided equally between Reece's relatives and the

Methodists. The Methodist share of £ 6749.15.3 1/2 was reinvested in the Reece estates to yield interest at the rate of 5% per year in perpetuity. According to the missionary's estimate, the Methodists were assured an income of some £ 342.5.10 annually. [20]

By the middle of the century, financial incapacity had begun to assume critical proportions in the progress of the Methodists in Barbados. In these middle years of the century, the wages of labourers were often quite low. Barbados, for instance, had the second lowest average daily wage in the West Indies for the period 1847-1848. By the year 1858 the small average wage of 7d. per day had risen to 10d. In the period between 1848 and 1848 there was a corresponding rise in the cost of essential items. The labouring population were badly off even when they were employed; in many cases they were faced with unemployment and consequent destitution. [21] Therefore the very group which constituted the bulk of the Methodist membership were in no position to render the financial support which that body needed. One of the missionaries, Henry Bleby, described such contributions as the people made as acts of self-denial. So bad were the conditions that some missionaries were even prepared to relax their financial discipline, [22] even though the Missionary Committee was anxious to see an improved performance in that area. Not only was financial support from England decreasing, but there was little hope of increasing the financial position locally.

In 1864, the Methodists were forced to face up to the real extent of their indebtedness. The District Meeting held in that year discovered that the interest alone on debts in Barbados amounted to some £ 436. In response to the desperate plight of the Barbados Circuits, that District Meeting suggested a number of possible courses for the consideration of the Committee in London. The first of these was that the annuity from the Reece bequest be applied to the liquidation of the debts, rather than merely to Circuit support. The second was that the Committee give a grant to the Barbados Circuits to enable them to cope with their heavy debts. In making these proposals, the District Meeting referred to the repeated requests which by then had been made to the Barbados legislature, and the great influence of the Established Church within that body. The Meeting urged on the Committee

> the importance of action being taken by themselves with the Home
> Government that these Anti-Methodistical Colonial Legislatures may

be instructed to act in a more friendly and just manner towards Methodism in these Colonies.

The third course was that the Committee's grant to the District be increased to £ 1150. Overall it is doubtful if the first proposal would have made much of a difference. If the debts had been paid, the recurrent revenue of the chapels would have been short to the extent of the transfer of funds.

The financial embarrassment of the Methodists was not restricted to Barbados by any means. Across the District, which included Trinidad, Tobago, Grenada and St. Vincent, the situation was regarded as so depressing as to be beyond the capacity of the people to deal with it. As a result the Superintendents often had difficulty paying their debts, for which they were pressed for payment by merchants who had given them credit. It was an experience which they shared with some of their Jamaican counterparts about this time. So disturbing was their financial situation that some of the ministers were not able to pursue their studies or carry out their pastoral duties effectively. [23]

The District Meeting stressed the hopelessness of their prospects unless they received help from London. Indeed, it lamented the inability of some persons in London to understand their plight. Their pleas notwithstanding, they did not get additional financial assistance from London, and such assistance as they had been receiving was eventually terminated. Some of the clergy of the Established Church were opposed to the legislatures in the various islands granting financial assistance to other denominations on the ground that the former was capable of providing all necessary religious services to the inhabitants. The Established Church had never in fact done so, and, even in the middle of the century, lacked the resources to do so.

The lack of sympathy on the part of the clergy of the Established Church was rooted in their prejudice against the Methodists. In addition, as an Established Church, they were funded by the legislature and may not have wanted to share that privilege with other denominations. The following table illustrates the level to which the Established Church was funded in Barbados.

Admittedly, the Established Church had a large number of clergy and churches, to the support of which this funding was applied. But the Moravians and the Methodists had several churches, and between four and six missionaries each during the same period. Yet neither of them received much funding from the legislature. This deprivation of assistance from revenue derived from taxes, which they themselves paid, would motivate them to challenge the prevailing system.

Table 10

Sample of Funding for the Established Church

Year	Amount (£)
1855	6865.11.8 1/4
1858	8867.18.10
1871	8761.15.1 1/2
1876	10601.19.8
1883	10493.13.2 1/2

Sources: *Blue Books* - 1855, pp. 32-39; 1858, pp. 36-45; 1871, pp. C1-12; 1880, pp. C1-12; 1883, pp. C1-12. Barbados Department of Archives.

For a long time after 1864 the Methodists had no respite from financial problems as Circuit debts persisted. These debts had accumulated largely as a result of the building and rebuilding undertaken in the seven or eight years previous to 1864. During that time the Methodists had either built or restored some six chapels in the island. In the same period the Moravians had established four, but seem not to have been carrying as heavy a debt as were the Methodists. For example, the Methodist First Circuit in Barbados had a debt of £ 3587 at the end of 1865, while the Second Circuit was indebted to the tune of £ 3358.0.0. Information for 1866 is lacking, but in 1867 the indebtedness of the Circuits stood as follows: for the First Circuit, £ 2220.16.4; for the Second Circuit, £ 2902.16.3; and for the Third Circuit £ 341.3.8. Barbados alone was responsible for nearly half the debt of the District. [24]

The financial state of the Barbados Circuits was no better in the years that followed. Regrettably, such records as are available state only what was paid rather than indicate the full extent of their indebtedness. However, the picture which is presented is far from encouraging. In 1869, for example, the Barbados First Circuit paid £ 912.10.0 in debts and still had a balance of £ 908.8.4. The second Circuit, on the other hand, paid £ 1009.15.16. In the following year, the same two Circuits paid respectively £ 910 and £ 315.9.0; while in 1871 the Second Circuit paid £ 1218.6.1, and the Third Circuit paid £ 241.1.8. [25]

The crippling debts facing the Methodists in Barbados posed a very serious problem. As long as they were insolvent they were in no position to ask merchants for credit. And as long as they were unable to obtain credit, much needed maintenance and repairs could not be done. Their difficulty was aggravated by the fact that neither the London Committee nor English Methodists generally seemed able to appreciate the seriousness of the problems they faced. The Missionary Committee in London kept urging economy on the missionaries in the West Indies. It was critical of their management of the finances, a criticism which drew strong responses from missionaries in Jamaica and Barbados. The plight of the missionaries in the West Indies was forcefully depicted by the Jamaican Chairman, Edmondson, who expressed his disapproval of the proposed changes. Henry Hurd in Barbados called for an end to the unfair comparison of missionaries in the West Indies with English ministers because their situations differed. He was not in favour of the reductions sought by the Missionary Committee – reductions in subsistence, provisions for horses, and other personal benefits. He was of the view that it would not be as easy to implement these changes as the Committee had thought. His opinions were supported by his colleagues in the island, who even more strongly expressed opposition to the proposals. All eventually undertook grudging compliance with the Committee's recommendations. [26]

We have already alluded to the complaints that the members were from the poorer classes. While poverty was partly responsible for the failure of some members to fulfill their obligations, there were others who were unwilling either to make regular contributions to the Church or to pay their pew rents. [27] Henry Hurd, for example, complained of the unwillingness of members to pay for those Sundays on which they were absent. [28] In 1876 another missionary complained that the bulk of their membership was "literally giving nothing" towards the support of the church. And he uttered the dire prophecy that such a church could not survive in Barbados. [29] Judging by their own descriptions of the resources of their members, one is forced to ask whether such strong criticisms of the performance of members is not unfair. The information we have, even from their own documents, does not suggest that the circumstances had changed to such an extent that the members could be called delinquent.

The lack of funds meant that various means had to be tried in order to reduce their deficits. As we shall see, later, there were several appeals to the legislature for help. In doing this, they had begun to receive and to rely on the support of some representatives in the House of Assembly. Isaac Reece of Christ Church, a nephew of the Methodist benefactor, became a firm supporter of their cause. By the mid-1860s they were also receiving the support of John Connell, one of the representatives for St. Philip. The list of those who voted in their favour whenever the House divided, shows that support for them in that institution was growing. It does not necessarily mean that the Assembly contained a large number of Methodists, but rather that some members of the Assembly were prepared to take a broader view of things than was previously the custom.

Increasingly during this period the Methodists sought to recoup their losses by holding regular bazaars and "Tea Meetings" as special fund raising efforts. These seem to have originated in the early 1860s as their finances declined. [30] By the mid-1870s these fund-raising activities had become virtual staples of the regular duties of the missionaries. These activities were not universally approved by the missionaries. One of them criticised them on the ground that their frequency made them less than special. [31] For those who had seen long service in these islands, as well as for those who had been recruited from the West Indies, such fund-raising had become a way of life. However, for those who had been newly recruited from England, such activities were regarded as demeaning both to the missionaries and to Methodism. Writing to one of the General Secretaries in 1876, a missionary criticised the amount of time devoted to fund raising as against that devoted to spiritual work. He concluded, therefore, that there was something radically wrong with Methodism – doubtless as practised. He scathingly criticised "Tea Meetings" which had the approval of the "native Brethren". When he developed his observations to their logical conclusions we get a glimpse of what the real problem was – the cleavage that was developing between the English missionaries and their local counterparts. Thus he wrote: "I think things will be much better if Englishmen were not so often under West Indian supers." [32] This suggests that his opposition to West Indian customs was coupled with an opposition to serving under West Indian leadership. It might also be seen to suggest the superiority of the Englishman as a leader of the Methodist body.

A position less hostile to West Indian leadership was taken by another missionary, who was also keenly sensitive to what he termed the "staple work of a Methodist preacher in the West Indies." His quarrel was that success in fund raising rather than diligence in one's pastoral duties had become the yardstick by which the missionary was judged. Financial concerns seemed to him to stifle the life of the missionary. Hence, he concluded: "to sustain ourselves without either state aid or help from the Committee is an utter impossibility." [33] It would have been more accurate to have said without increased state aid; for they had been in receipt of an annual grant at the time he wrote in 1876. The observation highlights the problem that what they had been receiving was far less than they needed. To the process by which they came to receive regular state aid we may now turn our attention.

While they benefitted from occasional contributions from individuals, the Methodists were never able to get any assistance from local institutions such as the vestries, with the single exception of the St. Michael Vestry which made a grant of £ 50 to them in 1860. This grant was made in response to their application for support for four of their schools in that parish. Their success was partly due to Henry Hurd's energy in lobbying most of the members before presenting his petition. [34] The small amount given them might have been due to the fact that the Vestry had, at the same time, to respond to victims of a fire, as Hurd indicates. It was also a small indication that they were beginning to gain favourable consideration. As yet, it could not be said that anti-Methodist prejudices had been broken down.

If we were to ask why the vestries were so unresponsive, the answer must be seen to lie in the nature of the vestries themselves. While they had certain civic functions to perform, they were very definitely a part of "the establishment." The rector of the parish was, since 1680, a member of that body, and sometimes he functioned as chairman. And so it is only in the wider context of the establishment that their lack of assistance can properly be discussed. For some reason, it was not until early in the year 1860 that the relationship between Methodism and the established Church was put forward as an item for serious discussion. And in that development Henry Bleby was not only actively involved, but had also provided the catalyst for it.

The 1859 Report of the First Circuit in Barbados had referred to "a powerful Church Establishment" as one of the causes of Methodist decline. That report further observed that, because the Methodists were a voluntary organisation, their survival was a matter of great difficulty. [35] Quite surprisingly, there was no reflection on this in the Minutes of the District Meeting of 1860. Whether it was because he was disappointed at the lack of response or because he wanted to ensure that the matter was not dropped, Bleby raised it with the Missionary Committee in London, as he was to do locally for the rest of his stay in Barbados. With typical forthrightness, he protested to the Committee against the privileged status of the Established Church in which the clergy were beneficiaries of the general taxation, while they tried to disrupt the functioning of another group within the island. And he asserted that being Methodists was costing their people too much. [36]

Some three years later Bleby was still fighting against the notion of establishment, but with what appeared to be greater sympathy from members of the public. In a strongly-worded letter to the Committee, Bleby harshly and with great exaggeration described the Established Church as the sole cause of Methodist retardation. In what was probably his only positive proposal on the matter, he indicated his willingness to fight for, and to support, concurrent endowment. Bleby further declared the exclusion of Methodists from the benefit of taxes to be unconstitutional. But his criticisms were not limited to the Established Church, whose clergy he somewhat scathingly and exaggeratedly denounced as immoral, utterly worldly, and utterly inactive save in their opposition to Methodism. He was also less than flattering in his criticism of current Methodist leadership, and of Henry Hurd in particular. In Bleby's view, Methodism would have progressed further had the right persons been chosen to lead the local mission. And he was firmly convinced of his own chances of success in getting an annual grant, had he been moved to Bridgetown instead of to Demerara. [37]

To put Bleby's frustration into perspective, we need to look at his efforts to obtain assistance for his Circuit from public funds. At this stage one needs only to notice the strange circumstance of such a request being made for a part of the body rather than for the whole; for Bleby was not seeking assistance for all Methodists. Indeed, the very nature of Methodist organisation made it easy for him to act unilaterally, because each Circuit was an independent entity. One also needs to observe that Bleby was not merely begging, cap in hand. He was seeking to press home the right of the Methodists to a share of the public funds. In the course of his struggles, it became noticeable that the legislature was on the whole not prepared to favour the Methodist cause. The refusals of that body, therefore, can be interpreted as an intentional policy to frustrate them.

Between 1858 and 1863 Bleby claimed authorship of five appeals to the legislature. The first of these was submitted in April 1858, in which he recited the efforts he was making towards the provision of schools at Ebenezer, Beulah, Shrewsbury, and the Crane. The provision of school places, he argued, would have had the effect of checking and eradicating evils among the youth, as well

as reducing the cost of detecting and punishing crime. Estimating that the overall cost of his projects would have been between £ 850 and £ 900, Bleby requested
a grant of £ 350 or such sum as the legislature felt able to award. Some four months
elapsed before the matter was dealt with by the Assembly, and they merely referred it to the Finance Committee of the House. [38] No further notice seems
to have been taken of it, even though Bleby had in the meantime written enthusiastically to London expressing optimism about the result. [39] It might well be
that, since he had also applied to the Education Committee for financial assistance, [40] the Assembly had chosen to ignore his petition to them. They would
seem to have quietly dropped a matter with which they were unwilling to deal.
In other words, if the members were not themselves hostile to Methodism, they
certainly lacked the courage to take such a bold step as Bleby's petition required.
And their apparent diffidence in this matter is thrown into relief by the fact that
grants were being made for the building or repair of chapels of the Established
Church. [41]

In presenting his second petition in March 1859, Bleby argued that the
members of his Circuit had been expending some £ 1000 from Church funds in
providing good schools for the public benefit. Moreover, his people had contributed to the public revenue from which grants were made to erect other places
of worship. He concluded that additional space for public worship was needed
in the parish of St. Philip, where the provision made by the Established Church
could not supply the needs of a quarter of the parish's population of 14,000. His
final observation was that the Methodist Church had expended thousands of
pounds throughout the island, and had exerted great influence on the labouring
classes. [42] This petition was immediately referred to the Finance Committee,
whose report recommended that no further grant be made "for church accommodation in that parish." The reason for that decision was that in 1857, and again
in 1859, sums had been granted for chapels in the parish. [43] Actually, the grants
had been made for work at St. Martin's church, a chapel-of-ease of the Established Church. In effect, therefore, the decision was one based on ecclesiastical
prejudice. Bleby's case was strong and had been well argued, and he had broached
the issue which lay at the heart of the system of establishment: the use of the revenue from all for the exclusive benefit of some. For such discrimination was the
inevitable result of a system of establishment.

Bleby delayed his third petition to the Assembly because of a recent
fire in Bridgetown, which would have rendered the needs of the victims more

urgent than those of the Methodists. [44] When that petition did come up for discussion in March of 1862, [45] the Assembly's response reflected a change from the intransigence which characterised that body in previous years. This was probably due to changes in the membership in the Assembly. This body contained the same personnel in 1859 and 1860; but there were eight new members in 1862, three years after the adverse vote of 1859. [46] In 1862, the Assembly, usually regarded as the most difficult and intractable of the two houses, passed a resolution granting Bleby's petition for £ 450. Two weeks later, the Council's unanimous rejection of the petition was communicated to the Assembly. [47] No reason was given for their rejection, and it was quite surprising that the Assembly made no attempt to ascertain the reason for the Council's action. Under the circumstances, one is left to conclude that the Assembly did not consider the matter sufficiently important to pursue.

The impression given by Henry Padgham, Bleby's colleague, is that Bleby was as much to blame for the rejection as the members of the Council. Padgham attributed the failure of the petition to a letter which Bleby had published, and which had been regarded as threatening. According to him, the ensuing public correspondence was "not calculated to advance the issues of Christianity in the community." And he concluded with the reflection that prudence and caution were the pre-requisites for dealing with the legislature, while anything resembling coercion was likely to have damaging effects. [48] Padgham's assessment was probably correct, for Bleby seemed determined to contest the issue publicly.

Notwithstanding the negative response to his previous petitions, Bleby submitted another for a grant of £ 872.9.3 or as much as the Legislature could give. If they were only able to give part, he asked for the balance as a loan to the Circuit. This was to be his last petition and it was signed by some 148 persons. One can sense his exhaustion as he reviewed the needs of the parish and the respective contributions of the Established Church and the Methodists, and as he pressed home the injustice of denying to the Methodists any share of "the revenue applied for ecclesiastical purposes." Before submitting his petition, Bleby had taken the precaution of securing interviews with the Governor, members of the legislature and planters in the St. Philip parish. His effort resulted in his obtaining the signatures of most of the landowners in the parish. [50] The extent of the support which he received represents a remarkable advance from the narrow conservatism of earlier years towards a refreshing liberalism. Yet there was nothing to warrant the optimism of his colleague, Henry Soper, who enthusiastically predicted that annual grants would become a reality before very long. [51] The truth is that up to the time of Bleby's departure from the island the matter had not been dealt with. It seems to have disappeared from the attention of the legislature. Again one can only conjecture that the likelihood of his having to leave the island provided the Assembly with an opportunity for doing nothing. At the same time, his somewhat irascible attitude had served to alienate persons who were in a position to determine policy; and, notwithstanding the justice of his claims, Bleby emerged the loser.

Other petitions were forwarded to the legislature at this time, in favour of the two chapels in Bridgetown. In the case of the James Street chapel, there were two petitions seeking the rescheduling of repayment of a loan on the chapel. That loan had been granted by the legislature in 1856 to enable the Methodists to complete a new chapel at James Street in Bridgetown. The loan was rendered necessary by the fact that, when work on proposed extensions began in 1855, the Methodists discovered that even the foundations of the existing structure were unsound. The legislature therefore granted a loan because the Methodists were unable to raise the additional funds. Because of heavy building commitments in the Circuit they were not able to make any repayments to date. The first petition sought a repayment schedule which would run from August 1859 for a period of five years. The Assembly passed the necessary enactment [52] without imposing any penalties on the Methodists. Another rescheduling was sought in 1863, and the petition was reluctantly granted. When the appropriate bill was brought before the Assembly, two attempts were made to thwart favourable consideration of the matter. The first came by way of a resolution seeking postponement of the discussion for six months, and would probably have resulted in the demise of the bill. The second attempt took the form of another resolution which sought to introduce a clause making the debt repayable at £ 100 per year. [53] Both resolutions were defeated, but in neither case was the margin of defeat substantial. Henry Bleby, a colleague of Henry Hurd who had sought the extension, saw the resolutions as reflecting a poor regard for Hurd, and therefore an adverse reflection on the leadership at James Street. [54] However, it was more a case of prejudice against Methodism than animosity towards Hurd. It must be remembered that the Methodists had failed to keep their payments up, and so could not expect too great enthusiasm for regular requests for rescheduling.

In the case of the Bethel chapel two petitions were also submitted. In this case, however, the petitioners sought assistance for repairs to the chapel. The arguments in support of the first petition were not unlike those put forward by Bleby for Ebenezer. The chapel had been built and maintained by private funds for twenty years; the Methodist membership had been exhausted by fund raising to build chapels and school houses across the island; and they had no assistance from the revenue of the island, although they had contributed to it. In requesting a grant of £ 400, they expressed the belief that the "Honourable House is ever disposed to respect the claims and promote the welfare of all classes of her Majesty's subjects for whose interest it may be required to legislate..." [55]

The language was courteous and might even be said to have been flattering; but it was an indirect challenge to the system of establishment, whereby one institution benefitted at the expense of others. So that by reminding the Assembly of its obligations to "all classes of her Majesty's subjects", the petitioners were also reminding the members that the system was discriminatory. Neither disestablishment nor disendowment had yet arisen as a topic of public debate. But concern was showing itself among the missionaries for an equitable distribution of the public funds. The petition was again unsuccessful.

A second petition from Bethel in 1863 fared no better than the first. Given its first reading in June 1863, the bill was not dealt with until some two months later. It was eventually withdrawn because its sponsor, a Mr. Yearwood, was "not prepared to proceed with the measure." There was no explanation of his action, and another member seized the opportunity to appeal to the Standing Orders of the House, [56] and force its withdrawal. The haste with which this was done suggests the persistence of an illiberal spirit towards the Methodists. As yet they had not been accepted by the dominant class in the island; and this class used to good effect a weapon which they had at their disposal - the power to grant or withhold such rights and privileges as the Methodists found difficult to fight against, given the numerical superiority of those who still supported the Established Church in the legislature.

Nevertheless times were beginning to change. A liberal spirit had begun to emerge in some quarters of Barbadian society. The coloured community had already gained representation in the House of Assembly, and could make their voices heard through a newspaper, *The Times*. Given the fact that Methodist lay leadership had always contained a large proportion of the coloured community, it is not surprising that public questioning of the discrimination emanated from this source.

One of the factors which contributed towards making this a live issue in the second half of 1863, was a resolution introduced into the House of Assembly by W.B. Griffith, the Auditor General. The resolution is sufficiently important to be quoted in full:

> That his house will receive no petition for any sum of money relating to the increase of salaries or proceed upon any motion for granting any money other than for the public service; or for releasing or compounding any sum of money owing to the public, but what is recommended from the Crown during the existence of the present House of Assembly. [57]

Griffith's argument was that the Governor was the person best informed as to the merits of any individual or groups, and that any request should be brought to the House by him.

In the course of his presentation, Griffith apparently made reference to the likelihood of a large number of petitions being received from the Methodists. This unfortunate remark was not only denounced as inaccurate, it led to an allegation that the real purpose of the resolution was to bar the Methodists from financial assistance. The editor of *The Times* alleged that the intention was to perpetuate the system of exclusiveness whereby the poor provided for the rich. The Established Church, he wrote, "will do little more than afford accommodation to the more wealthy class, and would not do that if all were churchgoers, and they are chiefly attended by persons of this class." This is an exaggeration which can easily be refuted by reference to the number of persons who attended the worship of the Established Church. However, he was basically correct in his contention that Griffith's resolution was motivated by prejudice. His point that the rejection by the Council of the bill to assist the Methodists in St. Philip had caused dissatisfaction beyond Methodist circles would suggest that a new mood was developing in the island. [58]

Alluding to the same matter, a pseudonymous writer questioned the policy of financial support for one religious group only. In the opinion of that writer, the poor were discriminated against in that they had to make provision for their own worship, because that was the effect of existing laws. In that case, the situation was one which required "early redress". The writer then ventured to draw the strangely optimistic conclusion that the Council would not have voted against financial support for the Methodists if the matter had been publicly aired. [59] Nothing in the conduct of such persons had shown that they were likely to succumb to such pressures. The writer was probably a Methodist, or a supporter of that body, and hence his conclusion. The Editor himself gave way to exaggerated claims, as he praised the Methodists for erecting a new chapel in Christ Church. This was to replace the old chapel on the Reece estates which was considered inadequate for their needs. Not only did he extol the Methodist influence as "powerfully conservative of peace and good order, and promotive both of the agricultural and commercial interests of the colony"; he added the further exaggeration that, had the Methodists been given financial assistance from public funds, "far less would be required to bring offenders against the law to punishment." [60]

For his own part, Henry Bleby joined in the debate to ensure that the claims of the Methodists did not escape attention. In a letter to *The Times* explaining the expenditure incurred in building the chapel in Christ Church, he drew reference to the extent of Methodist expenditure in St. Philip and expressed the hope that the legislature would respond positively to the St. Philip petition. The only intention of the Methodists, he explained, was to make the people "better subjects of the crown, better servants of their employers, and better in all relations which they are called to sustain in life." [61] A similar hope was expressed by another correspondent who, after summarising Methodist achievements, concluded that such a body had a claim on "the gratitude and finances of the community." [62] This spirit of liberality was a welcome change, though it was not yet sufficiently influential to ensure for them the financial support they were seeking. It is regrettable that this was the time at which Bleby was moved to Demerara, for it is possible that his doggedness was precisely what the situation required and might have achieved success eventually. Nevertheless, he had made a major contribution to the change that was taking place by enunciating Methodist claims and by challenging the system of establishment with its inherent discrimination and intolerance. The fact that he had not witnessed the success of his efforts is not very important. He had delivered sufficient shocks to the system to encourage the hope that the Methodists would be in receipt of regular grants within three or four years. Even that hope he made conditional on the "maintenance" of their claims. [63] Unfortunately, Methodist claims were not pressed after Bleby's departure and, not necessarily consequentially, they did not receive any grant for some time. It is only fair to observe that the persistence of prejudice was not the only factor that militated against Methodist success. Lack of unified action, as evidenced by their separate petitions, was also a major problem. By acting separately, the missionaries had made it possible for personality differences to be exploited. One gets the impression that Hurd and Padgham enjoyed greater favour in official circles than did the more outspoken Bleby, a factor which might have influenced his transfer to Demerara. [64]

On the other hand, one recognises the fact that relations between these missionaries were not always very cordial. Bleby was characteristically outspoken in his criticisms of Henry Hurd, for whom he had no high regard as a leader. Hurd seems to have harboured serious reservations about Bleby, especially as regards the latter's financial management. At the same time, Padgham had no very high regard for what he alleged was Bleby's lack of tact in dealing with the legislature. [65] Both Padgham and Hurd were inclined to defer to highly placed officials in an effort to gain help; and Bleby tended to see such help as a right. Conflict was therefore unavoidable with the latter.

As it turned out, the first non-conformist beneficiaries of public funding in the island were not the persistent Methodists but the Moravians. At a single sitting in April 1865, the Assembly voted to make a grant of £ 400 to the Moravians, probably as an act of generosity to them on the celebration of the centenary of their mission in the island. This circumstance was alluded to by William Haynes, one of the members for St. John, when he introduced a bill seeking financial assistance for them. But it was by no means the whole story. Haynes alluded to the fact that the Moravians belonged to an old church, and twice commended their cooperation with the Established Church in the island. On the second occasion he declared that they were entitled to such assistance because of all the good they had done. They rendered, said Haynes, "most hearty cooperation to the Established Church, not seeking to make proselytes but administering to the poor and those around them." Haynes' sentiments were strongly supported by Alexander Ashby, one of the members for St. James. As if to leave no doubt about his colleague's remarks, Ashby pointed out that the Moravians were never involved in stirring up strife, and that they were reluctant to intrude into the sphere of any other group. When J.R. Gooding, one of the members for St. Philip and a regular Methodist supporter, praised the Methodists for their zeal, his words fell rather flat in the Assembly. [66] But the debate did clarify an important point, which was that some members of the Assembly still harboured considerable prejudice against the Methodists. And it was largely for that reason that their petitions to the legislature received so little support. Not until October 1865 was a bill passed granting financial assistance to the Methodists. [67] They had been seeking it for seven years with little positive response; the Moravians were dealt with promptly. The Assembly members had made a distinction between the two groups, and this distinction in their perception of them was responsible for the differences in the treatment each received. Even so, the grant to each church was only for the year 1865.

Disestablishment and Disendowment

As we have already seen, the District Meeting of 1864 had recommended to the Missionary Committee the advisability of seeking the help of the Colonial Office with a view to obtaining for the Circuits some degree of financial help. [68] They had not as yet raised the question about the future of church establishment. However, this question had been raised in England, and had been debated there intermittently over a period of some twenty years. In England in the 1830s, the dissenting churches were almost wholly opposed to church establishment. A number of these bodies united to press for disestablishment of the Church of England, and for church organisation on the "voluntary principle." The Methodists stood aloof from this approach on the ground that they harboured no "hostile feelings towards the Church." [69] So strongly did they hold to this position that, when one of their ministers became involved in the activities of a branch of the Church Separation Society, he was suspended from his duties. [70]

Catholic emancipation in 1829 relieved the Roman Catholics of the various disabilities to which they had been exposed since the 16th century. But the removal of these disabilities only served to throw into relief the status of the Church of England in Ireland. The persistence of an established Protestant Church in Ireland was offensive insofar as it remained a symbol of English conquest. By the 1960s, however, there was a change of atmosphere, especially after the eminent W.E. Gladstone became a convert to disestablishment and committed himself to ending it. [71] Both Irish Catholics and English dissenters joined forces to bring about the demise of establishment. As progress was made towards dis-establishment in Ireland, neither Catholics not Protestants were prepared to support concurrent endowment.

The same concern for the end of the Irish system must have influenced the Imperial Government's attitude towards establishment in the West Indies. The Government decided to phase out the system of state support for the Established Church in the West Indies, and passed an Act to that effect in 1868. Granville, the Secretary of State for the Colonies, explained that the situation then was different from that which had obtained in 1824 when the first two bishops had been appointed to the West Indies. Furthermore, since the prejudice of slavery had in their opinion been wholly or partially obliterated, Parliament had judged the time opportune for discontinuing its assistance to the Established Church in the West Indies. [72] Granville further explained that the Government's intention was to bring about "complete religious equality." The best means towards that end was by way of "concurrent endowment." Religious equality was inconsistent with establishment, hence the state could not assist the ascendancy of any church. Grants were to be made to churches in proportion to their membership, and on the clear understanding that the body involved appropriated the funds in the manner approved by the Government. The despatch concluded, with unmistakable clarity:

> the two rules of universal disestablishment, and of distribution of state aid in proportion to numbers and voluntary exertion, should be invariably carried out. [73]

In various territories, efforts were made to comply with the general plan of the Colonial Secretary. Some governments such as those in Antigua, Jamaica and the Bahamas, disestablished and disendowed the Church. In other areas such as Trinidad and Guyana, the Governments arranged or maintained a form of concurrent endowment. [74] This meant a system of funding to denominations operating in the particular territory. In Barbados there was no disestablishment, as Caldecott implies; what resulted from the process was, as will be shown, a disservice to the dissenters and a discredit to the local government.

The course which the British Government had in view attracted considerable discussion in the local press. Opinions in favour of either establishment or disestablishment were heatedly canvassed by their respective supporters throughout 1870 and early 1871. [75] Although the Secretary of State's letter and the accompanying Act had been placed before the Council and Assembly in 1869, no further notice had been taken of the matter until June 1871. Meanwhile, Governor Rawson had received letters dated June 1870 and January 1871 urging him to deal with the matter. Why did he fail to proceed?

Rawson's explanation to the Assembly was that he had wanted to give the Church of England time to comment. [76] In view of this explanation, one would expect to find a comment from that body among the papers of the Assembly. That there are no such papers raises some doubt about Rawson's veracity on the matter. The second reason Rawson gave was that the delay was due to the expediency of separating Trinidad from the Diocese of Barbados, [77] an issue which evoked considerable discussion. His third reason, given to the legislature, was nearer to the truth in that it disclosed what must have been his real intention. In a message to the Assembly, he explained that the delay had given the legislature the opportunity of "spontaneously satisfying the reasonable claims of the only other two religious bodies, whose members give them a title to aid out of the public funds." [78] Obviously, he did not include the Roman Catholics who were not Protestant, and so were not qualified, even though they had over 300 members. The truth of the matter is that Rawson withheld the correspondence until the legislature had approved certain pittances to the Moravians and the Methodists. And even as he recommended to the Assembly what he considered a reasonable course of action, he must have been fully aware that his action conflicted with the objectives of the Colonial Office.

By way of clarifying this point, we need to look at two despatches by Rawson which were obviously not made public. The growing antipathy towards establishment, and the line taken by the Methodists, would have ensured for one of them a very hostile reception. The first despatch was an exhaustive examination of the proposals of the British Government, in which the Governor expressed his support for establishment. Somewhat illogically, he combined a number of reasons for continuing the *status quo ante*. For instance, he noted that Barbadians almost exclusively belonged to the Established Church. In stressing that some church would have a special position, he argued that the dissenters did not profess to provide a service for all and that the state could not impose the duties of burying, marrying and baptising on them. Therefore, there was no prejudice against the other communions simply because the State exercised control over one. And as if to crown the whole, he argued that the newly emancipated could not be expected to support their own church, if they were suddenly called upon to do so. Continuing his weak discussion, Rawson asserted that there was no reason to change the ecclesiastical arrangement in Barbados. The office of Bishop could not be reduced to "an equality with the highest officer of the Wesleyan body." The latter was merely a delegate of the London Committee, who stayed for a short time, and who would not have desired the social position which the Bishop was expected to maintain. [79] Amid all the illogicalities, two things stand out: Rawson was reluctant to give substantial financial assistance to the dissenters, though he favoured awarding both the Moravians and the Methodists the same amount of money. He was also opposed to the Methodists, whom he described as sheep stealers.

The second despatch must be discussed in the context of events which took place in Barbados in the last quarter of 1870. In September of that year, the Moravians approached the Governor for help with their mission. They were then faced with the daunting prospect of having their English support discontinued at a time when their local congregations were unable to make good the shortfall. Recommending them to the attention of the Assembly, the Governor reminded the House of the former's service to the island, and of their not having hitherto sought financial aid. The closure of their missions, he noted, would be a serious loss to the island. And so, as a mark of "wise liberality", he suggested a grant of £400 per year to them and a similar grant to the Methodists. [80] A bill to provide £400 per year to the Moravians was expeditiously dealt with by the Assembly, and was equally swiftly dealt with by the Council. [81] But at this stage, the Assembly did not discuss the proposal to assist the Methodists. Described as an unobtrusive but highly deserving Christian community, [82] the Moravians had received their mite from the Governor. The truth is that the award fell far short of the salaries of the four missionaries, each of whom received £170 per year. In the words of J.Y. Edghill, the Moravian Superintendent, it was only a token. [83] This was the treatment Rawson recommended for a group whose departure from the island he believed would be a loss. In the second of the two despatches, Rawson had declared that the Moravian Superintendent was perfectly satisfied with the measure - a satisfaction not evident from Edghill's letter in *The Times*. In it he indicated that the £100 per year granted for each missionary was less than the stipend each received. Two Colonial Office minutes were appended to the despatch and accompanying Act. The first surprisingly states: "This seems reasonable"; the second recommended that the Act be sanctioned. An unsigned draft despatch from the Colonial Office expressed satisfaction at the manner in which the legislature had met the Government's wishes on the subject. [84] It would seem, then, that the Colonial Office had given its sanction to the Governor's actions. But given the principle that grants were to be made in relation to the membership, [85] one must seriously question the extent to which this was in keeping with the original demand by the Colonial Office.

At the same time that the Governor had asked the Assembly to consider grants to the two dissenting bodies, he had written to Henry Hurd to invite proposals for funding from the Methodists. The latter in turn had referred the matter to his colleagues, being conscious of the fact that some of them were not favourably disposed towards state aid as a matter of principle. It was therefore not until January 1871 that their case properly came before the Assembly. The basic problem was the same as for the Moravians – that the parent body had planned to withdraw financial support, and their members were very poor. The statistical information submitted by Hurd showed the Methodists to be ministering to a larger constituency than the Moravians. [86] He did not ask for a specific sum, but he did indicate elsewhere his willingness to accept £ 100 for each missionary. [87] A petition urging the claims of the Methodists had only become necessary because the Assembly had failed to take action on the matter. Indeed, delay and opposition had been anticipated, to the extent that the Methodists were urged to "agitate as Mr. Bleby used to threaten to do." [88]

Unlike the situation with the Moravians, the bill to grant aid to the Methodists occupied the legislature for the better part of a year. One would have expected that, with the Act for the Moravians as a guide, it would have been a simple matter to pass a similar one for the Methodists. There was so little difference between the two, when a final Act was passed for the latter, that the delay has to be given some attention. A bill was read a first time in February 1871, a second time in April, and finally passed the Assembly in May. [89] The Auditor General, who had been a staunch opponent of aid for the Methodists some eight or nine years earlier, was among those who voted in favour of it. And the fact that it passed the House by 12 votes to 2 [90] indicates the tremendous change that had taken place in the Assembly. But unnecessary delays were caused by arguments as to the amount to be granted them, and by the fact that discussions were often broken off to deal with other matters.

The bill after being debated by the Council, was returned to the Assembly on the ground that it had made permanent provision for the Methodists. In this regard, it had done the same as the Act which made provision for the Moravians. Although the Council had no objection to the bill, that body asked the Assembly first to make similar provision for the curates of the Established Church. [91]

In effect this meant that the Assembly had to amend two Acts passed in 1862 and 1870 before that body could obtain the Council's approval of the provisions for the Methodists. The problem, if there was any, should have been as obvious to the Council when the Moravian bill was presented to them as it was when they received the one for the Methodists. It should also have been corrected with the earlier bill. As it was, the Assembly was only able to complete the changes in August, and the Council eventually passed the bill in November. [92] The result of this lengthy process was that the Methodists received a grant of £ 700 per year for their seven missionaries.

In the light of these circumstances, we can only conclude that Governor Rawson had carefully orchestrated events to ensure that the Moravians and Methodists had received the meagre provisions of the legislature before he took action on the issue of establishment. And this is reinforced by the fact that he forwarded the documents from the Colonial Office to the Assembly for their meeting on July 25, two months after the latter had passed the bill for Methodist support. In a speech to the legislature early in 1871, he had urged them to give the Methodists a grant similar to that given to the Moravians, "and thus to satisfy, as far as the island is concerned, the policy and desire of Her Majesty's Government, to establish religious equality throughout the West Indies." [93] But the main aim of disestablishment cannot be said to have been achieved in Barbados. What was done was merely a travesty of the imperial demands.

At the height of all their agitation for public funding in 1863, Henry Bleby had indicated a willingness to support concurrent endowment. Some six years later his colleague, Henry Hurd, forecast that the legislatures of the region would support that principle. [94] What resulted form the proceedings in Barbados was anything but concurrent endowment. It was, as one correspondent aptly observed, a discreditable act on the part of Governor Rawson. [95] It is not surprising that the Methodists soon began to feel that the apparent boon was not as helpful as they had anticipated. As early as 1876 they had raised the issues of their entitlement with John Pope Hennessey, the recently appointed Governor. This official had arrived in the island with a reputation for liberalism as is reflected in the Addresses presented to him by both houses of the legislature. [96]

And yet his reply to their Addresses suggests that he was somewhat attached to the Established Church. It expressed his conviction of the "importance of upholding establishments, whether Lay or Ecclesiastical, that are consonant with the wishes of the people." For this, among other things, the Assembly expressed their "most emphatic and cordial acknowledgment." [97] There is not enough here to indicate a community of interests between the two parties, but equally there is nothing to suggest that the Governor was likely to embark on a new policy with respect to dissenters.

The Methodists could only have been following the dictates of contemporary convention when, through Chairman Henry Hurd, their District Meeting presented an Address to the Governor in whose jurisdiction they were meeting. The Address expressed their reliance on him to protect and help them, and

> to sustain us in those islands where religious equality has been established on terms that are in harmony with the full enjoyment of that equality; and to secure for us in Barbados all the rights and privileges to which we are entitled.

Hennessey acknowledged the duty of securing their rights and privileges, but very smoothly changed the point of focus. In West Africa, he noted, Methodists had been his allies in relieving the Africans from oppressive taxes, and he expected Methodist support in Barbados for a similar policy. [98] As had been the case with President Skeete and Governor Lyon in the 1820s, the Governor had promised them nothing.

The disturbances which arose over Confederation in 1876, and the strained relations with the legislature which culminated with Pope Hennessey's recall, meant that nothing was done with respect to their entitlements. Indeed, nothing could have been done. The final lament was sung in one last petition in 1880. Signed on this occasion by all the missionaries in the island, it rehearsed all the old arguments. [99] Like some of its predecessors, this petition quietly faded from view – a final testimony to the outlook of those who comprised the islands's legislature.

The Methodists had not gained a great deal in terms of the quantity of funds they received from the local treasury. But they had stated emphatically their right to participate in the benefits derivable from the taxes of the whole population. Not only did their agitation ensure that they could not be completely left out of consideration, it could also be said to have helped the Moravians. The display of favouritism towards the Moravians could only have been intended to create a feeling of dissatisfaction and jealousy on the part of the Methodists towards the other group. They could, however, be satisfied with having raised public consciousness about the discrimination which had persisted in the island. That final vote on their petition for public funding shows that there was growing good will for the Methodists among those who made public policy.

Chapter 6

CUSTOMS, CONFLICTS AND CONTROVERSIES

During the period which preceded the abolition of slavery, the Methodists in Barbados were made to suffer the intolerance of a prejudiced society. That intolerance would not be completely eradicated, though it would show signs of diminution, in the latter part of the century. In this post-emancipation period, they would themselves be faced with internal as well as external conflicts. Three areas of concern are dealt with in the present chapter. The first of these is the problem of their relationship with the Established Church, which was exacerbated by their struggle for recognition by the legislature. The second of these is the problem of discipline among their members which caused a division at the James Street Chapel. The division, which began in the mid-1840's was never quite healed. It lingered on as a kind of subcutaneous infection ready to erupt at any moment. The third of these is the problem of a distinction between English missionaries on the one hand and their white and coloured local counterparts on the other. This distinction seems not to have operated in practice until the 1850's when the Missionary Committee began energetically to promote a local ministry as a form of economy. That course led to serious conflict involving two prominent West Indians on the one hand, and the District Chairman, Henry Hurd, on the other.

The problems which faced Barbadian Methodism constituted a part of the growing pains of a very youthful body. At emancipation, world Methodism was still less than one hundred years old, and the Missionary Committee, which framed policy for the West Indies, was merely twenty-one years old. The rapid changes then taking place in the West Indies meant that the Missionary Committee hardly had time to work out its strategies for one thing before it was overtaken by another. At the same time, Barbadian Methodism was forty-six years old – a substantial part of Methodism's first century. As the years progressed, there were increasing calls for the establishment of a Conference in the West Indies to manage the affairs of West Indian Methodism.

Church Relations

Relations between the Church of England and some Nonconformist bodies in the colonies were traditionally poor. This was particularly the case with respect to the Methodists who had broken away from the Church of England. The quality of relationship was basically the same in other colonies as it was in the West Indies. In Newfoundland, for example, they were categorized as "fanatic preachers", a term of contempt reminiscent of Sir Ralph Woodford's description of them in Trinidad as "Methodizzes". In another area of Canada, Anglican-inspired restrictions were interpreted as attempts to hinder the gospel or to retard the progress of Nonconformity. [1] Despite supporting the Established Church, the Colonial Office strove to ensure that the rights of other denominations were not trampled on.

In the West Indies, the comparatively small size of each island ensured that the various groups were frequently in some contact with each other. The hostility engendered by the anti-slavery campaigns exacerbated the antipathy which supporters of the Established Church felt towards the Methodists and kindred groups. Jamaica exhibited one of the worst examples of inter-church relations in the West Indies. For a large part of the eighteenth century, and until emancipation, there was active hostility against Nonconformists. Their ministers were harassed, imprisoned, and had their chapels closed. In 1832, following the slave rebellion of the preceding Christmas, they were to suffer even more at the instigation of the Colonial Church Union. [2]

In Trinidad, where the Church of England had not been established until 1844, there was a tendency towards assertiveness against Nonconformists. This showed itself in two ways in the early decades of the nineteenth century. One case involved a Methodist minister called Thomas Talboys, against whom a petition had been taken to the Council in Port of Spain. The petitioners were "inhabitants", whose complaints included the stock one of dangerous doctrines likely to subvert good order, and the charge of administering sacraments contrary to the rules of "our Established Religion". The Council restricted them to services before 8.00 p.m. with doors open, to prayers and sermons on the gospel. On the basis of these restrictions all other dealings with Nonconformists were decided, especially by Woodford. [3] Thus a Presbyterian and a Methodist were prohibited in 1816 "from interfering in any manner in the duties of the Rector of the Protestant Church". One year later Woodford sought the approval of Lord Bathurst, the Secretary of State, for continuing the restrictions as they affected "the administration of Sacraments or performing...Burial and Baptism to the prejudice of the claims of the Rector of Port of Spain". [4] In all of this the Governor and Council were responding to complaints from the same rector, who had hardly any parish or any claim to the privileges of establishment.

No objection was raised to Nonconformists in Barbados before the year 1823. They were not required by law to obtain licences to function, nor were they arrested and imprisoned. As indicated above, they were the victims of sporadic harassment which culminated in the destruction of their chapel. It was only in 1825 and later that their presence was challenged on the basis of a forgotten statute. By that time the first Bishop of Barbados , William Hart Coleridge, had already assumed office. Coleridge was an energetic official, who had been active in one of the missionary societies of the Church of England. He had formerly been secretary to the Society for Promoting Christian Knowledge, [5] one of the three large societies of the Church of England. Bishop Coleridge was also a high churchman, who was described as having "declared war" on dissent and having frowned on "brotherly relations between clergymen and Methodist Preachers". [6] This statement relates to the course followed by Coleridge in St. Kitts; it is unlikely that he followed a more sympathetic course in Barbados, but this is not easy to document.

One cannot say with certainty the extent to which Coleridge influenced the attitudes and activities of the clergy with respect to the Methodists. While as Bishop he might have given directions as regards church relations generally, the division among the clergy did not guarantee the cooperation of them all. Some of them were so independent as not to be "Bishop's men". The most that one can say is that Coleridge might have encountered kindred spirits among a section of the clergy. Nor can one determine the extent to which the Bishop of Barbados, as Visitor, influenced the training programme at Codrington College. But the Methodists regarded the College as a breeding ground for "popery" and shunned it, especially during the early period of teacher training. Codrington College had by this time produced a large proportion of the Anglican clergy who served in the island between 1835 and 1883, and some of these were serving in precisely those areas where the Methodists encountered difficulties. [7] There may therefore be a definite correlation between the presence of those clergy and the incidence of prejudice.

Competition for the attention and the souls of the newly emancipated Africans was keen, and would have aggravated such differences as there were between the churches. The Anglicans, despite their comparative lethargy, were convinced that they could cope with the evangelization of the ex-slaves and did not need others. The Moravians were prepared to work alongside others in the field. The Methodists were convinced that it was they (and to some extent the Moravians) who preached the true gospel. In such an atmosphere, allegations of religious prejudice need to be treated with caution. In the race to expand their work, it was impossible for the denominations to avoid bumping into each other.

Allegations of prejudice related to five areas in which the Methodists operated or sought to operate. One of these was in the vicinity of Speightstown where the Methodists experienced some difficulty establishing themselves. From the opinion of one missionary it would appear that the Church of England was highly respected by the people and that no useful purpose was served by hostility towards that body. Only a few months previously he had noted that the people in Speightstown were so afraid of Methodism that they were unwilling to receive Methodists. [8] Yet the same missionary and others accused the Church generally of seeking to destroy Methodism in the area. And one of them went so far as to accuse a rector of changing the times of his service to deter his members from attending the Methodist chapel. [9] Yet we do not know whether the alleged ploy was successful, or to what extent.

Similarly there were allegations of destructive intentions in the parish of St. Lucy, where the Bishop's appointment of a schoolmaster was regarded as an act directed against the Methodist school and hence Methodism itself. In Christ Church the rector, C.C. Gill, was accused of trying to annihilate Methodism. [10] However, there was no indication as to how this was being done. In the area of St. Mark's church in St. John, the complaint made by missionaries was against the peoples' preference for the high churchmanship or "popery" of the Established Church. On the other hand the complaint in St. James was that the rector of that parish had threatened the expulsion of his sexton if the latter had permitted Methodists to meet in his house. [11] The complaints are general for the most part and appear to relate to specific individuals only in one or two cases. But given the atmosphere of hostility before emancipation, the protraction of rivalry is not surprising. The Methodists were by no means accommodating towards the Established Church. Some of their denunciations have been mentioned in previous chapters. They were as anxious to impede the progress of their rivals when they purchased land at Bay Street in which they knew the Anglicans and Roman Catholics had taken an interest. [12]

Notwithstanding the general tensions between both churches, there was no open conflict until the early 1860s. It is regrettable that none of the newspapers for the year 1862 is available; in addition, neither the pamphlet written by Henry Bleby nor the reply by W.T. Webb any longer exists. [13] Nevertheless, from excerpts of newspapers for the year 1863 and a few fragments for 1862, we can piece together something of the dispute which took place at this time. Bleby's pamphlet, *True and False Apostles,* seems to have been motivated by the growth of a brand of theology which traced its roots to the Oxford Movement in England earlier in the century. This brand of theology emphasised, among other things, the fact that the Church of England was part of the ancient Catholic Church. It also put great emphasis on the sacraments of the church, especially the Eucharist, and on ordination. In the latter case, attention was given to apostolic succession through ordination by bishops who could be traced back to the first apostles. This notion of succession was always a sore point with persons of the evangelical persuasion. The main focus of Bleby's attention, therefore, was to demonstrate what he considered the proper qualifications of those called apostles. In so doing he also sought to demonstrate that the Methodists were true successors of the apostles in terms of their mission. However, he seems to have concluded that the apostles had no successors in terms of their function, which was to bear witness to one whom they had known as an individual. [14]

The challenge was taken up by representatives of the Established Church in the island, and the debate was sharpened by advocates of the Methodist cause. Two issues seemed to have emerged from all this. One was the right of the Methodists to designate themselves a "church". One writer expressed the view that the Methodists had "none of those essential marks, by which the visible Church of Christ is known". [15] But he did not say what those marks were, or why he considered the Methodists to be deficient in them. The other issue was that of "Apostolic Succession", described by one writer as a "papistical fallacy", and by another as "a cheat and an imposture, at variance alike with Scripture and common sense". [16] As the controversy progressed its range was widened. Members of the Established Church suggested that the Methodists had gone back on the stance of their founders, who had repudiated any separation from the Church of England. [17] Charges and counter-charges were not slow in coming, and eventually took the place of the theological niceties which had prompted the discussion. Thus, each side accused the other of indulging in sheep-stealing, and one of the Methodist writers accused a clergyman of the Established Church of bribing a Methodist layman to become his catechist. W.T. Webb, whose pamphlet evoked hostile criticism, is alleged to have urged that Methodists confine themselves to areas not served by the Established Church. But this was in turn criticised on the ground that Barbados would have been better off without the pupils of Dr. Pusey. These, said the writer, displayed the arrogance that was typical of those "leaning towards Romanism", and were "propagators of modern Pharisaism." Finally, Webb was criticised for allegedly stating that the revivalist religion of the Methodists was well suited to the black population, who, having itching ears, were likely to be led astray. Again the writer hazarded the opinion that Webb despised persons of dark complexion. [18]

It is very difficult to point to any positive merit in the disputes. No small proportion of the correspondence dealt with minor issues such as the lack of clarity on the part of certain of the disputants. Purely doctrinal differences were not clarified since neither Bleby nor Webb pressed the issues in public debate. As a matter of fact, Bleby's colleague commented negatively on his being the one who started the unseemly dispute. [19] One can say, however, that the dispute demonstrated three things. First of all, it demonstrated a considerable degree of intolerance on both sides. There was a strong feeling, on the part of the Methodists, against any group that was not narrowly "protestant". There were also strongly anti-Methodist sentiments on the part of a section of the Established Church. Secondly, it showed the extent to which the Methodists and the Established Church had actually grown apart from each other. The Methodists were no longer a sect of the Church of England, which might become re-united with the parent body. They were now asserting that they were a separate but equal contender for the consideration of the public. Even if Henry Bleby had started the controversy, and Henry Padgham had stood aloof, T.S. Gregory had joined the fray as a firm advocate of the cause of Methodism. The views expressed were not just Bleby's. Thirdly, it indicates the persistence of a virulent intolerance between the two groups. The language of the disputants cannot merely be dismissed as rhetoric; behind it lay the conviction that each considered the other to be inimical to the work of the Gospel. This dispute took place at the height of the debates over funding for the Methodists and, among other things, drew attention to the respective claims of the disputants.

The dispute was by no means a passing storm. The year 1863 also witnessed a prolonged controversy about the burial of children born to Methodist parents. Not having cemeteries of their own, it seems to have been the custom for such children to be buried in the churchyards of the Established Church. When therefore William Eversley, the vicar of St. Bartholomew's in Christ Church, declined to perform the necessary rites for a Methodist, Bleby protested strongly and publicly. Alleging that it was a reaction to successful Methodist open-air services in the area, Bleby charged the vicar with breach of his obligations to the public. He further accused Eversley of violating the law of Christian love, christian courtesy, and humanity, and of sowing anti-christian intolerance. [20]

In another incident Bleby detailed the story of a man who had taken his infant to the parish church of Christ Church for burial. As another service was in progress when the man arrived, the father went in leaving the infant's coffin outside. According to Bleby, when the father emerged at the end of the service, the coffin was missing – presumably buried. On the basis of an unspecified rumour, Bleby accused the rector of premeditated deception in clandestinely burying the infant. He therefore called for an exhumation of the corpse, and for the subsequent burial of the remains as a sign of good faith on the part of the Established Church. [21] There is no evidence of burial or of the exhumation having been performed, and nothing further was heard from him on the matter. What Bleby did not explain was why the clandestine act should have been undertaken after the curate had agreed to perform the burial service in the church.

Even though he did not prove the deception complained of, Bleby's airing of these grievances made the public aware of some very serious hardships which the Methodists occasionally encountered. [22] In addition to his public protest, Bleby took up the matter with the Bishop of Barbados, subsequently publishing the entire correspondence in *The Times*. [23] What the correspondence suggests is that the problem might have been settled with far less rancour than there had been. The Bishop acknowledged that Eversley had acted contrary to the law as far as Methodist baptisms were concerned. He did not make clear whether this was the civil law or the canon law. But the Bishop himself betrayed ambivalence when he expressed unwillingness to enforce conformity because the clergy were divided on the issue. He might also have avoided unnecessary rancour had he not made two offensive statements. One was to the effect that, if the Methodists wished to separate themselves with respect to the sacraments, they ought to have cemeteries of their own. The other was a re-commendation to the effect that they should cease to baptise until they had such cemeteries.

In response to the Bishop, Bleby made three very important observa-tions. First of all, he argued, no one should accept an office while harbouring "conscientious reluctance and pain about fulfilling the duties... (of) that office." Secondly, that having separate cemeteries offered no solution to the problem. It was neither reasonable nor just to require Methodists to relinquish their rights to cemeteries provided by their taxes. Thirdly, he rejected as unreasonable the Bishop's suggestion that they forego baptisms, claiming that by so doing the Methodists would be condoning intolerance. The clergy must do their duty, he emphasised. The problem was eventually solved when the Bishop proposed, and Bleby accepted, that a certificate of baptism be given by the Methodists to the minister who was being asked to do the burial. [24]

A second occasion of potential conflict between the Methodists and the Established Church arose in 1874. The immediate source was a Charge deliver-ed in the Cathedral by Bishop John Mitchinson on March 5, 1874. A very out-spoken and incautious person, [25] Mitchinson used the opportunity to comment on the Church's relations with non-conformists in the island. While he noted the absence of controversy which he attributed to "the absence of political grounds of feud, the moderation and piety of the superintendents of the two chief deno-minations, and the entire absence at present of an appetite for controversy", he was careful to point out that his understanding of the absence of controversy did not mean indifference to distinctive theological positions, nor the "complaisant assumption" that all denominations are equally excellent. He went on to thank the legislature for what he described as the establishment of "substantial religious equality" in the island. This obviously had reference to the financial arrangements of 1870 and 1871; but it is very unlikely that either the Moravians, Methodists or Roman Catholics would have shared his view on the matter. The provisions were manifestly unjust, but Mitchinson demonstrated insensitivity in his express-ion of support for the settlement. Mitchinson then went on to recognise the Mo-ravians as a branch of the "Catholic Church", but to regard the Methodists as schismatics with whom he was prepared to have very limited contacts. [26]

Mitchinson's remarks on this matter were unnecessary and disquieting because of the distinction he drew between the Moravians and the Methodists. By portraying one as a branch of the Catholic Church, and another as a schismatic pretender to being a "church", he can be said to have added fuel to the fires of prejudice which were smouldering at that time. It might well have been true, as a recent writer has stated, that the clergy followed Mitchinson's example in maintaining cordial relations with the Moravians. [27] But that in itself fails to deal with the broader issue of religious harmony which he claimed had existed in the island. Mitchinson's Charge had been neglectful of his own advice:

> nobody ever yet was won over to any creed by controversy;... like war controversy may at times become a stern necessity, but like war, we may well pray the good Lord to deliver us from it. [28]

The controversy his words might have started was not a necessity, stern or otherwise. His opinion still rankled when, in 1879, he was made President of the Education Board. The reaction to that appointment has already been recounted in a previous chapter. What all of this serves to show is that, at the very least, suspicion and distrust were dying hard in the island.

Church Discipline

Methodist discipline was very strict for all those who became converts to that body. Not only were members expected to be regular in their church attendance, but they were also expected to be exemplary in their lives. Even those portions of Sunday which were not occupied in actual worship could not be used for visiting others or receiving company. [29] Dances and other "frivolous" activities were frowned on by the rules of the church. One of their frequently quoted documents, the Liverpool Minutes of 1820, called upon Methodists to guard

> against all occupations of our time and thoughts, which have no direct connection with our great calling, and which would injuriously divert our attention from the momentous task of saving souls...[30]

In practice a watchful eye was kept over the activities of members to ensure their adherence to this exhortation as it was interpreted by the missionaries.

In 1845 a problem arose in the James Street chapel because of the association of some of the members with one of the lodges which operated in the island. This was the Oddfellows Society, which originated in England about the 1740s. The Society spread rapidly in the industrial north of England, the very areas where Methodism had a foothold. In addition, the Oddfellows met the needs of the lower middle class and the artisans who comprised the membership of the Society. Again the membership of the Methodists overlapped with the same groups. The organisation did not attract the patronage of the wealthy, as did the Freemasons, but developed into a large number of Friendly Societies. [31] In this regard, the Oddfellows were doing nothing different from the purposes served by the Methodist Friendly Society. This had been formed at Bethel in 1844 and restricted its membership to such persons as adhered to Methodist beliefs and practices. It was to that extent a church group, as those operated by Anglican churches could also be said to be church groups. Societies like the Freemasons and Oddfellows were secular, and therefore were not encouraged by the Methodists. One of the lay leaders encouraged other members of the chapel to associate with the Oddfellows, and two colleagues in dispute with the missionaries at least raised no objection. The opposition of the missionaries could be summed up in the words of Edward Branston who had only recently been appointed to James Street. He considered those who "for secular purposes united themselves to other Societies...(to be) convinced of sin." And no less an authority than the British Conference was cited in support of his abhorrence of such an association. [32]

The dissatisfaction which resulted from the way in which the missionaries handled this problem, lasted for two years and threatened to disrupt the harmony of Methodism in the island. It involved the Superintendent of the island and some of the lay officers in the James Street chapel. These persons were: a local preacher called Austin; another called Thomas, and the Circuit Steward, J. Hamilton. Its sudden emergence would suggest that the embers of dissatisfaction might have been smouldering for some time. It may also be that, in the anxiety to expand after emancipation, opinions and attitudes were being formed which had not been dealt with as they ought to have been. In addition to this, we shall notice in a limited form something of the conflict which existed between English customs and those which evolved in the West Indies.

It is only from the correspondence of the missionaries themselves that we get any idea of the nature of the problems that affected that congregation. Existing correspondence unfortunately does not include the letters written by the lay officers to London, and from that perspective is less than impartial.

These lay persons were accused by the missionaries in very general terms of being opposed to Methodist discipline. Writing to the General Secretaries, Fidler accused W.H. Austin (whom he described as an upstart local preacher) of nursing a grudge against the missionaries; Thomas of being negligent in his work; and Hamilton of "intolerable pomposity", and of adopting insulting manners towards the missionaries. These three he further described as worthless to the Methodist cause, and as turbulent demagogues. [33] Fidler's accusations appear to have been harsh and exaggerated, and to have been based largely on the leaders' open criticism of the missionaries and their policies.

For several weeks there was a battle of words between the antagonists, the Methodists making use of the *West Indian* newspaper, the other side making use of *The Liberal*. It is only in the pages of the latter that the details of the controversy are to be found. The most consistent opponent of the Methodists was the editor of *The Liberal*. He did not only consider the Oddfellows' Society to have aims consistent with christian principles, but he accused the Methodist ministers of encouraging enmity and discord. He accused them of arrogating to themselves the right to determine how others should conduct themselves – an accusation based on the advice given by them to their members to separate from those who had no proper sense of religion. But the editor was not the only critic describing a minister as a "self-conceited censor." The editor of *The Liberal* at the time was Samuel Jackman Prescod, but the other writers used a variety of pseudonyms which make identification impossible. The correspondence indicates that the uncompromising attitude of the missionaries would meet with stiff opposition from some quarters.

Part of the problem which Fidler identified at this time was the fact that certain leaders in the congregation embraced what he termed "Warrenite" opinions. The terms "Warrenite" and "Warrenism" as used by the missionaries, refer to a Dr. Samuel Warren who had sought to encourage a wider participation in the government of Methodism than that which obtained in England in 1835 when the Warrenite conflict began. This "rebel" leader was removed from the Methodist ministry, [34] and it was very unlikely that those who espoused his views would have been tolerated in Barbados. Methodism was a very autocratic system dominated by John Wesley, and, after his death, by the Conference of one hundred preachers which he established. Compliance with the decisions of this body was axiomatic for anyone who wished to remain part of the body or of the ministry. In Barbados, as elsewhere in the West Indies, the missionaries were required to conform with instructions regarding all aspects of Methodist activities.

The immediate response of the missionaries to the problem was prompt and severe. At the very outset, Fidler took steps to get rid of his antagonists. His approach was to refuse to the two lay preachers any future appointments and to assert his resolve not to nominate them for any office in his patronage. The third offender, the Circuit Steward, was also replaced. [35] Despite this, the matter had still not been resolved when we find Fidler writing to the Missionary Committee in May 1845. At most we can only say that the officers had been suspended. Branston at James Street had made use of the 1844 Conference Address to the Societies, which he was able to read to the congregation there. One section of that Address he considered particularly gratifying, "that part of it which seriously remonstrates with our members who for secular purposes unite themselves to other Societies, and which directs the pious attention of all to the faithful discharge of their duties towards each other, and towards the general community." In his view this had the effect of dissuading some of those who might otherwise have joined the Oddfellows Society, and inspired a greater diligence on the part of the members generally. [36]

Following the usual custom in such cases, disciplinary proceedings were instituted against the offenders in the Leaders' Meeting. This body played a significant role in the Methodist organisation. Apart from being responsible for their classes, the leaders had to be consulted and had to approve the appointment or removal of leaders. [37] In referring the matter to the Leaders' Meeting, Superintendent Fidler was faced with a serious problem in that a custom had evolved in the West Indies of permitting female leaders to participate in the disciplinary process. His concern was increased by the fact that these "inexperienced" female leaders, as he termed those involved here, were supporters of the dissidents. We have only Fidler's word that they were inexperienced. The chapel had long had female leaders, and one of those involved was Mrs. Ann Gill. [38] Apprehensive of his ability to maintain his own authority, he sought a ruling from the Missionary Committee. At the beginning of 1845 he reported having terminated the practice of having female leaders vote on matters of this nature; and asserted that all those with whom he had spoken had expressed satisfaction with that course. [39]

It is very unlikely that he would have spoken to any of those who sympathised with the cause, so his statement must be qualified. Far from effecting a settlement, as he claimed, his action served to aggravate the problem. Two of the male leaders refused to have their cases heard by male leaders only, and Fidler was forced to seek further advice from London. The suspended leaders had, in the meantime, refused to take their classes, causing Fidler to withhold their membership tickets on the ground that they had severed their connection with Methodism. [40] The action is strange, to say the least; for if they had been suspended for the reasons assigned, it is difficult to understand why they should have retained office as class leaders. This was one of the contradictions which Fidler did not explain. To ensure that the matter of the female leaders be laid to rest, he suggested to the London Committee that such leaders be barred from voting on disciplinary matters, and have only a restricted vote on matters of finance. [41] But the extent of the restriction was not spelt out. This conflict within a conflict was stirred up because an English missionary had rejected the variations which had taken place in local Methodism, and had insisted on the enforcement of the English practice.

The course favoured by Fidler did not have the support of his missionary colleagues. The Chairman of the District and others held to the local custom which in Fidler's view was "un-British, un-methodistical, but also unscriptural." It goes without saying that there was nothing scriptural about the practice in question, but the argument was still used. Fidler asked for either a notice in Conference Minutes clarifying the point, or a brief Circular "forwarded to every Station addressed to the female Leaders." [42] It is almost certain that the peculiar West Indian usage was a response to a situation in which the majority of the leaders happened to be female. Rather than examine it as a practical solution of a problem, Fidler was so myopic as to see it only as a departure from the letter of the law.

By the end of 1845, Fidler had gone to another Circuit, as had his colleagues in Barbados, Branston and Whitehouse. That the matter eventually petered out was due partly to the failure of the Committee in London to reply to correspondence, [43] and partly to the caution of the new missionaries. These latter were not only optimistic of an early restoration of peace, but were unwilling to take any steps which might reflect adversely on their predecessors. Part of their inaction derived from the fact that the "offenders" had been allowed by Fidler and his colleagues to continue functioning as leaders. [44] The new missionaries could not be sure how to proceed, and therefore allowed things to resolve themselves; but it is clear that they did not consider their predecessors' actions consistent or altogether wise. An uneasy peace therefore remained.

The early optimism of the new missionaries had given way to despair by the end of 1846. Early in the following year Henry Hurd, then a recent addition to the Barbados staff, reported dissatisfaction and uneasiness among the leaders and division among the congregation. Part of the dissatisfaction he attributed to the failure of the Missionary Committee to respond to a memorial of June 1845 from the leaders. Another part of the problem he attributed to the rigidity of the former missionaries. According to him, in insisting on Methodist usage, they had lost sight of "Christian courtesy and kindness". So that, even though some leaders were wrong, the overall effect was a disturbed leadership. It was in this context that he recommended a kind letter to the female leaders, particularly Mrs. Gill. [45]

Even as late as the middle of 1847 another missionary, John Corlett, reported things to be quiet, though he lamented the too free discussion of Methodist organisation and laws at James Street. [46] The persons likely to be involved in this discussion would on the one hand have been Englishmen living in Barbados, and on the other hand the elite among the coloured community. The former were likely to have had experience of Methodism in England, and to have been aware of the roles of the leaders. The latter would have embraced persons who were either rising to positions of prominence in the community, or seeing their counterparts rise. The combination of these two groups meant that the James Street chapel would have had a large proportion of the educated and social elite among the Methodists. They considered themselves a cut above the Bethel congregation, as has already been shown. Because of their education and social position, they felt that they should play a greater role in Methodist affairs. This early desire to participate in Methodist administration was not supported by the missionary in 1847. On the contrary, he expressed his preference for dealing with "spiritual matters", [47] and let the matter rest there. Thirty years later, when consideration was being given to the establishment of an autonomous Conference, the laity were not yet playing a significant role in the church. As a result, the Missionary Committee deferred granting the change until the laity had been allowed a greater share of responsibility in the church.

The West Indian Ministry

During the period of slavery there were no coloured or black clergy within the ranks of the Established Church in the West Indies. There were precious few within the ranks of the missionaries of the Nonconformist bodies. The Baptist Church was originally organised by blacks in Jamaica, and was served by a number of black leaders until 1814. In that year the first missionary arrived from England and the movement split. A native Baptist group persisted with black leaders, while the main body was led by missionaries from England. [48] This latter group did not include persons of African descent among its ministerial staff, though it contained a large African lay leadership. The Moravians and Methodists also had strong lay leadership as did the Baptists; but only the Methodists had then appointed a coloured man to the ranks of the missionaries. This was John Hodge, who served in the Antigua District from 1818 until his retirement in 1840. The Moravians had their first coloured minister in the Eastern Caribbean in 1856 in the person of John Andrew Buckley. [49]

The number of coloured Methodist ministers began to increase after the end of the system of slavery. By that time the struggles of the free coloureds in the 1820's had resulted in their being relieved of disabilities they had suffered in the past. The grant of the franchise to such as met the rigid qualifications meant that a number of them became eligible for election to the assemblies. In Jamaica in the 1840's coloureds were elected to the Assembly through the efforts of the Baptists. In Barbados, Samuel Jackman Prescod was elected to the local Assembly in 1843 and remained for some time the only coloured person there. [50] He was not representative of the views of blacks and coloureds in Barbados, nor were coloureds and blacks united in their outlook. Even as late as 1876, there was considerable division within this broad grouping during the Confederation disturbances. [51]

Between 1833 and 1845 there were 12 coloured Methodist missionaries out of some 90 in the West Indies, and these 12 were designated "Assistant Missionaries." The paucity of blacks or coloureds in the ministry may be attributed to a number of factors. One of these was the reluctance of many missionaries to encourage blacks or coloureds to enter their ranks. These missionaries thought that the persons available were not of the stamp or, in the case of the freedmen, that they needed more time to develop properly. For example, a young Jamaican recommended for the itinerant ministry in 1834 was not accepted. Some missionaries considered him better suited for the role of schoolmaster. The issue contributed to the schism which resulted in the Methodist Church in Jamaica, in which Thomas Pennock played a major part. [52] On the other hand, the society itself and some officials objected to having Africans as preachers. There was opposition to George Lisle, Moses Baker and a number of others in Jamaica. Sir Ralph Woodford in Trinidad objected to a Methodist missionary allowing slaves to preach. [53] If the white missionary was considered irresponsible and unacceptable to him, it is not to be expected that coloured missionaries would have found favour with him. Colonial prejudice was so strongly against Africans in the role of preachers that the missionaries would have thought their caution justified.

The paucity of coloured missionaries, which was so noticeable in the West Indies as a whole, was for some time characteristic of all the churches in Barbados. The Moravians did have a local white minister in the person of James Young Edghill, who had begun serving in 1853. They were not to have a coloured local minister until 1871, when Henry Moore returned to the island after ten years' service in Tobago and Antigua. In striking parallel to the experience of W. H. Griffith, a coloured Methodist minister, the local Moravian Conference had recommended Moore as "a fit and proper person to be appointed our Assistant in the Mission in any of the sister islands." [54] When one considers that Edghill spent his entire ministry in Barbados, the difference in policy is remarkable. Although they were ministering to blacks and coloured persons, it would appear that they did not want to take a step that was unusual at that time. White Caribbean society, and white Barbadian society in particular, was strongly resistant to the upward mobility of the coloured person. W. G. Sewell noted in 1859 the strict observance of a caste system in the island, with all the distrust born of such prejudices. [55] It would therefore have been difficult to deploy coloured ministers in the island at that time. Such coloured ministers as the Methodists accepted for work were being posted to other islands.

According to John Gilmore, such non-whites as were ordained to the Anglican ministry by the late 1850's were destined for the less remunerative parishes of the Windward Islands. He assigns two basic reasons for the paucity of coloured clergy in Barbados. One of these was the prejudice of the laity themselves, expressed in the following passage, the source of which he has not given:

> ...while the planters actually contemn a black clergyman, however exemplary in character and respectable in attainments, the negroes feel

themselves slighted whenever they have a shepherd of their own colour. [56]

Though Gilmore has not attempted to explain the contradiction in the attitude of the black congregants, one can reasonably conclude that their attitude reflects that depreciation of themselves which was the tendency of the slave system. The other reason Gilmore assigns for the paucity of coloured clergy is the "gentlemen heresy." This heresy consisted of a bias in favour of university-educated clergy. This bias was certainly there under Bishop Coleridge, and was the reason for his failure to ordain candidates recommended to him by the Church Missionary Society. [57] The "gentlemen heresy" is reflected in the Ordination Tables which Gilmore compiled for the Diocese of Barbados for the years 1842 –1873. Of the 85 candidates whose backgrounds are studied, 30 are listed as "Not Ascertainable." Of the balance, only 17 are listed as having fathers in the areas of the trades or teaching; and only one these is listed as belonging to the class "Free Person of Colour."

Even though the formal organisation of Methodism in the West Indies dated back to 1786, there were very few West Indian ministers by the last third of the nineteenth century. Henry Hurd estimated in 1872 that there were nine in the Jamaica District, nine in the St. Vincent District, six in the Antigua District, and five in the Demerara District. [58] Recruitment of West Indians was a slow process, and was spurred on by pressure from the Missionary Committee in London. We have already seen that the Committee sought to encourage the recruitment of "Native Agents" to effect economy in financial matters. While it would appear that the term was used for West Indians generally, the predominant usage seems to have been in reference to black or coloured ministers. Thus when William Bannister wrote to the Committee in 1853 about pastoral problems, he spoke of the likelihood of the "Native Agents" setting themselves up if no missionary was appointed to Ebenezer. Similarly, when a coloured minister, John Horsford, protested inequalities in 1867, he spoke of native youths who had recently been recommended for the ministry. [59] The only "native youths" on record turn out to be coloured. It means therefore that while some of the issues affected white West Indians, the inequities complained of more frequently applied to the black and coloured ministers.

That the English missionaries were not very eager to encourage a "Native" ministry can be stated with some confidence. Two circumstances may be cited by way of illustrating this. The first of these was the case of W. H. Griffith, a coloured Barbadian, who had offered himself as a candidate for the ministry. The District meeting of 1852 recommended him "cordially and unanimously" to the Missionary Committee. The Minutes then added:

> The Brethren are of opinion that he would make a good missionary to any part of Africa...

The Missionaries also made the sympathetic recommendation that, if so appointed, he should be allowed to marry, as his fiancee was eminently suitable. No explanation was given for recommending him for work in Africa, especially since there were openings in the West Indies. Nor did these minutes indicate whether he had expressed a desire to serve in Africa. We are also not told why he was not eventually sent to Africa, and the minutes for the time of his acceptance no longer exist. In the only other case on record of such proposed or actual posting, the candidate is said to have requested to go to Africa. [60]

The District Meeting of 1854 provides the second circumstance. When that Meeting discussed the issue of local ministers, it did so with a strong sense of impatience on the part of the Missionary Committee in London. And so members sought to clear themselves of any suspicion the Committee might have had about their opposition to the idea, and to impress on that body their inability to find suitable candidates as well as their concern to safeguard the respectability of the ministry. Their reply to the Committee ended with this argument:

> We should justly incur the censure of the Committee if, in our zeal, we were to recommend men who were not competent and who consequently would bring our ministry into disrepute. [61]

The Secretary of that Meeting was Henry Hurd, who was later to serve as Chairman of the District at a time when the issue assumed much greater proportions. What is interesting is that the minutes reflect the position consistently taken by Hurd. Whether they actually reflect what was said, or whether Hurd framed them as he would have preferred is a question to which no conclusive answer can be given. Others continued to offer themselves to the ministry and were accepted as "Assistant Missionaries."

The term "Assistant Missionary", to which objection was taken by a prominent West Indian minister, first appeared in the Minutes of the District Meeting for 1847. There it was used with respect to two former probationers, who were being recommended for full ministerial status. The minutes record the request from the District Meeting that the designation be no longer applied to the two missionaries, William Heath and William Cleaver. The next available minutes, those for 1849, omit the term in listing the missionaries in question. This would suggest that the term applied at that time to probationers. The term next appears in the minutes for 1854, at which time it referred to a coloured Barbadian, William H. Griffith, who had just completed the first year of his probation. Thereafter, the term is used for black and coloured West Indians, with the single exception of Jonathan Richardson who was white. However, it ceased to be used of Richardson after he finished his probation.

The correlation of this usage with a steady trickle of coloured personnel into the ministry suggests that there was a note of inferiority attached to it. When James E. Chase offered himself for the ministry in 1858, the District Meeting recommended his acceptance as a permanent "Assistant Missionary". This recommendation may have been influenced by the fact that Chase was then a widower with four children, [62] and that it was not customary to accept as a missionary one who already had a family. But we cannot be sure of this. One possible clue to our understanding of the distinction can be found in the address presented to him on the eve of his departure from Barbados for Tobago. This address, presented by persons who had been in his class for several years, stressed that the West Indies possessed suitable material for the Methodist ministry. The group then went on to express the hope

> that we may regard your appointment (together with that of Mr. Shrewsbury and others recently admitted from this and other West India Islands) as the dawn of a brighter era in the history of our Church in these islands than any which has hitherto attended it, and you will prove the precursors of many to follow, if not the nucleus of a native ministry, not indeed as such to cause the subversion of a European Agency, but by a strict union, and active co-operation therewith, to promote the interest of Christ's kingdom, as well as supply a want more generally felt in the Antilles than is often expressed.

While thanking Hurd and Heath for their efforts in fostering Chase's vocation, they asked why there were not more native ministers. By way of partial response they reflected:

> Happily for the dignity of our race, the stigma heaped upon it of mental incapacity and intellectual inferiority has long since been removed by the genius displayed by many of its members in every walk of life where opportunities presented themselves...

Concluding that if they had not improved the "Wesleyan Missionary enterprise" would have been a failure, the group expressed the prayer that the Head of the Church would enable her

> to perceive the want of the times, and adopt and carry out such measures in accordance with the improved state of society, as cannot fail to tend to her internal strength and external prosperity. [63]

The nature of the Address, which spoke of the disabilities which had been removed from "our" race, suggests that colour was a major obstacle here. When this is compared with what the Ministers were saying about the absence of suitable material, it also suggests that the writers harboured a suspicion of racism on the part of the ministers who led the church.

In the early nineteenth century, it was customary for missionaries recruited in the West Indies to be paid at the same rate as missionaries recruited in England. This policy had been followed with the knowledge and approval of the Missionary Committee. It was only in the second half of the century that a change came about when the Committee itself used the distinction in rates as a means of effecting economy. The Committee was of the view that "Native" ministers were likely to have fewer needs and be more adaptable to local hardships than their European counterparts. This new policy drew sharp criticism from Jonathan Edmondson, the Chairman of the Jamaica District. [64]

Two other reasons may be suggested for the new policy. In the first place, the demands of the "home" missions were increasing and the English Circuits were no longer producing the personnel to fill the inevitable gaps. And as the century progressed, there was an increasing shortage of trained ministers such as the recently established Theological Institution [65] was expected to produce. This necessarily meant a shortage of personnel for the West Indian missions. In the second place, English Methodism was continuing its thrust into Africa and the Far East. The basis for the Committee's course was that the West Indies could no longer be regarded as an infant to be constantly supported by the parent body. Part of the self-sufficiency they expected, therefore, was its ability to produce the manpower necessary for its on-going development.

Stipends and allowances constituted only one area in which distinctions existed between the West Indian and the English missionaries. Another area related to the "Itinerant Preachers Fund", what was in effect a pension fund for the ministers. It would appear that, before any minister was able to join the fund, the Missionary Committee was required to pay into it a sum of £ 4.4s. This sum the Committee was also to pay annually, while the missionary himself was required to pay £ 7 annually. A problem arose in 1863 because the Missionary Committee refused to make any payments for some West Indian born ministers, and the Directors of the Fund were unwilling to admit any new West Indian missionary until the deposit had been paid. After discussing the matter, the District Meeting of that year made very forceful representations to the Committee. On the one hand the Meeting was of the view that the Missionary Committee should not allow local ministers to be placed at a disadvantage as against their English counterparts. The Meeting therefore advised the Committee to ensure that the local ministers were placed on the same footing as ministers in England. On the other hand the Meeting noted that the Committee had previously paid for some local ministers. Members deplored the injustice of refusing to pay for others at that time, and called for a removal of all disabilities. [66] The differentiation seems to have been twofold: one was a differentiation between English and West Indian ministers, the other was a distinction between West Indians. One suspects that the latter distinction was one of colour, that is, between white and coloured or black West Indian ministers.

The issue of the status of West Indian ministers had been raised somewhat earlier by John Horsford, a coloured minister, in a book entitled *A Voice from the West Indies.* A brief notice of the positions taken in that book is made with a view to indicating the reasons for Horsford's unpopularity with some church officials. One point may be regarded as fundamental to all that Horsford wrote on the subject: colour can neither enhance nor diminish worth. Horsford expressed clearly his abhorrence of colour prejudice whose basis was nothing more than the "hereditary connexion with a race whose progenitors were black." On this premise, he argued strongly for a local ministry which he considered necessary both to avoid excessive outlay from Britain and to prove that a good foundation had been laid. He himself was not in favour of the withdrawal of European ministers, whom he was prepared to retain if only "to perpetuate brotherly reciprocity." This local ministry, he argued, must be undertaken "deliberately, energetically, and perseveringly." Overall, his emphasis was on the equality of the ministers. [67] In his later pronouncements he would reject the idea that West Indian ministers needed less money than their English counterparts.

It was while he was on the last stage of his Methodist ministry that Horsford most severely criticised the system which had hitherto prevailed. In broaching the subject, Horsford made reference to the practice of limiting the functions of some West Indians to those of catechists. This was aggravated, he claimed, by the fact that such catechists were not allowed to function in every chapel. Although he acknowledged that the practice had been confined to the Antigua District at that time, it would appear that he feared its extension to the St. Vincent District of which Barbados was a part. This led him to take a broader view of the issue, and to seek to ascertain the Committee's position. "I am confident", he wrote, "that you and your respected colleagues will not sanction anything that would wilfully disparage or deliberately degrade any person simply because he may be a West India." [68] In a subsequent letter, Horsford would take issue with this distinction which in fact originated with the Committee.

A second area which Horsford criticised concerned the designation of the ministerial staff. Horsford's quarrel was that, despite having been admitted to "full connexion", some West Indians were still being designated "Assistant Missionaries", while less experienced Englishmen were not so designated. Either they were qualified, in which case it was improper to reduce them to an inferior status while they did the same work as Englishmen; or they were unqualified, in which they would not have been recommended for admission to full ministerial rank. [69] What was an even greater offence to him was that no West Indian was considered eligible for the highest office – the Chairmanship of the District. On the contrary, they were being superseded by persons of less experience than themselves. In asking the Committee to change its policy, he remarked:

> I feel that natives deserve consideration at your hands, that equality of status is just; and that invidious distinctions instead of doing good can only lead to discord between brethren which I have every desire to avoid. [70]

On the basis of Horsford's letter, one can attribute the discrimination to the Committee itself. Their policy was responsible for the entrenchment within the ministry of those same prejudices which had for long been present in West Indian society.

A third area of complaint concerned the remuneration of the missionaries, with Europeans being more amply rewarded than their West Indian counterparts. It is with respect to this practice that Horsford opposed the view that the Europeans' needs were greater than those of their West Indian counterparts. In the first place, he observed that the duality of scales implied an invidious distinction which remained a formidable barrier to equality of status. In doing so, he made the point, not likely to be well received, that the European missionary was not necessarily superior to the West Indian. Citing the equality among the Moravians and in the Established Church, in the latter of which all were rectors, he pleaded for a system similar to that in England where the salary was related to the means of the Circuits. His point was only partially sound. By referring to rectors alone, he did not take into consideration the problem of those who ministered at the chapels-of-ease. These latter, while their stipends were equal, were paid substantially less than the rectors. In any case, they were not entitled to the glebes which were the perquisites of the rectors. In 1867, the rectors were receiving £ 320.10.3 sterling per year, while the other clergy were receiving £ 200. [71] In 1877 the coloured Moravian minister Henry Moore complained of receiving only £ 145 per year. But even in 1870, the white local Moravian minister Edghill noted that his own stipend was £ 170 per year – the same as his other colleagues. [72] Moore's complaint implies either a reduction since 1870, or that he was being paid at a lower level than his colleague Edghill who was white.

Quite apart from the difference in treatment of Europeans and West Indians, Horsford detected a difference in the treatment of two West Indian ministers. These were James Chase and Jeremiah Shrewsbury, who had both been recruited in the West Indies as mature candidates, and whose salaries were supposedly fixed. However, a decided preference had been shown for young Shrewsbury, [73] who was the son of the missionary driven out of Barbados in 1823, and who had been born in St. Vincent. The obvious answer to the query being raised by Horsford was that Shrewsbury was white and Chase was coloured. But another case makes it necessary to review this response. It transpired from the correspondence that another coloured minister called Trotman had been granted an increase, while Chase had remained at the same stipend for twelve years. Trotman, though junior to Chase, had succeeded in pressing his case for consideration. Shrewsbury, however, had been accorded the same recognition given missionaries coming from England. The Committee were the ones to blame for the situation which developed, since they had been responsible for the distinction. They had also rejected Hurd's plea for financial assistance for Chase. [74] Even so, we note that Hurd's plea was for financial assistance, and not for all to be put on the same footing.

Hurd's attitude to this matter could be described as ambivalent. He would have insisted that he was as eager to have an indigenous ministry as anyone else. Yet he seems frequently to have demurred at precisely that point at which concrete action was expected. For example, Hurd pleaded that local men not be sent into ministerial work without first undergoing proper training. He further stressed:

> When I consider that so little has been done in the way of education and training I am surprised there are so many Native Ministers in the West Indies as there are. [75]

In fairness to Hurd, his attitude reflected the changes which were only then beginning to appear in the Methodist body as a whole, in that more emphasis was being placed on training prior to beginning work. In the past a candidate was accepted for the ministry and placed as a probationer under a senior minister who guided his reading and study, as well as supervised his functions. So that after a period of some four years the candidate was accepted into "full connexion" and ordained. At this time Hurd would have been aware that several of the English ministers lacked the training he was advocating.

In response to Horsford's criticism about salaries and the likelihood of its deterring would-be candidates, Hurd adopted a patronising attitude which could be described as unfair. This was particularly the case in his remarks about three candidates who were presented for work in the mission, one of whom was from the St. Vincent District. According to him, the latter individual, though surprised at the small stipend, was by no means deterred from offering himself. Hurd asserted that the candidate's interest was in preaching the Gospel, not in remuneration. The young man seems to have had some talent to the extent that Hurd was prepared to recommend him for training in England. In so doing, he assured the Committee: "he is most worthy of your fostering care, and...you would be amply rewarded by the gratitude and diligence and usefulness of the young man, for the benefits conferred." He then went on to assert that some people had been trying to turn the young man from his purpose, but that "nobler sentiments influenced him." [76] There is a patronising ring to the words of Hurd. The candidate might well have opted for the small stipend, notwithstanding the discrimination. It does not necessarily mean that he was satisfied with the provision. That there was dissatisfaction, and that it was spreading, is fairly certain. Less than two years after Hurd wrote this letter, the Committee took cognizance of the extent of dissatisfaction among the ministers. They reported that a newly ordained minister "could only consent to remain in the work on condition that all financial distinctions be removed." Four other young men, according to the Minutes, "offer themselves only on this condition, and are recommended on this condition alone." [77] It was an unusual rebellion, and the Committee eventually won the day; but it shows that concern over the discrepancy was quite serious.

The fact that the differential in remuneration between local and English ministers originated with the Committee, and the fact that the differential implied the inferiority of a section of the West Indian ministers, indicates that the Committee was not in favour of equality among the ministers. Part of the Committee's stance was attributable to Marmaduke Osborn, one of the General Secretaries. It was he who seems to have persuaded the Committee of the need for a differential in the scales of remuneration. His explanation was that

> Unless...the Ministry to be raised in the West Indies could be supported on a more economical scale, and the means of their support be provided by the resources of the islands, there was no alternative, but that the work must decay. It was therefore with deep concern that the Secretaries found that the Districts insisted on an entire equality between the European and the Native Ministers not of ministerial capacity and standing, which have never been questioned, but of pecuniary allowances. [78]

The Committee supported Osborn in making the distinction, on the ground that "To lay upon the people the burden of supporting a Native ministry at European rates is in effect to discourage and prohibit a Native Ministry." The Committee also expressed "in the strongest manner their concurrence" with instructions sent out on the matter. Those instructions were the financial arrangements concerning which ministers objected in 1864 and after.

Another of the architects of the new policy was Elijah Hoole, one of the General Secretaries. And several missionaries expressed shock and surprise that he had been a signatory to such a letter as had come to them in 1864. One of the points to which Horsford had taken strong exception was Dr. Hoole's suggestion of a strong desire to confine the Europeans to a few leading positions, leaving the West Indians to survive on such support as they were able to muster from the local societies. This suggestion so horrified Horsford that he felt unable to deal with it for some time. [79] As the architects of the new policy, the Committee would not have been able to understand his sensitivity to the matter. They were too far removed, both by distance and by origin, to see his point. Influential members of the Committee itself had intended local ministers only for inferior positions. And his opposition to that was the reason for Horsford's unpopularity among Methodist policy makers.

Henry Hurd himself was not amenable to the views being expressed by Horsford and others. Quite apart form his annoyance at the ventilation of this subject, Hurd was unfairly critical of two persons who were its principal advocates. These were Horsford himself and Jonathan Richardson, a white West Indian minister recently transferred to the District. Both of these he regarded as having extreme views on the subject. He accused both men of being "Utterly opposed...to all" of the Committee's recent measures, which would suggest that Richardson was as vocal in his opposition to this discrimination as was Horsford. However, Hurd presented no evidence to substantiate his accusation. He even went so far as to say that it was not in the best interests of the Committee to have both men in the same District, and so he urged the Committee to separate them. [80] Given the fact that Horsford was coloured, the fact that a white West Indian held views similar to his would indicate that the problem was far more serious than Hurd wanted to acknowledge. What he seems to have wanted was an end to the discussion.

So great was the emotion generated by this matter that Horsford eventually resigned from the Methodist ministry in order to seek ordination in the Established Church. [81] At that time, he had already completed some 32 years as a Methodist minister. Somewhat maliciously, Hurd expressed his joy at Horsford's departure; [82] while the author of the 1869 Report for the Ebenezer Circuit alleged that the Circuit had begun to revive immediately after his departure. [83] The Report was no more than an additional jab at Horsford. There had not been enough time for any change to have become evident; and unless there was a resident minister, the normal pattern was for the performance of the Circuit to decline. Since a successor was not appointed until the following year, the Circuit was managed from Bridgetown. It could not have received the kind of attention which a resident minister might have provided, the lack of which attention had previously been given as a reason for its failure to perform.

What this debate did was to expose the fragility of the relationship between English and West Indian ministers. That fragility was expressed by one of their missionaries, John Wesley Genge, who, after some adverse comments on the way in which the missionaries raised funds for the work, went on to say:

> I know I could do much to improve matters in my own society, but my hands are tied. I can inaugurate nothing, any suggestion or remark as to how we manage at home is ignored... Whenever Mr. Hurd retires from the Chairmanship I earnestly hope you will appoint some English minister to succeed him one who will have some depth of piety and large experience. [84]

The recommendation went beyond the mere difference between English and West Indian customs. What is evident here is not just an English minister being unwilling to accept West Indian adaptations to English Methodist practice; on the contrary, we see a resentment against having as superiors persons originating in the West Indies. So that by the time the West Indian Conference became a reality, some Englishmen were ready to withdraw from service in the West Indies.

The inauguration of the Conference in 1883 coincided with certain changes in the staff serving the Barbados Circuits, and with an unfortunate controversy over an appointment to the James Street Chapel. At the centre of this controversy was an English minister called William Parker, and a West Indian called Jonathan Richardson. Originally an ardent supporter of Richardson, or so he claimed, Parker became so opposed to being superseded at James Street by Richardson that he left the Methodist ministry. Parker's letters on this issue were numerous and contradictory and they illustrated three things. First of all, they showed that Parker believed James Street to be the proper place for him. To be moved, in his opinion, suggested demotion, so he turned down the offer of the Kingstown Circuit in St. Vincent. At one time the premier Circuit in the St. Vincent District, Kingstown had gradually yielded pride of place to James Street, but it still remained an important circuit. With the Eastern Conference having its headquarters in Barbados, the James Street Circuit became even more attractive. Parker therefore believed that he was the man for this Circuit, and that it was his special function to raise Methodism in the eyes of the upper classes in Barbados. He wished to "stamp" his name on Barbados as Hurd and others had done. [85] He was disappointed in that he was being deprived of the opportunity to realise that ambition.

The second thing illustrated by the correspondence was that Parker was an individual who harboured very deep prejudices. Behind what he wrote must be seen a devaluation of the West Indians and an exaggerated sense of what was due to an Englishman. One sees this, for example, when he recommended the transfer of the coloured minister Allan Campbell from Providence in Christ Church to Berbice in British Guiana, in which latter station he asserted no Englishman ought to have been located. [86] In addition, Parker seems to have made common cause with persons he called "the whole of the most respectable of our people", whose support he claimed for his right to remain at James Street. Indeed, Parker boasted of being the only Superintendent educated at a Theological College. [87] Yet the reports which the annual District Meeting of 1872 made on his examinations as a probationer do not show him as an outstanding person. Parker merely expected as an Englishman to be given preference.

The third feature illustrated by the correspondence was Parker's arrogance. He complained that Richardson had accused him of being "inconsistent, illogical" and of demonstrating "undue love of self." [88] The last is perfectly true, so far as the correspondence illustrates. In one of his letters, Parker spoke of himself as an acceptable preacher anywhere in Barbados. In another he noted the need for "more cultured" Methodist preachers in the island, observing that neither Chairman George Sykes nor Wright – a senior minister – knew the needs of Barbadian pulpits. [89] Parker's assessment of the needs of Barbados must be judged against his own assessment of what he had to offer. It is therefore not a fair indication of the state of things in Barbados. In spite of all he did, Parker failed in his efforts to secure the James Street Chapel for himself; but he was successful in being accepted for the ministry of the Established Church. He became the minister of St. Philip-the-Less at Boscobel in St. Peter, from 1885 to 1892. [90] His defection was the second in less than two decades, but the circumstances were by no means as aggravating as those which had prompted the departure of John Horsford.

The West Indian Conference

In the closing years of the nineteenth century, three of the largest denominations in the West Indies were involved in processes to attain autonomous status. For the Anglican Church, the process was carried through to its completion in 1883 and has survived without interruption. Discussions had actually begun among the West Indian bishops as early as 1873, and concluded with the formation of the Province of the West Indies some ten years later. The Bishops were concerned about financial difficulties facing the church following disestablishment in all the territories except Barbados. [91] However, the Anglicans already had a solid financial base and were still recipients of financial support from the S.P.G. in London. For various reasons, the chief of which was cost of travel, it was decided to institute a Provincial Synod which comprised bishops only, with provisions for clerical and lay representation as soon as circumstances permitted. [92]

The Moravian process dates back to 1848, and was prompted by the concern of their Mission Board in Europe to detach its oldest mission so as to direct funds elsewhere. The objective of the Mission Board was threatened by a number of problems which successfully retarded the attainment of full autonomy by its West Indian missions. Of great significance was the fact that the missions were unable to attain complete self-support. This was due in large part to the economic conditions which from time to time were of a depressing nature. In addition to this, they lacked a sufficiently large West Indian staff of ministers to prevent them depending on European recruits. Lacking the facilities to train their own staff in the West Indies, they were dependent on Codrington College since their own College in Pennsylvania was diffident about admitting coloured candidates. In 1880 their General Synod in Herrnhut, Germany, recommended increased lay participation in the management of church affairs as a prerequisite to autonomy. In the end the General Synod could only grant limited autonomy until the deficiencies mentioned above had been corrected. [93]

In the case of the Methodists, it is not possible to say precisely when the idea of a Conference began to take shape. It appears to have been the intention of the Missionary Committee as early as 1845. Findlay and Holdsworth note that in that year the Committee expressed the hope that they would soon be rid of their West Indian burden whom they could leave to get by on their own resources. The attitude of the Committee was based on their loss of revenue in England and their desire to respond to new missionary challenges. [94] In this regard the Methodist approach was similar to that of the Moravians. But whereas the latter were prepared to allow their West Indian missions a grace period during which to improve their finances, the Methodists forced their missions to conform with their financial arrangements.

Individual missionaries in the West Indies did not give expression to any desire for a conference – at least as far as the records indicate. The only exception to this was Horsford who, in a moment of frustration, urged that the sooner the West Indies was separated from London the better it would be. [95] However, one cannot build a case on this solitary outburst which was aggravated by the issue of discrimination against West Indian ministers. If others shared the outlook of Horsford, they did not venture to express it.

The idea of a West Indian conference began to emerge at the District Meeting of 1872, in which the Meeting responded to a letter from the Committee. In their response the Meeting assured the Committee of their desire to attain to self-support as quickly as possible, and of their efforts to prepare the people for that goal. [96] One gets the impression that pressure was being brought to bear on them. The following year the District Meeting asserted that the time had come for a distinct conference or two conferences as seemed appropriate. Reporting that all chapels had become free of debt, the Meeting thanked the Committee for their financial support in the past. [97] This would suggest that the Meeting felt ready to take on the responsibilities of self-support and self-government. The votes in the Meeting of 1883, by which time the personnel had changed somewhat, convey a contrary opinion as will be shown later.

The idea of a West Indian Conference was seriously addressed by the St. Vincent District Meeting of 1875. From that discussion it would appear that the Committee wanted to have a wholly "native" ministry first. The District Meeting regarded that course as unattainable in the absence of an institution for training the candidates. The District Meeting also expressed disagreement with a view, which they attributed to the Committee, to the effect that the ministry should be African. In the light of those concerns, members stressed that

> while they desire to see many more raised up of that class, they would remind the Committee that West Indian Society is more mixed than perhaps that of any other part of the world, and this mixed society means that the Ministry must necessarily be mixed also, as any other

course would tend to uphold rather than to overthrow the abominable class prejudices that still prevail. [98]

The distinction between "native" and "African" indicates that persons of West Indian origin were contemplated, and incidentally reinforces the view that "native" could include both groups.

In 1879 the Committee decided to send the Rev. Marmaduke Osborn on an extensive visit to the West Indies to obtain information on a number of areas. First of these was the necessity for, and the possibility of, self-government on the part of the West Indian Districts. In the second place, Osborn was to investigate the desirability of creating an Affiliated Conference in the West Indies. And finally, he was to discover the arrangements which were being made by the Districts for liquidating the chapel debts. [99]

The visit of Osborn to the Meeting of the St. Vincent District in 1879 showed up a series of weaknesses as far as the Committee was concerned. London had made clear its demand for "a well organised lay element" before Conference status could be granted to the West Indies. The Meeting insisted that there already was a lay element in the churches, and that if their desire was granted things would sort themselves out. The normal practice was for the ministers to dominate the Methodist organisation. No lay person usually attended the District Meetings, though lay officers from James Street attended when the Meeting was held in Barbados. Even so these laymen had no rights, but were only present as guests. At the Circuit level, the ministers often functioned as Chapel and Circuit Stewards with responsibility for the finances. The Missionary Committee insisted on the appointment of lay officers, and the District Meeting agreed to promote at once the appointment of Poor Stewards, Society Stewards, and Circuit Stewards. [100] In itself this concession on the part of the District Meeting was an admission that they had not been promoting lay participation at this level.

The first step in the new process had been taken in Barbados some months later when a missionary reported the implementation of the recommendations, and his relief from responsibility for Chapel Finance. [101] The missionary had been stationed at James Street Chapel, the best endowed in terms of potential lay leadership. Even here the change was not as easy as there was a challenge against the activities of the missionaries in that they did not conform to English practice. The challenge did not amount to much and was not effective. The same relief which the James Street minister felt was reported to be general in the District. Osborn's visit had therefore set in motion the kind of development for which the means, if not the will, had been available for some time. The District Meeting of 1879 had made certain recommendations by way of easy stages towards implementing the Conference arrangements, though members were not happy to be put off by the Missionary Committee. As an experiment for the two years, they agreed that the District be subdivided and that there be annual representative gatherings to conduct the business then undertaken by the District Meeting. The members thought that the Circuits would be well supplied with lay officers, and that the experience gained would be valuable when the Conference was actually formed. In this way the transition to a Conference was expected to be easy. [102] After discussing Osborn's Report, the Missionary Committee concluded that the establishment of a West Indian Conference would be premature, and repeated its demand for "an improved Circuit and District organisation" with laymen sharing those "privileges and responsibilities which hitherto belonged to ministers only." The Committee further decided to review the matter in three years. [103]

It is only in 1881 that the District Meeting opened the way for the Circuit Stewards to be allowed full participation in their deliberations. The Circuit Stewards to be so honoured were those who were willing to assume financial responsibilities. What these entailed were fourfold: that they should keep the mission houses in good repair and furnished without any additional grant from the District Meeting save that for ordinary deficiencies; that they should keep the Circuit Accounts, receiving and disbursing the funds of the Societies; and finally, that they should endeavour to help forward the work of God and to promote the general interests of the Societies. [104]

The majority of the English ministers were opposed to the establishment of a Conference in the West Indies. There were three grounds for their opposition. First, they cited the financial incapacity of the West Indies, due to general poverty and the indebtedness of the Societies. Second, they drew attention to the need to depend on European ministers for some time to come, arguing that the class of persons composing West Indian congregations generally were not such as to supply the best material for the "Native Ministry". Third, they considered that there was a lack of sufficient British laymen in the West Indies, [105] a deficiency which they regarded as militating against the success of the venture. In short, the ministers did not believe the local laymen capable of managing the affairs of the church, and further feared the deterioration of Methodism under such leadership. In effect, they condemned all but English laymen. The point is that each new group of English ministers from the 1860s onwards saw defects in those usages which one could identify as West Indian. The need to preserve British Methodism was their primary intention – and that required British laymen.

What gave impetus to the implementation of the Conference plan was the return to England of an English minister called George Sergeant in 1881. He had experience of the West Indies, having served in Antigua - and more recently in Jamaica - over a period of some twenty-one years. He was drafted into the Missionary Conference, which he seems to have persuaded that the West Indies was ready for a conference. By this time, Osborn seems also to have changed his view on the matter; and the establishment of a Conference in South Africa, a land of mixed races like the West Indies made the Committee more amenable to establishing one in the West Indies. Above all, dissatisfaction over the cost to British Methodists of the West Indian missions prompted the Committee to begin planning in earnest for casting off its burdensome progeny. George Sargeant, who was so influential in getting the idea accepted, was either fortunate or influential in being appointed the first President of the West Indian Conference. [106] The Missionary Committee, on the assumption that the Conference should be established along the same lines as that established in South Africa, sought no specific proposals from the West Indian Districts. [107] The latter did have an opportunity to comment on the proposals as they were developed. Strangely enough, the Moravians also related the West Indian situation to that in South Africa when they were considering proposals for a Conference in the region.

By the time the matter was brought to a head, there was a great cleavage within the ranks of the ministers in what was now the St. Vincent and Demerara District. The meeting of this newly combined District illustrates how far apart Englishmen and West Indians had grown on the matter. It also illustrates the differences which had arisen within the ranks of the West Indians. At the District Meeting of 1883 three resolutions were considered. One of these stated that a Conference was premature and likely to be detrimental to work in the area. This resolution, moved by John Grimshaw and Henry Adams, English missionaries in British Guiana, received eight votes with support from two West Indians, J.P. Owens and E. D. Jones, both white Barbadians. By way of a counter resolution, one by West Indians Walter Garry and Allan Campbell, urged that the time was opportune for establishing a Conference and called on the Committee to make the necessary arrangements for effecting it. All six supporters of this resolution were coloured West Indians. The third resolution sympathised with the Committee's intention to form a West Indian Conference, promised not to oppose it, but asked for details of the scheme prior to its implementation. Moved by Englishmen David Wright and Frederick Miller, this resolution received nine votes including those of three West Indians. [108] The three West Indians were all coloured.

The pattern of voting we see here indicates that the ministers were divided not simply into West Indians and Englishmen; but that the West Indians themselves were divided. The two white West Indians were opposed to the establishment of a conference, the coloured West Indians were either wholly or partially in support. The level of positive support for a West Indian Conference in the St. Vincent and Demerara District was very small – approximately 25 percent. Elsewhere in the West Indies there was division on the issue. In the Antigua District, the Chairman, Thomas Chambers, and his colleagues rejected the idea on the ground that the scheme would be "cumbrous and expensive." In the Bahamas the Chairman, Jonathan Richardson, remained resolutely in favour of the conference while his District was as resolutely opposed to it. [109] Lack of consensus in the West Indies did not prevent the plan being implemented. At its meeting at Hull in England in 1883, the British Conference reported that the West Indian mission had reached "that stage of growth when the demand for a conference is imperative." Therefore the Conference decided that the establishment of a West Indian Conference was "the only safe way" of meeting the West Indian demand. [110]

The arrangement for the West Indies consisted of a General Conference which was to meet every three years, along with two Annual Conferences. One Annual Conference comprised the three existing Jamaica Districts and the Haiti District, and was known as the West Indian Western Conference. The other consisted of the Antigua, St. Vincent and Demerara Districts, and was known as the West Indian Eastern Conference. As far as structure was concerned, the General Conference was composed as follows: When dealing with ministerial affairs the President, who was also to be President of each of the Annual Conferences; the Vice-President of each Annual Conference; the Chairman of each District in the West Indies; and ten elected ministers, five from each Annual Conference. When dealing with more general matters, the General Conference comprised all the ministers mentioned above, together with the Treasurer of each Fund, and ten laymen elected in the same way as the ministers. The Annual Conferences were structured in two sections as was the General Conference. For the discussion of ministerial matters each Annual Conference consisted of the President and Vice-President; the Chairman of each District within the jurisdiction of the Annual Conference; and one out of every three ministers, to be elected at the District Meeting preceding the Conference. For more general matters, the Annual Conference was to consist of all the ministers just mentioned, together with two lay General Treasurers, and elected laymen equivalent to those ministers elected at the District Meetings.

The functions of the Conference were also clearly set out. The General Conference was to have the sole power of legislation and to "exercise full oversight and control" of Methodist work in the region. Its task involved responsibility for Literature, Worship, Temperance, and the review of Methodist Missionary affairs. It was also responsible for the transfer of ministers from one Annual Conference to the other. However, it had no power to hear appeals from the Annual Conferences with respect to the supervision or discipline of ministers or members. Such matters of discipline were restricted to the Annual Conferences which constituted the final courts of appeal. The Annual Conferences were also responsible for the selection and deployment of ministers, general educational affairs, all matters relating to property, as well as the funds of the Districts. English ministers on probation were given the option of staying or returning to England when their probation ended.

The last chapter in the series of events was to come soon after the new President arrived. When Sargeant arrived in the island, there were seven ministers, only two of whom were English. Following the custom on such occasions, a polite Address was presented in which the signatories pledged their support and cooperation. They expressed their confidence in Sargeant, whose long service in Antigua and Jamaica they felt sure would give him a thorough knowledge of the West Indies and its needs. They looked forward to a proper organisation of Methodism in the West Indies, with due regard to "self-support, self-government, and self-perpetuation." [111]

The variation in outlook between the ministers is indicated by a list of topics appended to the Address. Whether they were intended for public lectures, or merely as resolutions for reflection, is not indicated anywhere. Searches have failed to reveal any reports suggesting that discussions had been held on them. While the topic of Rev. Lavender is general, that of Rev. Denham may be making a point to those who advocated the Conference: do not depend on England. Rev. J.C. Richardson was not among those who voted on the Conference in 1883. His topic reflects what were known to be his views on the ministry, though his concept of suitability might have been influenced by his being white. Rev. Irvine's topic reflects the hesitation with which he voted, but the same cannot be said for Rev. Tull who voted with Irvine. Revs. Campbell and Aguilar voted that the West Indies was ready for the Conference, and their topics reflect this. [112]

As things went, the Conference did not bring the blessings which were anticipated by its advocates in London or in the West Indies. Financial problems continued to be a severe burden, while the shortage of West Indian born ministers rendered adequate staffing difficult. As Barbados illustrated, some of the English missionaries were not yet ready to accept West Indian leadership even if that leadership was white. Barbados also illustrated division among the ministerial staff such as was seen at the District meeting of 1883. So that one can say that the atmosphere was not the most favourable for the introduction of the new system.

Chapter 7

CONCLUSION

The Methodist Society was one of those missionary bodies which began to establish themselves in the West Indies in the late eighteenth century. At the time they arrived in Barbados, the tension caused by slave amelioration had not yet appeared on the scene. Nevertheless, their start was not a particularly auspicious one. There was a pervasive atmosphere of hostility which sometimes broke out into acts of harassment. Their experiences in the West Indies, particularly the destruction of the Barbadian chapel and the expulsion of the missionary Shrewsbury, helped to arouse public opinion in England against the atrocities of West Indian slave society. They therefore played a significant part in the story of the termination of West Indian slavery. That role was an indirect one, since Methodists in Barbados were not the vocal champions of emancipation that the missionaries in Jamaica were.

Methodist adherents in Barbados were small in numbers before emancipation. The Methodists seem not to have made any great impression on the slave population in the island. Even after emancipation, their level of growth was neither as great nor as sustained as they themselves had anticipated. In 1883, after nearly one hundred years in the island, their full membership was still less than 2000. While strict discipline was one possible cause of their continued small size, the tendency of the labouring classes not to embrace Methodism must certainly be a more likely cause.

Despite their small size, the Methodists had played an important part in religious developments in Barbados. While they suffered spasmodic harassment before 1823, in the period from 1825–1832, they felt the full extent of efforts to frustrate the re-establishment of their mission. In part, this was due to the planter/legislators, who invoked an unused seventeenth century law against them. In part it was due to officials like Governors Warde and Lyon, and President Skeete, all of whom showed an unwillingness to help the Methodists gain recognition and authorisation to function in the island.

The fight to register their chapels as places of worship was only the beginning of a long process to gain acceptance in the island. The kind of attitude which resulted in the expulsion of Shrewsbury in 1823 was not likely to be easily changed. In the early post-emancipation period, the attitude of some planters was changing very slowly and Methodist work began to receive some support from liberal elements within the society. Their membership, as they often remarked, continued to be predominantly of the labouring class. This naturally meant that their financial base was a weak one, since that class could not meet their financial obligations to the Methodist Society. They were anxious to attract members of the planter and professional classes as part of their desire for respectability.

The continued shortage of funds led them to seek assistance from the public treasury. Not only were their attempts unsuccessful for some time, but in the process of providing funds for the non-established churches, the Governor and legislature added to the discrimination which Methodists and others suffered. It was not only that the sums awarded were small; they bore no relation to the size of the Methodist congregations in the island. Their efforts to obtain financial support from public funds also demonstrated that they were perceived far less favourably than the Moravians. The reasons were that the Methodists were less co-operative than the latter, and were also more inclined than the latter to be adversely critical of the Established Church.

That tendency of the Methodists to engage in adverse criticism displayed itself during the efforts to establish a popular system of education. Their suspicions of the clergy of the Established Church led them to withdraw some of their teachers from the training and examination process. Admittedly, some of the Anglican clergy were not sympathetic towards Methodism, but Methodist aloofness, even from examinations, did not help them. One also has to admit that the Inspector of Schools, whose tenure of office spanned the thirty-three years of popular education noticed here, seemed too short of patience in his dealings with the Methodists. On the other hand, their own incompetence was partly responsible for the Inspector's poor assessment of themselves.

Internal dissension did nothing to help their cause. The disputes at the James Street Chapel, where conflicts erupted between the minister and leaders, was a source of embarrassment because of their persistence. This problem of discipline raised the twin issues of local as against English usage, and the role of the laity in the government of the church. The issue of local usage was never really faced, and it remained dormant to raise its head intermittently in the latter half of the nineteenth century. The issue of lay responsibility was only dealt with because it was part of the change demanded by the Missionary Committee prior to the establishment of a Conference. The expatriate ministers' unwillingness to introduce this change reflects the view that the laity was not ready for it. Perhaps it reflects even more the view that only persons of a certain social standing were capable of administering the affairs of Methodism.

No issue was potentially more explosive than that which related to the fostering of a local ministry. With a free coloured population of means, some of whom were members of the Methodist body, the issue was bound to arise. And as the coloureds fought and won recognition for themselves in civil matters, it was inconceivable that they would not seek similar recognition within the church. The Missionary Committee, while expressing its interest in this ministry, tied the issue to its desire for economy in the local operation. This was not likely to win support among local personnel, especially since they were being designated "Assistant Missionaries" in spite of their years of service. To compound the problem even further, there were certain English ministers who considered themselves superior to their West Indian counterparts. So that, when the establishment of a West Indian Conference was approved by the English Conference, there were prognostications of a lack of Englishmen to serve in the West Indies if West Indians became leaders. Unfortunately, the prophecies became true. In Barbados, the controversy at James Street which led to the withdrawal of William Parker from the Methodist ministry, was an example of the kind of tension which threatened Methodism.

In the sixty years which this study covers, the Methodists had established themselves firmly in the island. They had less than 2000 full members, but over 12000 claimed to be Methodists when the census of 1881 was taken. They had also some twenty-one schools across the island. In these years, they had struggled against religious prejudice in the island. That they survived was a credit to their ability to fight against the prevailing spirit. But they had problems among themselves which still needed to be dealt with, and they still had to adjust their style of operation to one less hostile to their counterparts in the Established Church. The latter needed to make adjustments of their own in order to recognise the rights of others to function in the island. But this required the removal of the system of establishment, the continuation of which rendered religious co-operation a difficult proposition.

In reviewing the period under discussion, it is clear that the Methodists did not succeed nearly to the extent that their leaders had envisaged, especially in the post-emancipation era. On the other hand, while they were often disappointed, they did not perceive themselves as failures. It was, of course a matter of perspective. But the Methodists could look back on the period and receive some consolation from the fact that they had become the second largest congregation in the island, surpassing the Moravians who had established themselves in the island some years previously. They could also count a total of about 12000 persons declaring themselves to be adherents to Methodism, even though actual membership was a modest 2000. This suggests that the Methodist impact and influence were much broader than the actual statistics of membership imply. The fact that Methodists fought institutionalised prejudice and not only survived, but became firmly established by the last quarter of the century, is a tribute both to their tenacity and to their capacity to influence some of the members of the plantocracy towards a more liberal way of thinking. While religious prejudice was still very much in evidence in 1883, it had at least lost some of its sting by that date and Methodist determination in Barbados must partly account for that circumstance.

Methodist work in the field of education must also be viewed as a positive achievement, though again on a more modest scale than they had hoped. In a situation in which the colonial legislature took some years before accepting in principle its obligation to foster and finance popular education, and a much longer period to put that principle into practice, the efforts of private philanthropic and religious groups to promote education must be commended. In several instances Methodists set up schools in rural areas, offering sometimes the only opportunity for the children of ex-slaves to receive their early education. What is perhaps most remarkable is that, in spite of the vicissitudes the Methodists experienced at these early attempts at education, they did not give up, and in the end could boast of twenty-one schools in various parts of the island. Their contribution, therefore, to the development of a national system of education was commendable. It must also be remembered that their efforts were attended with great sacrifice, both on the part of the teachers and the students. In this respect, too, they were helping to lay the foundation for later years.

REFERENCES

CHAPTER 1

1. Edward Brathwaite, *Creole Society in Jamaica, 1770–1820.* Oxford: Clarendon Press, 1971, p. 105.

2. Jerome Handler, *The Unappropriated People.* Baltimore: Johns Hopkins University Press, 1974, p. 66.

3. For the persistence of certain families in the island, see Ronnie Hughes, "The Origins of Barbados Sugar Plantations and the Role of the White Population in Sugar Plantation Society", A.O. Thompson (Ed.), *Emancipation I: A Series of Lectures to Commemorate the 150th Anniversary of Emancipation,* Barbados, 1984, p. 31. Karl Watson, *The Civilised Island Barbados: A Social History.* 1979, pp. 43–45, discusses the subject of endogamy.

4. E. Long, *History of Jamaica.* (1774) London: Frank Cass and Co. Ltd., 1970, II 246, where he condemns the practice.

5. George Pinckard, M.D., *Notes on the West Indies.* London, 1806, was critical of this characteristic of the Barbadian. See II.75f., 79, 132. Karl Watson, *op. cit,* pp. 34f. senses a lack of empathy in such writers, but he does not deny the characteristic.

6. For the slave population in Barbados, see Handler, p. 20; for the Leeward Islands, see E.V. Goveia, *Slave Society in the British Leeward Islands at the End of the Eighteenth Century.* (1965) Greenwood Press, Westport, Conn., 1980, p. 203; and for Jamaica, Brathwaite, op. cit., p. 152.

7. Handler, *op. cit.,* pp. 144–146.

8. Handler, *op. cit.* p. 141. cf. Brathwaite, *Creole Society,* p. 169, for a similar development. Goveia, *op. cit.,* p. 227.

9. The subject is discussed in Handler, *op. cit.,* pp. 76–81.

10. Handler, op. cit. pp. 90–93; cf. Cox, *Free Coloureds in the Slave Societies of St. Kitts and Grenada.* Knoxville: University of Tennessee Press, 1984, p. 95, on the distinguishing of themselves in the two islands.

11. C. Palmer, *Human Cargoes.* Chicago: University of Illinois Press, 1981, pp. 98f. Spanish manifests recorded slaves as *piezas.* A *pieza* did not necessarily mean one slave; any disability could result in a slave being

considered part of a whole. See also D.P. Mannix and M. Cowley, *Black Cargoes*. London: Longmans, Green and Co., 1962, pp. 125–127 on the Zong case, in which a court ruled that a cargo of slaves could not simply be treated as merchandise.

12.   On this, see Orlando Patterson, *The Sociology of Slavery*. Granada Publishing, 1973, pp. 43, 44. Also see Richard Sheridan, "An Era of West Indian Prosperity, 1750–1775", *Chapters in Caribbean History*. London: Caribbean Universities Press, 1973, p. 104.

13.   Handler, *op. cit.*, p. 70. On the penalty in Barbados, see E. Goveia, *The West Indian Slave Laws in the 18th Century*. London: Caribbean Universities Press, 1973. The fine for killing one's slave was £ 15, for killing someone else's slave £ 25 currency.

14.   These cases are discussed in P.M. Sherlock, *West Indian Nations*. Kingston: Jamaica Publishing House, 1973, pp. 179–180; also in F.J. Klingberg, *The Anti-Slavery Movement in England*. 1926. Hamden, Conn.: Archon Books, 1968, pp. 179–180; and W.L. Mathieson, *British Slavery and its Abolition, 1823–1838*. 1926. New York: Octagon Books, 1967, pp. 96–97.

15.   Pinckard, *op. cit.,* I. 369.

16.   Pinckard, *op. cit,* I.263, 264.

17.   See Albert J. Raboteau, *Slave Religion*. London: Oxford University Press, 1980, pp. 30–31, 44–45, for burial traditions among the Africans. On p. 44 Raboteau cites a nineteenth century witness to the effect that a variety of items were buried with a little child. These included a "miniature canoe ... and a little paddle" and several personal items by which the infant would have been recognised by relatives when it arrived among them.

18.   Pinckard, *op.cit.,* I. 271f., 274.

19.   Watson, *Civilised Island,* p. 89.

20.   See, for example, Handler, *op. cit.,* p. 154. Also see E.G. Parrinder, *African Traditional Religion*. London: Sheldon Press, 1976, pp. 113–119.

21.   Orlando Patterson, *op. cit.,* pp. 190–192. Patterson following a late 19th century writer ascribes the healing to myal men. But myalism emerged only in 1842 and 1860. His source, therefore, is not a strong one. Brathwaite, *op. cit.* pp. 162, 163, suggests that leadership of the slaves had shifted to black Baptist preachers, with both them and the obeah men being seen as a threat to the planters.

22. See, for example, Brathwaite, *op.cit.* pp. 44, 45, cf. Edward L. Cox, *op. cit.*, p. 95.

23. Brathwaite, *op. cit.* p. 22.

24. Helen T. Manning, *British Colonial Government after the American Revolution, 1782–1820.* 1933. Hamden, Connecticut: Archon Books. Repr., 1966, pp. 154, 156, on the system.

25. H.N. Coleridge, *Six Months in the West Indies in 1825. 1832.* New York: Negro Universities Press, 1970, p. 296.

26. Goveia, *op. cit.*, p. 218.

27. The resolution is cited in Schomburgk, *History of Barbados.* London, 1848, p. 417. The address by a group of free coloureds, led by Jacob Belgrave, Sr. is discussed in Handler, *op. cit.*, pp. 90–93, and 198. For the free coloureds in St. Kitts and Grenada, see Cox, *op. cit,* pp. 101, 102. For a contemporary review of free coloured experiences in Trinidad, see J.B. Philippe, *An Address to the Right Hon. Earl Bathurst, by a Free Mulatto,* (1823). Trinidad: Paria Publishing, 1987.

28. See Handler, *op. cit.*, pp. 102–105. Schomburgk, *op. cit.*, pp. 431f. makes no reference to the change discussed by Handler, but projects the provision as a boon – "a tardy act of justice."

29. Handler, *op. cit.*, p. 29.

30. H.F. Durham, "Laws of Barbados Aimed at Quakers, 1676- 1723", *Journal of the Barbados Museum and Historical Society,* Vol. XXXIV, May 1927, No. 2, pp. 73–75.

31. The abolition of the slave trade is well documented. See for instance Klingberg, *op. cit.*, Chs. III and IV.

32. G. Smith, *op. cit,* Vol. 111, pp. 86ff.

33. G.G. Findlay and W.W. Holdsworth, *The History of the Wesleyan Methodist Missionary Society.* London, 1921, Vol. 1 pages 36–55 trace the origin of the Society, which was launched in Leeds on October 6, 1813.

34. For a discussion of the characteristics of a sect, see Bryan Wilson, *Religious Sects.* London: World University Library, 1970, pp. 7, 17. Cf. W.F. and M.F. Nimhoff, *A Handbook of Sociology.* 5th ed. London: Routledge and Kegan Paul, 1968, p. 477.

35. Findlay and Holdsworth, *op. cit.* 1. 65–67.

36. It was the custom of the Methodists to describe their body as the "Methodist Society" during the 18th and early 19th century. It was only

later in the 19th century that they described themselves as the Methodist Church.

37.   Robert F. Wearmouth, *Methodism and the Working-Class Movements in England, 1800–1850.* London: Epworth Press. Repr. 1947, pp. 6ff. A similar point is made by E.P. Thompson, *The Making of the English Working Class.* 1963. London: Gollancz, 1965, p. 352. One senses an undue harshness in Thompson's presentation.

38.   This movement, led by a self-styled Captain Ludd, aimed at uniting factory workers against poor working conditions in the Lincolnshire area. See Wearmouth, *op. cit.,* pp. 41f. for Coke's action.

39.   Wearmouth, *op. cit.,* p. 37. Cf. G. Smith, *History of Wesleyan Methodism.* London, 1861, Vol. 2, p. 513. Michael Watts, *The Dissenters.* Oxford: Clarendon Press, 1978, p. 446 points out that John Wesley was opposed to the registering of Methodist chapels as belonging to "Protestant Dissenters". Some magistrates seemed unwilling to licence them without the offending designation.

40.   Wearmouth, *op. cit,* p. 51.

41.   J.M. Whiteley, *Wesley's England,* 4th. edn. London: The Epworth Press, 1954, p. 304.

42.   For a general discussion of the clergy, see Whiteley, *op., cit.,* pp. 298–307.

43.   Edward Long, *History* II. 1 shows Middlesex with eight parishes in over 1.3 million acres; II.102, Surrey with seven parishes in over 670 000 acres; and II.182 Cornwall with five parishes in over 1.5 million acres. By contrast, Barbados with 106 000 acres had eleven parishes.

44.   Long, *op. cit.,* II.238. Mary Turner has regrettably attributed to *all* the clergy what Long limited to *some.* See *Slaves and Missionaries.* University of Illinois Press, 1982, p. 10.

45.   E.V. Goveia, *Slave Society in the British Leeward Islands at the end of the Eighteenth Century.* 1965. Westport, Conn.: Grennwood Press Publishers, 1980, p. 265.

46.   H.E. Holder, *A Short Essay on the Subject of Negro Slavery.* London, 1788, pp. 9, 19, 31.

47.   Fulham Papers, XV, f. 80: Robertson to Porteus, Harbour Island, June 17, 1790; ff. 87–93; Gordon to Porteus, Sept. 7, 1792; XVI. ff. 174–5; Clergy of Barbados to Bishop Porteus, Sept. 26, 1788; XVIII, ff. 157–8: C. Donaldson to Mrs. Monk, Highgate, St. Mary's, Oct. 18, 1808.

48.   Noel Titus, *The Church and Slavery in the English Speaking Caribbean*. Caribbean Group for Social and Religious Studies, Barbados, No. 2, 1983, pp. 10–12.

49.   W. Dickson, *Letters on Slavery*. London, 1789, p. 58.

50.   W. Dickson, *Mitigation of Slavery*. New York: Negro Universities Press, 1970, p. 77.

51.   M. Craton, *Sinews of Empire*. London: Temple Smith, 1974, pp. 174f; J.H. Bennett, *Bondsmen and Bishops*. University of California Press, 1958, p. 95, where a bishop reportedly queried whether slaves could be reclaimed from paganism as long as planters equated baptism with manumission.

52.   A. Dorner, *History of Protestant Theology*. (1871) New York: AMSPress, 1970, 11 246. See also Ernst Troeltsch, *The Social Teaching of the Christian Churches*, Vol. II, New York: Harper Torchbooks, 1960, pp. 719–720.

53.   Troeltsch, *op. cit.*, 11, 720. Cf. Goveia, *op. cit.*, pp. 274–280 on the strategy of the Moravian missionaries, and J.E. Hutton, *A History of Moravian Missions*. London: Moravian Publication Office, 1922, p. 40.

54.   J.T. & K.G. Hamilton, *History of the Moravian Church. 1722–1901*. Bethlehem, Pennsylvania: Moravian Church of America, 1901; Hutton, *History*, p. 41.

55.   Goveia, *op. cit.*, pp. 277–279; cf. Turner, *op. cit.*, pp. 39, 65, 71f.

56.   Goveia, *op. cit.*, p. 180.

57.   *The Times*, May 5, 1865. This article was part of "A History of the Moravian Church" which it is believed was the work of Rev. J.Y. Edghill, a minister of the Moravian Church.

58.   *The Times*, May 16, 1865.

59.   J.E. Hutton, *op. cit.*, p. 41.

60.   O.W. Furley, "Moravian Missionaries and Slaves in the West Indies", *Caribbean Studies*, Vol. 5, No. 2, pp. 4, 6. Buchner was critical of this development as having been an embarrassment. See *The Moravians in Jamaica*. London, 1854, p. 21.

61.   *The Times*, May 16, 1865.

62.   The sources for what follows are: William Peirce, *The principles and Polity of the Wesleyan Methodists*. London, 1873, pp. 328–331; and MMS Box 129, No. 1. This is an untitled compilation of material, the relevant section of which is headed: "Leaders and Leaders' Meeting."

63.   Peirce, *op. cit.*, p. 328.

64. Thomas Coke, *History of the West Indies,* (1808–11) London: Frank Cass, 1971. II. 43. Note: the term "missionary" is used synonymously with "minister" throughout this thesis.

65. On this see Coke, *op. cit.,* I. 414–416 (Jamaica); II. 253–259 (St. Vincent); III. 12, 13 (Nevis).

66. Coke II. 185 for opening. For debt, MMS Box 142, Letter 5 of a series from John Corlett to a friend, June 1 1848.

67. MMS Box 142 (File 1848). Letter 5. John Corlett to (A friend), June 1, 1848. Corlett sought, in a series of letters, to give his correspondent a brief history of Methodist Missions in Barbados. Cf. Coke II. 145–147, 149.

68. Coke, *op. cit.,* II. 139; Findlay and Holdsworth, *op. cit.,* II. 190.

69. Coke, *op. cit.,* II. 151.

70. MMS 113 (File May–Aug. 1818) No. 20. Rayner to Committee, June 17, 1818.

71. E. L. Cox, *op. cit.*

72. Mary Turner, *Slaves and Missionaries,* pp. 15–18.

73. On these restrictive Acts see Southey, Capt. Thomas, *Chronological History of the West Indies.* 1827. London: Frank Cass, 1968, III. 73, 110, 165, 182. Cf. also Winston McGowan, "Christianity and Slavery: Reactions to the Work of the London Missionary Society in Demerara, 1808–1813", *A Selection of Papers Presented at the Twelfth Conference of Caribbean Historians.* Edited by K. O. Lawrence, 1980, pp. 35f. for Governor Bentinck's Proclamation against the LMS.

74. Coke, II, 141; cf. 11. 151 citing Lumb, another missionary.

75. Hamilton, *op. cit.,* p. 249; cf. Hutton, *op. cit.,* pp. 53f.

76. *Op. cit.,* II. 59.

77. Southey, *op. cit.,* III. 29.

78. MMS Box III (File 1812–1813) No. 39: Whitworth to H. E. The Governor, Feb. 15, 1813.

79. C. T. Abbey & J. H. Overton, *The English Church in the Eighteenth Century.* London, 1878, Vol. II, p. 119.

80. E. A. Wallbridge, *The Demerara Martyr.* 1848. New York: Negro Universities Press, 1969, p. 17.

81. *Ibid.,* pp. 16 and 18.

82. MMS Box 113 (File May–Aug. 1818) No. 20; Rayner to the Committee, June 17, 1818.

83. MMS Box 113 (File Sept.–Dec. 1818), No. 39: Francis Brown to the Missionary Committee, October 17, 1818.

84. Findlay and Holdsworth II. 197.

85. MMS Box 111 (File 1812–1813), No. 92: reply of Francis Brown, senior, December 15, 1813. the writer's spelling has been retained in the quotation.

86. MMS Box 118 (File Jan.–March, 1820) No. 26: District Meeting to the Missionary Committee, Barbados, Feb. 9, 1820.

87. MMS Box 118 (File July–Dec., 1821) No. 92: Shrewsbury and Nelson to the Committee, April 27, 1821; cf. Box 116 (File 1820) No. 16: Shrewsbury to the Committee, June 20, 1820.

88. MMS Box 112 (File 1814) No. 65: Richard Beck to Samuel Thomas, July 21, 1814. There is no indication as to who Samuel Thomas was. Cf. Findlay and Holdsworth, *op. cit.,* II. 192, where the missionary, Jeremiah Boothby, was described as a young man on his first appointment. Cf. II. 162, where in 1816 Boothby was described as a probationer in his fourth year.

89. MMS Box 114 (File April–June, 1819), No. 29: Rayner to the Committee, May 3, 1819.

90. MMS Box 113 (File Sept.–Dec., 1818) No. 37: Rayner to the Committee, December 5, 1818.

91. MMS Box 118, No. 146: Shrewsbury to the General Secretaries, Oct. 24, 1822.

92. Eric Williams, *Documents on British West Indian Slavery,* Trinidad Publishing Co., 1952, p. 243 document 376.

93. William Peirce, *op. cit.,* p. 305.

94. MMS Box 111 (File 1803–1804) No. 59: Bradnack to Coke, October 28, 1804. MMS Box 111 (File 1803–1804) No. 60: William Harding, Richard Chapman, and Francis Brown to the Committee, November 2, 1804.

95. MMS Box 113 (File May–August 1818) No. 20: Rayner to the Committee, June 17, 1818.

96. MMS Box 113 (File Sept.–Dec. 1818) No. 17: Francis Brown to the Missionary Committee, October 17, 1818.

97. MMS Box 115 (File Jan.–March 1820) No. 62: William Shrewsbury and John Larcom to the Committee, March 28, 1820.

98. For these details, see Findlay and Holdsworth, *op. cit.,* II. 136, 176f. 181.

99.   The full text of the instructions is to be found in Peirce, *op. cit.,* pp. 745–751.

100.   This is a quotation from Section VII. 7 of the instructions. See Peirce, *op. cit.,* p. 749.

101.   J. H. Bennett, *op. cit.,* pp. 81, 83, 88, 92.

102.   Fulham Papers, Vol. XVI, fols. 174–5.

103.   Holder, *Short Essay,* pp. 9, 19 and 31.

104.   MMS Box 118 (File 1822) No. 41: Shrewsbury to the General Secretaries, April 19, 1822.

105.   See Klingberg, *op. cit.*

106.   This subject is treated in two places: by H. Beckles, *Black Rebellion in Barbados.* Bridgetown: Antilles Publications, 1984, pp. 86–120; also in "Emancipation by Law or War? Wilberforce and the 1816 Barbados Slave Rebellion", in David Richardson (Ed.) *Abolition and its Aftermath.* London: Frank Cass, 1985, pp. 80–104. See also Michael Craton, "Emancipation from Below? The Role of the West Indian Slaves in the Emancipation Movement" in Jack Hayward (Ed.) *Out of Slavery.* London: Frank Cass, 1985, pp. 112–115.

107.   Kingsley Lewis, *The Moravian Missions in Barbados, 1816–1886.* Verlag Peter Lang, 1985, pp. 132–136.

108.   Hutton, *op. cit.,* p. 233.

109.   Richard Watson, *A Defence of the Wesleyan Methodist Missions in the West Indies.* London, 1817, pp. 10, 11, where reference is made to the accusation.

110.   MMS Box 116 (File 1820) No. 29: Shrewsbury and Nelson to the Committee, Sept. 11, 1820; Box 117 (File 1821) No. 2: Shrewsbury & Nelson to the Committee, Jan. 10, 1821; No. 11; Shrewsbury & Nelson to the Committee, June 25, 1821; Box 117 (File 1822) No. 5. Nelson to the General Secretaries, Jan. 12, 1822.

CHAPTER 2

1.   For his date of birth, see J. V. B. Shrewsbury, *Memorials of the Rev. William J. Shrewsbury.* 2nd. edn. London, 1868, p. 2.

2.   MMS Box 116 (File 1820) No. 16: Shrewsbury to the Missionary Committee, June 20, 1820.

3. MMS Box 117 (File Jan. to July 1821) No. 2: Shrewsbury and Nelson to the Committee, January 10, 1821. Cf. Box 116 (File 1821) No. 92: Shrewsbury to the Committee, April 27, 1821; and Box 117 (File July–Dec. 1821) No. 15: Shrewsbury to the Committee, August 7, 1821. Also No. 14: Shrewsbury and Nelson to the Committee, and No. 11: Shrewsbury and Nelson to the Committee, both dated August 8, 1821.

4. MMS Box 117 (File Jan.–July 1821), No. 2: Shrewsbury and Nelson to the Committee, January 10, 1821. (File Aug.–Dec.) No. 83: Shrewsbury and Nelson to the General Secretaries, November 8, 1821. Their letter stated that there was not one righteous person in the Speightstown population of about 700. They also expressed their willingness to abandon the area. Cf. Box 118, No. 92: Shrewsbury to the General Secretaries, July 31, 1822; Box 119, No. 4: Shrewsbury to the General Secretaries, January 27, 1823; Box 119, No. 24: Shrewsbury to the Secretaries, April 3, 1823.

5. William J. Shrewsbury, *Sermons Preached on Several Occasions in the Island of Barbados.* London, 1825, Sermon VIII, p. 251. The emphasis is his own.

6. *Ibid.,* p. 252.

7. *Ibid.,* Sermon XIII, pp. 408f., 412, 416.

8. *Ibid.,* Sermon VIII, p. 267.

9. MMS Box 118 (File July–Dec. 1821) No. 92: Shrewsbury and Nelson to the Committee, April 27, 1821; cf. Box 116 (File 1820) No. 16: Shrewsbury to the Committee, June 20, 1820.

10. MMS Box 116 (File 1821) No. 38: Shrewsbury to Marsden, March 1, 1821.

11. This subject is treated extensively in two places by H. Beckles, *Black Rebellion in Barbados.* Bridgetown: Antilles Publications, 1984, pp. 86–120; also in "Emancipation by Law or War? Wilberforce and the 1816 Barbados Slave Rebellion" in David Richardson (Ed.) *Abolition and Its Aftermath.* London; Frank Cass, 1985, pp. 80–104.

12. For the details of the programme, see Vincent Harlow and Frederick Madden, *British Colonial Developments, 1774–1834.* Oxford: Clarendon Press, pp. 562–564. Cf. Klingberg, *op. cit.,* pp. 335–339 for Bathurst's circular despatch of May 1823.

13. Klingberg, *op. cit.,* pp. 210f., 215f., 217.

14. *Barbados Mercury and Bridgetown Gazette,* August 9, 1823.

15. MMS Box 119, No. 134: Shrewsbury to the Secretaries, August 25, 1823.

16. The Court of Policy was an advisory body, which also had the power to make regulations for the colony. It consisted of both selected and elected members. See D. J. Murray, *The West Indies and the Development of Colonial Government, 1801–1834.* Oxford: Clarendon Press, 1965, pp. 69, 70.

17. C. Northcott, *Slavery's Martyr.* London: Epworth Press, 1976, pp. 52f.

18. MMS Box 119, No. 134: Shrewsbury to the Committee, October 18, 1823. Findlay and Holdsworth are in error when they assert that Shrewsbury himself published the letter.

19. The Governor gave the date of Shrewsbury's verbal request as Wednesday, October 16. Since all sources give Sunday, October 19 as the date of the destruction, the date of Wednesday is incorrect.

20. October 21, 1823, in Minutes of the (Privy) Council, 1821–1825, Lucas Manuscripts, Vol. 34. The manuscript volumes are closed, but the minutes are on microfilm at the Barbados Public Library.

21. At a meeting of the Privy Council on April 12, 1825, the members, in a communication to the Governor, took responsibility for the investigation. On this occasion, they sought to emphasise a positive role on their own part and their displeasure with the magistrates.

22. The Legislative Council consisted of the same personnel as the Privy Council. They acted in different capacities when they were constituted as one or the other. Renn Hamden pertinently observed that the objects of the Committee could have been attained by the Governor's direct approach to the magistrates.

23. The minutes for this date are to be found in the Minutes of the Council, 1821–1825, Lucas MSS, Vol. 34.

24. The expression "very culpable dereliction of duty" was the Council's in a communication to the Governor dated April 12, 1825. This communication went on to state, however, that they had advised the Governor against further action. See Minutes of the Legislative Council for that date. Lucas MSS, Vol. 34, p. 511. The original decision is in the Minutes of February 23, 1824.

25. MMS Box 121, No. 1: Printed Paper entitled "RIOTS IN BARBADOS". Apart from a general report, the paper included copies of letters written by the missionary. One of these was written from St. Vincent "To the Members of the Wesleyan Methodist Society, Barbados" on October 24, 1823.

26. Findlay and Holdsworth, II. 203, note that Mary Roach had been Shrewsbury's servant and that she was the victim of some hostility.

27. Mary Turner, *Slaves and Missionaries,* pp. 17f.

28. MMS Box 120, No. 96: Exley et al. to Taylor, February 14, 1824.

29. Bathurst to Warde, February 14, 1825. In *British Parliamentary Papers, Slave Trade,* Vol. 67. Shannon: Irish University Press, 1969, p. 10.

30. The report is to be found in the Minutes of the Barbados Privy Council for October 1824. Reference to it is made in *The Barbadian* newspaper of May 20, 1825. This issue gives details of the Minutes of the Assembly for April 5, 1825, when one of the magistrates was called.

31. MMS Box 121, No. 129: John Gill, R. S. Wickham, E. H. Moore and W. H. Grant to Mrs. Gill, October 21, 1824. All four magistrates were among those investigated with respect to the demolition of the chapel in 1823. Moore was one of the two whose conduct was not censured by the Barbados Privy Council.

32. MMS Box 121, No. 185: Gill to Morley, March 4, 1825. For other accounts of their hardships, see No. 31: Ann Gill to Shrewsbury, October 30, 1824. The letter was copied to the Rev. George Morley by the recipient, who added some comments of his own. See also Box 122, No. 97: Gill to Morley, May 18, 1825; No. 123: Gill to Morley, Cabbage Tree House, Bridgetown, July 2, 1825; and No. 133: Thomas to Morley and Watson, July 11, 1825. These letters refer to Mrs. Gill's being examined by the Council and Assembly.

33. MMS Box 148: Minutes of the St. Vincent District, 1824.

34. D. J. Murray, *op. cit.,* p. 131.

35. *The Barbadian,* April 5, 1825.

36. *Ibid.,* April 8, 1825. The emphases are those of the writer.

37. *Ibid.*

38. *Ibid.,* May 20, 1825, for a report of the meeting of the Assembly.

39. Minutes for April 8, 1825 in Minutes of the (Privy) Council, 1821–1825, Lucas MSS, Vol. 34. Reels 14 and 15.

40. Minutes for April 12, 1825, Lucas MSS Vol. 34.

41. Stiv Jakobsson, *Am I not a Man and a Brother?* Gleerup, Uppsala, 1972, p. 385, suggests that Rayner preferred the easier task, hence his return to St. Vincent.

42. *The Barbadian,* May 20, 1825.

43. Substance of the Debate in the House of Commons, June 23, 1825, on Mr. Buxton's Motion, Respecting the Destruction of the Methodist Chapel in Barbados, p. 10.

44. Buxton said, for instance, that Shrewsbury was "for some years" a missionary in England, which he was not; implied that Shrewsbury was sent to Barbados because he was West Indian by virtue of marriage, but he was only married in 1823. He also implied that the magistrates interfered with the riots by summoning Shrewsbury to explain his failure to enrol in the militia. The summons preceded the riots; but the way it was presented reflected worse on the magistrates.

45. *The Barbadian,* December 16, 1825.

46. *Ibid.*

47. MMS Box 123, No. 80: Rayner to Morley, March 25, 1826.

48. Rayner's peaceful landing may well have been due to the uncertainty of arrival times.

49. Findlay and Holdsworth, II. 208 erroneously gave the month of February.

50. This position was reported in MMS Box 123, No. 80: Rayner to Morley, March 25, 1826.

51. Lucas MSS, Minutes of the Legislative Council (1821–1827) October 11, 1826, including Rayner to Skeete, March 15, 1826.

52. Lucas MSS, Minutes of the Legislative Council (1821–1827) April 16, 1826.

53. *Ibid.* See the Minutes of September 5, 1826 for Bathurst to Warde, July 7, 1826.

54. MMS Box 123, No. 80: Rayner to Morley, March 25, 1826.

55. For the provisions of this Act – 52 Geo. III, Cap. 155 – see *Halsbury's Laws of England,* 4th edn., London: Butterworths, 1975, Vol. 14: "Ecclesiastical law", pp. 1275–1292.

56. This statute will be found in Hall's *Laws of Barbados,* 1643–1762, No. 2, where it is given without a date.

57. MMS Box 123, No. 87: Rayner to Morley, March 31, 1826. In his letter, Rayner expressed himself as follows:

> I cannot think that the Archdeacon's advisor could imagine that the Colonial law, alluded to by the President could invalidate the Toleration Act of 1812.

58. MMS Box 123, No. 88: Rayner to Morley, March 31, 1826; cf. Rayner to Skeete, April 21, 1826, to be found in the Lucas MSS, Minutes of the Legislative Council (1821–1827).

59. MMS Box 123, No. 106: Rayner to the Committee, April 20, 1826.

60. MMS Box 123, No. 130: Rayner to the Rev. John Mason, May 13, 1826.

61. MMS Box 123, No. 139: Rayner to the Rev. John Mason, June 1, 1826.

62. MMS Box 123, No. 146: Rayner to Morley, June 7, 1826.

63. MMS Box 123, No. 186: Rayner to the Secretaries of the Wesleyan Methodist Missionary Society, August 3, 1826.

64. This is reported in MMS Box 123, No. 224: Rayner to Morley, September 28, 1826.

65. Rayner to Warde, September 15, 1826, in Minutes of the Legislative Council, September 26, 1826, Lucas MSS 1825–1827, Vol. 35.

66. *Ibid.,* September 26, 1826.

67. Minutes for January 2, 1827, in Minutes of the Council, 1825–1827, Lucas Manuscripts, Vol. 35.

68. MMS Box 123, No. 146: Rayner to Morley, June 7, 1826.

69. MMS Box 125, No. 189: Rayner and Stephenson to Morley, August 1, 1827.

70. MMS Box 124, No. 27: Rayner to Morley, February 28, 1827. Cf. No. 29: Stephenson to the General Secretaries, February 28, 1827.

71. MMS Box 124, No. 27: Rayner to Morley, February 28, 1827.

72. MMS Box 125, No. 189: Rayner to Morley, August 1, 1827. Findlay and Holdsworth, II. 210, have not accurately represented the arrangement made.

73. MMS Box 125, No. 162: Rayner to the Rev. John Mason, July 8, 1827.

74. MMS Box 126, No. 127: Rayner to Morley, March 31, 1828.

75. MMS Box 126, No. 188: Rayner to the Secretaries, June 7, 1828; cf. No. 222: Rayner to Morley, June 29, 1828. Rayner was accused of neglecting his duties.

76. MMS Box 127, No. 208: Rayner to Morley, May 28, 1829. Cf. Box 128, No. 60: Jno. Briddon to Morley, July 28, 1829.

77. MMS Box 127, No. 208: Rayner to Morley, May 28, 1829.

78. MMS Box 123, No. 139: Rayner to the Rev. John Mason, June 1, 1826.

79. MMS Box 123, No. 186: Rayner to the Secretaries of the WMMS, August 3, 1826.

80.   MMS Box 123, No. 224: Rayner to Morley, September 28, 1826.

81.   MMS Box 124, No. 85: Rayner and Stephenson to the General Secretaries, April 18, 1827.

82.   MMS Box 125, No. 215: Stephenson to the General Secretaries, September 17, 1827.

83.   Mary Turner, *Slaves and Missionaries,* pp. 21f.

84.   MMS Box 126, No. 28: Rayner to the Committee, December 1, 1827.

85.   According to Schomburgk, *op. cit.,* p. 492, Sharpe was made Attorney General in 1839. See p. 432, where Sharpe was mentioned as Solicitor General.

86.   MMS Box 131, No. 1: Edmondson to James, January 5, 1832. Sharpe's opinion is contained in Box 130, No. 259: Sharpe to the Bishop of Barbados, December 3, 1831.

87.   Turner, *Slaves and Missionaries,* pp. 86, 120–122.

88.   This Act was passed on October 17, 1826.

89.   Huskisson to the Officer Administering the Government of Barbados, September 3, 1828. *British Parliamentary Papers, Slave Trade,* Vol. 76, pp. 544–6.

90.   For a discussion on the Act see Claude Levy, "Barbados: the Last Years of Slavery, 1823–1833", in *Journal of Negro History,* 44 (1959) pp. 317–321; and the same writer in "Slavery and the Emancipation Movement in Barbados, 1650–1833", in *Journal of Negro History,* 55 (1970), pp. 9, 11. On Huskisson's response to the Jamaican Assembly, see Turner, *op. cit.,* p. 121.

91.   The spelling in the original has been retained.

92.   "Returns from all Slave Colonies belonging to the British Crown", 1831–32 (660) *British Parliamentary Papers, Slave Trade.* Vol. 80, Irish University Press, 1969.

93.   *Ibid.*

94.   Handler, *Unappropriated People,* p. 159.

95.   See Olwyn Blouet, "Education and Emancipation in Barbados, 1823–1846; A Study in Cultural Transference", Ph. D. Thesis, University of Nebraska, 1977, pp. 67–70, for a summary of educational facilities in Barbados in 1830.

96.   Mary Turner, *Slaves and Missionaries,* p. 102.

CHAPTER 3

1.   An Act for the Abolition of Slavery throughout the British Colonies; for promoting the Industry of the manumitted Slaves; and for compensating the Persons Entitled to the Services of Such Slaves. 1833. Clauses 1, 2, 4 and 5.

2.   Circular Despatch addressed by Mr. Secretary Stanley to the Governors of His Majesty's Colonial Possessions transmitting the Act passed for the Abolition of Slavery (3 & 4 William IV. c/73), and a Proclamation for giving effect to the same. The despatch is dated September 5, 1833, and the last paragraph discussed religion. See "Papers presented to Parliament by His Majesty's command in explanation of the measures adopted by His Majesty's Government for giving effect to the Act for the Abolition of Slavery Throughout the British Colonies. 1835 (177) Vol. L, in *British Parliamentary Papers*, Slave Trade, Vol. 81.

3.   W. A. Green, *op. cit.*, p. 131.

4.   Cited in Douglas Hall, "The Flight from the Estates Reconsidered: The British West Indies, 1838–42", *Journal of Caribbean History*, Vols. 10 & 11, 1978, p. 23.

5.   W. K. Marshall, "The ex-slaves as Wage Labourers on the Sugar Estates in the British Windward Islands, 1838–1846", pp. 18f.

6.   W. K. Marshall, T. Marshall, B. Gibbs, "The Establishment of a Peasantry in Barbados, 1840–1920", *Social Groups and Institutions in the History of the Caribbean.* Papers presented at the VI Annual Conference of the Association of Caribbean Historians, April 4–9, 1974. Association of Caribbean Historians, 1975, pp. 86ff.

7.   W. E. Riviere, "Labour Shortage in the British West Indies after Emancipation", *Journal of Caribbean History*, Vol. 4, May 1972, p. 59; Mathieson, *op. cit.*, pp. 42–46; B. Gibbs, "The Establishment of the Tenantry System in Barbados", W. K. Marshall, (Ed.) *Emancipation II: A series of Lectures to Commemmorate the 150th Anniversary of Emancipation.* Barbados: Department of History, U.W.I. and National Cultural Foundation, 1988, pp. 31–35.

8.   W. F. Burchell, *Memoir of Thomas Burchell.* London, 1849, p. 260.

9.   MMS Box 135, No. 53: Lofthouse to Bunting and Beecham, August 8, 1834. The emphases are mine. Henry Bleby had similarly explained to ex-slaves in Jamaica the implications of the change.

10. Hall, "Flight from the Plantations" p. 23. For a general discussion on this point, see pp. 17–24.

11. Reply No. 7577 from John Candler, in the "Report of the Select Committee on West India Colonies", 1842, Session 1842, Vol. XIII. *British Parliamentary Papers, Colonies, West Indies,* I, Irish University Press, 1968.

12. J. H. Hinton, *Memoir of William Knibb,* London, 1849, p. 180. Cf. MMS Box 134 No. 71: Beard to Beecham, Calliqua, St. Vincent, March 29, 1834.

13. MMS Box 149: Barbados Society Report, 1833, submitted to the District Meeting of 1834; cf. MMS Box 134 (File Jan.–March) No. 40: Penny to Bunting, Beecham & Alder, Harbour Island, Bahamas, March 8, 1834; Box 135 (File April–June) No. 47: Britten to the Missionary Committee, Tortola, June 30, 1834.

14. MMS Box 149: Barbados Society Report, 1834. For the responses of the Methodists, see C.O. 28/115: Smith to Spring Rice, January 28, 1835, enclosure 2.

15. MMS Box 150: Minutes of the St. Vincent District, 1836. For the missionary's comment, see Box 138, No. 148: Aldis to Beecham, June 29, 1836.

16. C.O. 28/115: Smith to Spring Rice, January 28, 1835, enclosure 1.

17. *Ibid.,* enclosure 3.

18. W. A. Green, *op. cit.,* p. 329.

19. For their building programmes in this period see MMS Box 149: Barbados Society Report, 1834, cf. *Ibid.* Barbados Society Report, 1835. MMS Box 139, No. 87: Fidler to the Committee, April 3, 1837; and No. 130: Phelp to Beecham, May 25, 1837. The first Ebenezer chapel was built in 1845. See Box 141 (File 1845) No. 49: Fidler to Hoole, August 7, 1845.

20. Kingsley Lewis, *op. cit.,* p. 227.

21. See W. A. Green, *op. cit.,* p. 327, where education is shown to have been subservient to sectarian or denominational interests in England.

22. MMS Box 141 (File 1845), No. 49: Folder to Hoole, August 7, 1845.

23. MMS Box 149: Minutes of the St. Vincent District, 1834. The classification into slaves and free persons naturally ended in 1834 with the coming into effect of the Act for the Abolition of Slavery. The details of

membership are taken from the Minutes of the District Meetings held usually in January or February each year. The Minutes for 1837 to 1839 are on microfilm at the Barbados Public Library, reel Bs. 52.

24. The heading used in the returns was: "Attendants on Public Worship, including Members and Scholars". Invariably the figures returned in the column exceeded the aggregate of all the columns.

25. For William Sharpe's view that few freemen were not christian, see "Report of the Select Committee on West India Colonies, 1842", Answer 1577. Answers 1776 and 1777 by G. Carrington attest to the connection between schools and church attendance.

26. MMS Box 134 (File Jan.–March) No. 5: Phelp to the Committee, Providence, January 20, 1834; cf. No. 73: Phelp to the Committee, March 31, 1834. An icrease was reported in Box 135 (File April 14–Sept.), No. 19: Rathbone to Beecham, August 23, 1834; also see No. 34: Phelp to Beecham, September 10, 1834; and (File Oct.–Dec.), No. 80: Phelp to Beecham, December 31, 1834.

27. MMS Box 138, No. 236: Moister to Beecham, October 10, 1836.

28. MMS Box 141 (File 1844), No. 59: Whitehead to the General Secretaries, Providence, October 3, 1844.

29. MMS Box 137, No. 141: Fidler to Beecham, November 14, 1835. The other person would have been Mortier, who was sent to Georgetown in Demerara.

30. MMS Box 140 (File 1838), No. 9: Fidler to the Committee, February 1, 1838.

31. MMS Box 140 (File 1839), No. 11: Phelp to the General Secretaries, March 4, 1839; (File 1840), No. 11: Biggs to the General Secretaries, April 10, 1840; (File 1841), No. 26: Hudson to the General Secretaries, Speightstown, April 28, 1841.

32. MMS Box 140 (File 1841), No. 26: Hudson to the General Secretaries, Speightstown, April 28, 1841.

33. MMS Box 141 (File 1845), No. 60: Fidler to the General Secretaries, November 4, 1845. Cf. No. 43: Fidler to the General Secretaries, June 17, 1845, for his willingness to give way to Cullingford, the new missionary.

34. MMS Box 139, No. 87: Fidler to the Committee, April 3, 1837. For complaints about dilatoriness, Box 136, No. 123: Aldis to Beecham, April 23, 1835; and Box 138: No. 250: Aldis to the Committee, Speightstown, October 21, 1836.

35.   On the *Sugar Duty Act* and its consequences, see Richard A. Lobdell, "Patterns of Investment and Sources of Credit in the British West Indian Sugar Industry, 1838–97", in *Journal of Caribbean History,* Vol. 4, 1972, pp. 39–46; W. A. Green, *op. cit.,* pp. 230–234; C. Levy, *Emancipation,* pp. 103–110, 113.

36.   For details of Methodist membership, see Appendix II.

37.   See, for example, MMS Box 158: Report of the Second Barbados Circuit, 1862, which lists 126 expulsions for that year. Other Reports noted the need for increased pastoral oversight in the area. See MMS Box 154; Report of the Barbados Circuit, 1846, where expulsions for immorality were reported and where a missionary was said to be needed at once. Cf. Box 155: Report of the Barbados Circuit, 1851, where again a minister was requested without delay.

38.   MMS Box 156: Report of the Barbados Circuit, 1854.

39.   MMS Box 158: Report of the Second Barbados Circuit, 1859.

40.   MMS Box 158: Reports for the First and Second Circuits, 1859; and for the same Circuits for 1862; Box 159: Report of the Second Circuit, 1863.

41.   MMS Box 155: Report of the Barbados Circuit, 1851.

42.   MMS Box 154: Society Report of the Barbados Circuit, 1846.

43.   Reporting on this station, the missionaries noted: "The society is small and not very lively. We held a Missionary meeting there since the year came in and brought the matter before them, but we left with the impression that the Ark must find another place, a foreboding that we had sung the requiem of Methodism in Scotland."

44.   MMS Box 155: Barbados Society Report for 1853.

45.   MMS Box 141 (File 1846), No. 20: William English to the General Secretaries, March 20, 1846.

46.   MMS Box 141 (File 1847), No. 29: Corlett to the General Secretaries, June 24, 1847. For the fear of secession, see (File 1846), No. 93: English to General Secretaries, November 4, 1846. For a complaint about shabby treatment, see (File 1846) No. 98: George Ranyell to the Secretaries, December 19, 1846.

47.   MMS Box 142 (File 1848) No. 21: Corlett to the Committee, April 7, 1848. This matter will be discussed in some detail in the last chapter.

48.   MMS Box 142 (File 1849), No. 11: Corlett to the Secretaries of the Conference and the Missionary Committee, March 10, 1849.

49.   MMS Box 156: Letter appended to the Report of the Barbados Circuit, 1854, Bleby to the General Secretaries, Barbados, February 24, 1855. Bleby was acting as Chairman of the District at that time. Bleby had previously served in Jamaica, being there at the time of the rebellion of 1831/32.

50.   MMS Box 156: Report of the Barbados Circuit, 1855.

51.   MMS Box 161: Report of the Barbados First Circuit, 1870.

52.   MMS Box 142 (File 1848), No. 21: Corlett to the Committee, April 7, 1848.

53.   MMS Box 142 (File 1849), No. 34: Corlett to Beecham, September 15, 1849. In this letter, Corlett alleged that the mission had been mismanaged. A similar allegation was made by him in No. 35: Corlett to the General Secretaries, October 9, 1849.

54.   MMS Box 142 (File 1849), No. 16: Corlett to the Committee, April 27, 1849; cf. Box 154: Report of the Barbados Circuit, 1848, where the failure to have a minister resident at Speightstown is lamented.

55.   MMS Box 229 (File 1862), No. 106: Bleby to Hoole, December 24, 1862. Cf. No. 107: Soper to Hoole, December 24, 1862. Reece's proposals were set out in Bleby's letter.

56.   MMS Box 229 (File 1863), No. 12: Bleby to Boyce, February 24, 1863.

57.   MMS Box 158: Minutes of the St. Vincent and Demerara District, 1863.

58.   This was Bleby's son, John, who, in the interest of economy, was asked to share his father's home. The arrangement was not altogether acceptable to the elder Bleby, since his son seems to have been denied some of the allowances to which he would otherwise have been entitled. See MMS Box 229 (File 1863), No. 12: Bleby to Boyce, February 24, 1863; No. 21: Bleby to Hoole, March 10, 1863; and No. 46: Bleby to Hoole, May 25, 1863.

59.   MMS Box 142 (File 1852), No. 74: Butcher to Beecham, October 6, 1852.

60.   MMS Box 143 (File 1855), No. 76: Wilson to Osborn, November 20, 1855. Wilson was a newcomer to Barbados, having only arrived earlier in the year.

61.   MMS Box 157: First Barbados Society Report for 1857.

62.   The image of the dry bones is from the Old Testament of the Bible, where it represents a totally dispirited people. See Ezekiel, Ch. 37.

63.   MMS Box 229 (File 1863), No. 51: William Watson to the General Secretaries, June 9, 1863. Watson was severely critical of local Methodism for which he had little complimentary to say.

64.   MMS Box 229 (File 1862), No. 107: Soper to Hoole, December 24, 1862.

65.   The term "Tractarian" was given to the early leaders of the Oxford Movement, because they disseminated their beliefs in a series of publications called "Tracts for the Times".

66.   MMS Box 159: Report of the Barbados First Circuit, 1863.

67.   MMS Box 161: Barbados First Circuit Report, 1869.

68.   The Barbados Societies were further divided in 1868 into three Circuits, the third being the Speightstown Circuit.

69.   See, for example, MMS Box 161: Report of the First Barbados Circuit, 1869 and 1870.

70.   MMS Box 161: Report of the First Barbados Circuit, 1870. The Report also noted their inability to raise sufficient local preachers.

71.   MMS Box 161: Barbados First Circuit Report, 1870.

72.   MMS Box 231 (File 1872), No. 31: Aguilar to the General Secretaries, November 9, 1872.

73.   MMS Box 161: First Circuit Report, 1869, concerning Bethel; First Circuit Report, 1870; Box 162: James Street Circuit Report, 1872; Box 163: Ebenezer Circuit Report, 1874; Box 164: James Street Circuit Report, Bethel Circuit Report, and Providence Circuit Report, 1877. The only exception was the Ebenezer Circuit which reported improvement.

74.   MMS Box 161: Barbados First Circuit Report, 1870. The Report was written by Henry Hurd, though it was signed only by his assistants Gleave and Choate.

75.   MMS Box 164: Providence Circuit Report, 1877.

76.   Findlay and Holdsworth, II. 372.

CHAPTER 4

1.   Mary Olwyn Blouet, "Education and Emancipation in Barbados, 1823–1846: A Study in Cultural Transference". Ph. D. Thesis, University of Nebraska, 1977. In 1833 the British Parliament began making grants for school building in England, Scotland and Wales. See W. A. Green, *op. cit,* p. 328.

2.   Carl Campbell, "Towards an Imperial Policy for the Education of Negroes in the West Indies after Emancipation," in *Jamaica Historical Review,* Vol. VII, 1967, pp. 72, 90.

3.   Carl Campbell, "Imperial Policy", pp. 78–86.

4.   Olwyn Blouet, *op. cit.,* p. 85.

5.   On Catholic Emancipation see Elie Halevy, *The Liberal Awakening (1815–1830).* London: Ernest Benn, 1961, pp. 257–274.

6.   On the political development, see James Millette, *The Genesis of Crown Colony Government.* Trinidad: Moko Enterprises Ltd., 1970, Chapter II. On the appointment of the Bishop, see J. T. Harricharan, *The Catholic Church in Trinidad.* 1498–1852. Port of Spain: Inprint Caribbean Ltd., 1981, p. 50. Fr. Harricharan does not link the appointment to the wider issue of loyalties; he limits it to British dominance in a culturally and institutionally non-British island.

7.   Carl Campbell, "Imperial Policy", p. 73. For Sterling's views, see Gordon, S. C. (Ed.). *Reports and Repercussions in West Indian Education, 1835–1933.* London: Caribbean Universities Press, 1968, p. 63.

8.   F. J. Klingberg, "The Lady Mico Charity Schools in the British West Indies, 1835–1842", *Journal of Negro History,* Vol. XXIV, 1939, pp. 295, 296. Cf. Carl Campbell, "Denominationalism and the Mico Charity Schools in Jamaica, 1835–1842", *Caribbean Studies,* Vol. 10, No. 4, p. 153.

9.   Klingberg, "Lady Mico Charity Schools", pp. 297ff.

10.   Carl Campbell, "Denominationalism", pp. 162, 164, 166.

11.   Campbell, "Denominationalism", pp. 155, 164–167.

12.   W. A. Green, *op. cit.,* p. 330. Carl Campbell, "Social and Economic Obstacles to the Development of Popular Education in Post Emancipation Jamaica, 1834–1865", *Journal of Caribbean History,* Vol. 1, Nov. 1970, p. 57 suggests that the annual grant for the period 1835–1845 was £30 000. But cf. his "The Development of Primary Education in Jamaica, 1835–1865", p. 10 where the amount is given as £25 000, and p. 21 where the grant for 1838–1841 was £30 000.

13.   Olwyn Blouet, *op. cit.,* p. 142. For the S.P.G. grants to 1845 see C. F. Pascoe, *Two Hundred Years of the S. P. G.* London: 1901, p. 195.

14.   Campbell, "Obstacles", pp. 72–74; Fay Williams "The Work of the Anglican Church in Education in Jamaica, 1826–1845", U. W. I., M. A. Research Paper, 1987, p. 66; W. A. Green, *op. cit.,* pp. 335, 336.

15.   W. A. Green, *op. cit.,* pp. 332 and 412, n. 12; Campbell, "Denominationalism", p. 155.

16.   R. V. Goodridge, "The Development of Education in Barbados, 1818–1860", M. Ed. Thesis, University of Leeds, 1966, p. 70. For Jamai-

ca, see Fay Williams, "The Work of the Anglican Church", pp. 55, 56 and Campbell, "Primary Education in Jamaica", p. 64.

17. See Gordon, *Reports and Repercussions,* p. 63.

18. Campbell, "Denominationalism", pp. 155–165. Blouet, *op. cit.,* p. 145; H. Cnattingius, *Bishops and Societies.* London: S.P.C.K., 1952, pp. 151–158.

19. Coleridge's statement is cited in Goodridge, R. V. "Development of Education", pp. 106f. Sterling reported that children were being taught three or four hours per week. See Gordon, *Reports and Repercussions,* p. 61.

20. Campbell, "Imperial Policy", pp. 80, 81; on Coleridge, see Blouet, *op. cit.,* p. 187; cf. Colbert Williams, *The Methodist Contribution to Education in the Bahamas.* Gloucester: Allan Sutton, 1982, p. 150.

21. MMS Box 149: Minutes of the St. Vincent District, 1835; cf. Box 151: Report of the Barbados Society, 1840, and Box 152: Report of the Barbados Society, 1842.

22. MMS Box 153: Report of the Barbados Society, 1843.

23. MMS Box 155: Report of the Barbados Society, 1851.

24. MMS Box 158: Report for Day and Sabbath Schools for the Second Barbados Circuit, 1859. The comment was made about the Rice's Methodist School.

25. MMS Box 160: Report of the First Circuit Day Schools, 1865.

26. *Ibid.*

27. Maynard, *op. cit.,* p. 130.

28. Kingsley Lewis, *op. cit.,* pp. 115–117. R. Goodridge, pp. 113f. discusses Moravian views on education.

29. For a report on the Established Church's influence, see MMS Box 152: Report of the Barbados Day Schools, 1842.

30. MMS Box 140, No. 26: Hudson to the General Secretaries, April 28, 1841.

31. S. J. Curtis, *History of Education in Great Britain.* 7th Edn. London: Tutorial Press Ltd., 1968. pp. 237ff.

32. MMS Box 151: Report of the Barbados Day Schools, 1840.

33. MMS Box 152: Minutes of the Demerara District 1843. The emphasis was indicated in the Minutes by means of an enlarged script.

34. Gordon, *A Century of West Indian Education,* p. 25. "An Appeal to the Friends of Education on Behalf of the Negroes in the British Colonies", January 1836.

35. C. R. McCarthy, "The Imperialist Motive in the Introduction of Popular Education in Barbados, 1833–1876", M. Ed., 1983, University of Alberta, p. 222. McCarthy appears to be overstating his case when he asserts that moral and religious education was an attempt to infuse the "stock knowledge and values available in English elementary education into Barbados".

36. Millicent Whyte, *A Short History of Education in Jamaica.* London: Hodder and Stoughton, 1983, p. 11.

37. S. C. Gordon, *Century,* p. 171, "Prime Minister to the Treasury, 21 July, 1835".

38. Gordon, *Reports and Repercussions,* p. 61.

39. Blouet, *op. cit.,* p. 220.

40. S. S. Goodridge, *Facing the Challenge of Emancipation.* Bridgetown: Cedar Press, 1981, p. 65.

41. Kingsley Lewis, *op. cit.,* pp. 127, 128.

42. MMS Box 149: Minutes of the St. Vincent District, 1835.

43. See MMS Box 150: Minutes of the St. Vincent District, 1836, for Grogan's candidature; Box 151: Report of the Barbados Day Schools, 1840, for his death.

44. MMS Box 151: Report of the Barbados Day Schools, 1840.

45. MMS Box 153: Report of the Barbados Day Schools, 1843.

46. Gordon, *Century,* p. 171.

47. Blouet, *op. cit.,* p. 218.

48. The inability of the poor salaries to serve as an attraction to persons of talent was expressed early in the programme. See Gordon, *Century,* pp. 34, 175. The problem persisted for many years into the late nineteenth century.

49. MMS Box 153: Report of the Barbados Circuit, 1843.

50. Latrobe, "Report on Negro Education", enclosure to Schedule A. Only the school at Mangrove in St. Philip charged a similar rate. Others charged as high as 31/2d sterling per week.

51. MMS Box 139, No. 164: Phelp to Beecham, September 30, 1837.

52. MMS Box 140, No. 83: Phelp to the General Secretaries, November 20, 1838.

53. Population returns tend to be somewhat piecemeal. More detailed returns are given in the 1850's, showing paupers and children engaged in

agriculture. In 1844, the highest number of persons tried for misdemeanours outside of Bridgetown came from District E. See Blue Book, 1844, pp. 180ff.

54.   MMS Box 133, No. 132: Phelp to Beecham, July 12, 1833.

55.   See the Latrobe Report, p. 62. According to R. Goodridge, the Moravians at Mt. Tabor found the people too poor to pay. See R. Goodridge, "Education in Barbados", p. 122.

56.   MMS Box 153: Report of the Barbados Society, 1843. Cf. Box 140, (File 1840) No. 38: Biggs to the General Secretaries, September 3, 1840: and No. 60: Biggs to the General Secretaries, December 24, 1840, in both of which the flourishing state of the school is recorded. Phelp was probably too impatient.

57.   Campbell, *Primary Education in Jamaica,* p. 77. As a rule the General Superintendent was the same person as the Chairman of the District.

58.   See Gordon, *Century* p. 38, for the Secretary's letter and the response by the Mico Charity.

59.   Green, *op. cit.,* p. 328; cf. Wood, *op. cit.,* p. 214.

60.   F. R. Augier and S. C. Gordon, *Sources of West Indian History.* London: Longmans, Green and Co. Ltd., 3rd. Imp., 1967, p. 219. The Secretary did not consider that the ex-slaves could not yet have acquired the wherewithal to provide for their children's education.

61.   Fay Williams, "The Work of the Anglican Church", pp. 66, 69; cf. Campbell, "Obstacles" pp. 73ff.

62.   On the allocation of the fund, see C. Campbell, *The Development of Education in Trinidad, 1834–1870,* unpublished Ph. D. thesis, U. W. I., 1973, pp. 146, 147, where the effects of the new policy on various territories are mentioned. Cf. Klingberg, *Mico Charity,* pp. 308, 315.

63.   Barbados Blue Book, 1846, p. 23.

64.   Notwithstanding the increasing grants, they continued for some years until formally abolished in 1876. See the *Official Gazette,* October 5, 1876, where the House of Assembly on September 26 passed a resolution (No. 10) calling for the discontinuance of the grant of £800.

65.   These were in the years 1846 and 1856. In the former, the grant was for schoolhouses, in the latter for the Foundation School.

66.   MMS Box 154: Report of the Barbados Day Schools, 1846.

67.   *Ibid.,* Cf. Box 154: Report of the Barbados Day Schools, 1848.

68.   The Report will be found in the Minutes of the House of Assembly for July 28, 1857. Appended to this Report is a letter from Rawle to the Clerk of the Assembly dated February 14, 1857. This letter embodies Rawle's proposals for the Training Institution.

69.   For the view of the Trinidad planter, see Donald Wood, *Trinidad in Transition.* London: Oxford University Press, 1969, p. 227; cf. W. A. Green, *op. cit.,* p. 338 where the opinion of the Stipendiary Magistrate is cited.

70.   Levy, *Emancipation,* p. 91; cf. Campbell, "The Development of Vocational Training in Jamaica: First Steps", in *Caribbean Quarterly,* Vol. II, No.s 1 and 2, March and June 1965, pp. 25, 26.

71.   Gordon, *Century,* pp. 44, 59; cf. Campbell, "Vocational Training", pp. 18, 19.

72.   Clauses 8, 9, 11, 12. Cf. Gordon, *Century,* p. 48, where provision is made in Trinidad in 1851 for a Training College.

73.   K. Lewis, *op. cit.,* p. 128. The discussion in Lewis is so confused as to leave doubt about what was being challenged.

74.   For a discussion on the Bahamian situation, see Colbert Williams, *op. cit.,* pp. 151–154. Cf. Mary Turner, "The Bishop of Jamaica and Slave Instruction" in *Journal of Ecclesiastical History,* October 1975, p. 11; and Campbell, "Denominationalism", p. 155 for Jamaica.

75.   See Wood, *op. cit.,* p. 223. The Trinidad Board could have included others beside members of the legislature.

76.   The necessity for the approval of the Bishop had been opposed in the Committee of the House of Assembly by S. J. Prescod. A change to "assent" was passed. See Minutes of the Assembly, August 13, 1850. The approval of both officials was reported to the Committee on January 7, 1851. In Committee of the House the question of toleration was raised in that the Bill required the Authorised Version of the Bible to be read, and this was felt to have the effect of excluding Roman Catholics. The amendment for the removal of that reference was lost. See Minutes of the Assembly, August 20, 1850.

77.   The rules were approved at the Committee's Meeting on January 7, 1851. New rules were approved by the Education Committee on November 24, 1865, and came into force on January 1, 1866.

78.   Minutes of the Education Committee, March 2, 1852. The Minutes, which are located at the Barbados Department of Archives, are now closed.

79.   These figures are taken from Methodist Reports to their District Meet-
       ings. In 1871, 1874 and 1875, no schools were reported to be under the
       average. No Reports are available for 1858, 1860, 1861, 1864, 1866, 1868,
       1872 and 1873.

80.   Campbell, "Obstacles" p. 86; S. Wilmot, "Baptist Missionaries and
       Jamaican Politics, 1838–54", in K. O. Lawrence (Ed.), *A Selection of
       Papers Presented at the Twelfth Conference of Caribbean Historians,*
       1980, pp. 48–59. Cf. Colbert Williams, *op. cit.,* pp. 150–154 for the
       Methodists in the Bahamas.

81.   These figures are compiled from the quarterly grants entered in the
       Minutes of the Education Committee.

82.   Minutes of the Education Committee, November 29, 1853; and
       February 16, 1854.

83.   Minutes of the Education Committee, March 2, 1852. The Inspector
       seems to have had a dislike for the Methodists.

84.   Minutes of the Education Committee, May 4, 1866.

85.   Minutes of the Education Committee, January 28, 1864.

86.   Minutes of the Education Committee, July 22 and October 28, 1862.

87.   Minutes of the Education Committee, April 28, 1857. Bleby had writ-
       ten to the Committee on March 16 defending Kirton. His letter forms
       part of these Minutes.

88.   This complaint was made in the Report of the Second Circuit Day
       Schools, 1864, MMS Box 159. With respect to the Belmont School,
       Padgham had written to the Education Committee to the effect that no
       proof of Mr. Carrington falsifying the records had been established,
       "and I beg to add that I believe he had not done so…".

89.   Minutes of the Education Committee, October 23, 1857.

90.   Minutes of the Committee, May 21, 1858. This decision was based on the
       Inspector's verbal report to that effect.

91.   Minutes of the Committee, May 21, 1858.

92.   MMS Box 228 (File 1858), No. 14: Bleby to Hoole, February 26, 1858;
       No. 31: May 11, 1858; No. 87: December 26, 1858; (File 1860), No. 7:
       Bleby to Hoole, January 26, 1860.

93.   Minutes of the Committee, May 6, 1859.

94.   Minutes of the Committee, July 28, 1859. The money was eventually
       granted at the meeting of October 20, 1859.

95. Minutes of the Committee, February 12, 1861.

96. Minutes of the Committee, November 17, 1859.

97. Minutes of the Committee, July 23, 1869.

98. Minutes of the Committee, January 10, 1861.

99. Minutes of the Committee, October 27, 1863; January 28, 1864; July 27, 1866. Henry Padgham, the Methodist minister, was listed in the first of these.

100. Gordon, *Century,* pp. 61–63.

101. MMS Box 158: Report of the First Circuit Day Schools, and Report of the Second Circuit Day Schools, 1859.

102. For his complaint to the Education Committee, see Minutes for October 28, 1862. In his Report on the Circuit, Bleby stated: "We have no confidence in the Government Inspector, or the reports which from time to time he makes concerning our schools". See MMS Box 158: Second Barbados Day School Reports, 1862.

103. Minutes of the Committee, August 1, 1861; and July 22, 1862. The Methodists in the Bahamas had a difficult struggle to participate in public funding because of the aggression of the Church of England.

104. Minutes of the House of Assembly, January 10, 1860; August 13, 1861.

105. Minutes of the Legislative Council, January 4, 1867.

106. The Report is in the Minutes of the House of Assembly, January 10, 1860.

107. The disparaging remarks were made about the teacher of the Belmont Methodist School. He added "little could be looked for but less is found". See Minutes of the House of Assembly, August 13, 1861.

108. Minutes of the Education Committee, August 18, 1859.

109. Minutes of the Committee, October 20, 1859.

110. The figures are compiled from the Reports submitted by the Inspector from time to time.

111. MMS Box 155: Barbados Schools Reports, 1853. The teacher was described as knowing his profession but lacking energy.

112. MMS Box 156: Barbados Circuit Day School Report, 1855.

113. MMS Box 157: Barbados School Report, 1856, for Speightstown; for Bethel, First Barbados School Report, 1857; and for Ebenezer, Second Barbados Day School Report, 1857.

114. MMS Box 158: Barbados First Circuit Day School Report, 1859; Box 160: Barbados Second Circuit School Report, 1867.

115.   Minutes of the House of Assmebly, November 3, 1863.

116.   Gordon, *Century,* pp. 38, 80; *Repercussions,* pp. 79f.

117.   "Rules to be observed by Schools in connexion with the Education Committee", sections 8–21. The rules were passed on November 24, 1865. A copy is enclosed in MMS Box 232.

118.   "Report of Schools for the Poor in connexion with the Education Committee of Barbados, for the year ending 30th September, 1867", included in the Minutes of the Assembly, Session 1868/69.

119.   The Report is enclosed in the Minutes of the House of Assembly, May 21, 1872.

120.   Minutes of the Education Committee, January 23, 1872.

121.   *Ibid.*

122.   *Ibid.*

123.   Minutes of the Committee, March 22, 1872; Minutes of the House of Assembly, May 21, 1872.

124.   Report of the Commission on Education, 1875, see Gordon, *Repercussions,* pp. 99–106.

125.   See *Laws of Barbados,* Session 1877/78, Barbados, 1878: An Act to Establish a General Education Board and to Provide for the Improvement and Extension of the Educational System of the Colony. Cap XLI.

126.   Colbert Williams, *op. cit.,* pp. 151, 152. Similar problems were forestalled in Trinidad in 1870 when Governor Gordon successfully curbed the desire to have equal representation of Anglicans and Catholics on the Board of Education. See Campbell, "Education in Trinidad", p. 489.

127.   *Barbados Agricultural Reporter,* August 12, 1879.

128.   *Ibid.* May 2, 6, 9, 20; July 22, August 19, 1879. Numerous pseudonymous letters were published on the subject of Mitchinson's bigotry.

129.   *Barbados Agricultural Reporter,* August 12, 1879, letter signed "NO BIGOT".

130.   For the correspondence between the Governor and the Bishop, see the *Official Gazette,* August 14, 1879. For the criticism of the Governor, see the *Barbados Agricultural Reporter,* August 19, 1879.

131.   See section XXI.

132.   Minutes of the Education Board, May 15, 1879. In Trinidad the system of centralisation had been instituted from the beginning to reduce the

influence of the Roman Catholic Church. See Campbell, "Education in Trinidad", pp. 65–76.

133. Minutes of the Education Board, May 19, 1879.

134. MMS Box 232, No. 14: Garry to Osborn, May 28, 1879; cf. No. 18: Wright to Osborn, June 9, 1879.

135. Minutes of the Education Board, August 18, 1879.

136. Minutes of the Education Board, September 15, 1879. The decision was notified to the Board in a letter from Garry to the Secretary of the Board dated August 21, 1879.

137. The rules of the Board were published in the Official Gazette for March 6, 10, 13, 18, 20, 25, 1880. These rules were finalised by the Education Board on December 11, 1879, and approved by the Executive Council on February 24, 1880.

138. For those in 1880, see Minutes of January 28 and February 8, 1880; for those in 1882 see the Minutes of January 25 and April 5, 1882.

139. See Minutes of the Education Board, February 8, 1880 and January 25, 1882.

140. *Ibid.,* October 20 and November 19, 1879; January 25, 1882.

141. Minutes of the House of Assembly, Session 1879/80, Document 80–27: Report of Primary Schools in connection with the Education Board, for the year 1879.

142. Minutes of the Assembly, Session 1882/83, Minutes of April 10, 1883, Document 208: Report on Primary and Combined Schools for the year 1882.

143. Minutes of the Assembly, February 13, 1883, Session 1882/83, Document 180: Report of the Infant Schools in connexion with the Education Board for the year 1882.

144. Minutes of April 10, 1883, Document 208: Report on Primary and Combined Schools for the year 1882.

145. Minutes of the Education Board, September 24, 1879; see also Minutes for September 29, 1879.

146. *Ibid.* September 15, 1880.

147. *Ibid.* January 28 and March 1, 1880.

148. *Ibid.* July 28 and August 18, 1880.

149. *Ibid.* March 16, 1881.

150. *Ibid.* February 16, 1881.

151. This came before the Board on August 7, 1880.

152. Minutes of the Board, April 4, 1883. See Minutes of April 25, 1883 for his appointment.

153. *Ibid.* June 6, 1883.

154. *Ibid.* May 3, 1880.

155. Minutes of the Board, January 28, 1880. The school was the Wilson's Village School operated by the Methodists.

156. *Ibid.* August 31, 1881; cf. August 24, 1881. What Wright's explanation was is not stated in the Minutes.

157. Minutes of the Standing Committee of the Board, April 24, 1882, cf. also May 23, 1882 and April 25, 1883.

CHAPTER 5

1. MMS Box 549: Minutes of the Missionary Committee, Dec. 5, 1851.

2. This was the position of the Missionary Committee as cited by Findlay and Holdsworth, II. 362. For the decline in funds and membership, *ibid;* I.190. Cf. Michael Craton, *Sinews of Empire.* London: Temple Smith, 1974, p. 285, where it is said that "pure philanthropy" was dead by 1840.

3. See, for example, MMS Box 149: "Report of the Barbados Station", 1835.

4. MMS Box 129, No. 1. This document has no title, but is a resume of the practices of the Methodists. The document briefly states the existing practice, with parenthetical references to either Conference Minutes, Instructions, or District Minutes dealing with the topic. The compilation is probably the work of the Chairman or Secretary of the District. The work ist undated, but was done about 1828, the same date as the rest of the material in that box. The relevant section here is that entitled "Accompts and Allowances", referring to "Accounts and Allowances".

5. These figures were extracted from the Accounts attached to the annual Society Reports.

6. MMS Box 143, No. 53 (File 1856): Hurd to the General Secretaries, August 27, 1856.

7. The Colonial Office tried to establish a Confederation of the Windward Islands in the 1870's. This was not supported by the Barbadian legisla-

tors, who feared a diminution of their traditional institutions and a loss of their control.

8.   MMS Box 164: Minutes of the St. Vincent District, 1876. The new James St. Chapel yielded £220 in 1857. See MMS Box 157: Minutes of the St. Vincent and Demerara District, 1857.

9.   K. Davis, *Cross and Crown in Barbados.* Frankfurt am Main: Verlag Peter Lang, 1983, pp. 74 and 66 respectively.

10.   For the Circuit Accounts between 1835 and 1845, see Appendix IV.

11.   "Bethel Society Reports and Accounts, 1873 to 1891" in Pulic Library, Barbados, Microfilm Bs. 54.

12.   See Maynard, *Moravian Church,* pp. 144, 145.

13.   MMS Box 138, No. 12: Fidler to Beecham, January 12, 1836.

14.   MMS Box 141 (File 1845), No. 8: Fidler to Beecham, January 22, 1845; No. 10: Whitehead to Beecham, February 6, 1845.

15.   MMS Box 141 (File 1845), No. 8: Fidler to Beecham, January 22, 1845. For the establishment of free villages see Rawle Farley, "The Rise of Village Settlements in British Guyana", *Caribbean Quarterly,* Vol. 10, No. 1, March 1964, pp. 52–60. For similar activity in Jamaica, see J. H. Hinton, *Memoir of William Knibb.* London, 1849, pp. 304–306.

16.   MMS Box 141 (File 1845) No. 10: Whitehead to Beecham, Providence, February 6, 1845.

17.   For the career of Abraham Reece see J. E. Reece and C.G. Clark-Hunt, *Barbados Diocesan History.* London: The West India Committee, 1925, pp. 79, 114, 116, 118.

18.   MMS Box 143 (File 1854), No. 10: Bannister to the Secretaries, January 25, 1854.

19.   MMS Box 142 (File 1852), No. 55: Corlett and Butcher to the Missionary Committee, July 12, 1852.

20.   MMS Box 143 (File 1854), No. 5: Bannister to the General Secs., January 24, 1854.

21.   See Levy, *Emancipation,* 113f., 119f.

22.   MMS Box 158: Report of the Second Barbados Circuit, 1859; Box 228: (File 1860) No. 19: Bleby to Hoole, March 26, 1860.

23.   MMS Box 231 (File 1876) No. 15: Hammond to Punshon, April 29, 1876.

24.   The sources for these accounts are as follows: for 1865, MMS Box 160: Minutes of the St. Vincent District, 1866; for 1867, Minutes of the St.

Vincent and Demerara District, 1868, same box. The District had by this time been enlarged to include Demerara.

25. MMS Box 160: Minutes of the St. Vincent District, 1870, for 1869; Minutes of the St. Vincent District, 1871, for 1870; and Minutes of the St. Vincent District, 1872 for 1871.

26. For a full discussion of this subject, we are dependent on the letters of the missionaries. Efforts to trace letters sent to the West Indies, even at SOAS, have not been successful. For the missionaries' letters, see MMS Box 229 (File 1864) No. 59: Hurd to the General Secretaries, June 9, 1864; No. 67: Hurd to the Gen. Secs., June 23, 1864; No. 68: Dixon to the General Secretaries, June 24, 1864; No. 69: Heath to Hoole, June 24, 1864; No. 94: Hurd to the General Secretaries, September 9, 1864; No. 99: Hurd to Boyce, September 22, 1864; No. 118: Hurd to Boyce, November 8, 1864; No. 128: Dixon to the General Secretaries, December 22, 1864. Also Findlay and Holdsworth, II.363–65. Edmondson had previously served in Barbados.

27. See, for example, MMS Box 230 (File 1865) No. 59: Dixon to the General Secretaries, October 23, 1865; No. 40 (File 1866), Horsford to Hoole, October 24, 1866.

28. MMS Box 231 (File 1873) No. 43: Hurd to Boyce, Ebenezer, November 7, 1873.

29. MMS Box 231 (File 1876) No. 15: Hammond to Punshon, Bethel Mission House, April 29, 1876.

30. The Minutes of the 1864 District Meeting spoke of their efforts to raise funds between 1861 and 1863 to meet shortfalls in revenue.

31. MMS Box 229 (File 1863), No. 58: Padgham to Hoole, June 25, 1863.

32. MMS Box 231 (File 1876) No. 14: Genge to Boyce, April 29, 1876. The word "supers" was obviously an abbreviation for "superintendents".

33. MMS Box 231 (File 1876) No. 15: Hammond to Punshon, April 29, 1876.

34. MMS Box 228 (File 1860) No. 38: Hurd to the General Secretaries, May 22, 1860. Hurd claimed to have been personally acquainted with most of the members.

35. MMS Box 158: Barbados First Circuit Society Report for 1859.

36. MMS Box 228 (File 1860) No. 19: Bleby to Hoole, March 26, 1860.

37. MMS Box 229 (File 1863) No. 67: Bleby to Boyce, July 25, 1863. Bleby had obviously exaggerated when he described establishment as the

sole cause of their decline. It is interesting to find that Methodists, Moravians and Anglicans associated regularly in organisations such as the Bible Society. For a list of participants, see the *Barbados Almanac,* 1860, pp. 64 and 65.

38.   Minutes of the Assembly, April 27, 1858. For the action see the Minutes for August 10, 1858.

39.   MMS Box 228 (File 1858), No. 31: Bleby to Hoole, May 11, 1858.

40.   Minutes of the Education Committee, May 21, 1858. Bleby's letter, which was incorporated into the minutes, was dated April 1858. The Education Committee was established in 1850 by the first Education Act. The Committee was not empowered to make grants for buildings; but in any case this application was not as extensive as that to the legislature, being confined to the Ebenezer School.

41.   In the same year, the Assembly had made grants to St. Barnabas of £150, to St. Patrick of £200 and St. Clement of £400.

42.   Minutes of the Assembly, March 22, 1859.

43.   Minutes of the Assembly, April 26, 1859.

44.   MMS Box 229 (File 1860) No. 63: Bleby to Hoole, July 25, 1860. Cf. No. 64: Hurd to the Committee, July 25, 1860 which also mentions the fire of 1860.

45.   Minutes of the Assembly, March 26, 1861. At the same meeting, John Gooding gave notice of a bill to grant the Methodists' petition.

46.   For these details, see the following Blue Books: 1859, pp. 89–90; 1860, pp. 76–77; 1862, pp. 90–91 where the lists of Assembly members are printed.

47.   This information was conveyed in a terse communication to the Assembly. See the Minutes for May 13, 1862. For the Assembly's action, see the Minutes for April 29, 1862.

48.   MMS Box 229 (File 1862) No. 81: Padgham to Hoole, October 9, 1862. The letter to which Padgham referred cannot be traced by the present writer. There are no extant newspapers for 1862 save a copy of *The Times* in the H. A. Vaughan collection at the Barbados Archives. This is in poor condition and is closed. A pamphlet written by Bleby in 1862 aroused considerable discussion. Such extracts of its contents as are cited in the press are all that can be obtained of it.

49.   Minutes of the Assembly, December 16, 1862. For an editorial comment, see *The Times,* April 28, 1863.

50.   Box 229 (File 1862) No. 106: Bleby to Hoole, December 24, 1862. Cf. *The Times,* June 19, 1863. According to the 1861 census, there were 91 landholders in the parish of St. Philip. This petition seems, therefore, to have had the support of members of the Established Church. It gave as one reason for Methodist support the impracticability, presumably on the part of the Established Church, of catching up with the "religious wants of the people by increasing places of worship to the extent required". But it overstated the case when the position usually taken by the missionaries was that the clergy of the Established Church did not preach the Gospel. That Bleby forwarded a petition with that statement suggests that in his eyes, the advantage it offered outweighed its inaccuracy.

51.   MMS Box 228 (File 1862) No. 107: Soper to Hoole, December 24, 1862, reports this fact.

52.   Minutes of the Assembly, July 5, 1859; and September 27, 1859. The bill was passed *nem. con.*

53.   Both amendments were introduced by Thomas Gill, one of the members for the City, and H. Stuart Mayers, one of the members for St. Joseph. This petition is to be found in the Minutes of the Assembly for May 12, 1863. For the passage of the Bill, see the Minutes of July, 14, 1863.

54.   MMS Box 229 (File 1863) No. 67: Bleby to Boyce, July 25, 1863. Cf. No. 77: Bleby to Boyce, September 8, 1863; and No. 127: Bleby to Hoole, December 25, 1863.

55.   The petition was incorporated into the Minutes of the Assembly for June 11, 1861.

56.   There is only one copy of Standing Orders in existence for this period, and that is for 1867. Section 56 of this declared that a motion may be put at the bottom of the order if not ready to be proceeded with. On any second occasion, if it is not ready, the motion must be expunged unless a satisfactory explanation was given to the House. See "Rules, Orders and Forms of Proceedings of the House of Assembly of Barbados Relating to Public Business", Barbados 1867, at the Barbados Archives.

57.   Minutes of the Assembly, June 9, 1863. The resolution was printed in part in *The Times,* June 16, 1863. Except for the year 1867, Griffith was a member of the Assembly from 1861–1876. From 1861–1866 he repre-

sented St. George, while from 1868–1876 he represented St. Joseph. In 1876 he became a member of Council.

58. *The Times,* June 9, 1863. The editor of *The Times* was pro-Methodist as a rule in his religious comments.

59. See, *The Times,* June 26, 1863. The writer styled himself "One of your Constant Readers".

60. *The Times,* October 2, 1863.

61. *The Times,* October 13, 1863. Just in passing, it might be pointed out here that Bleby's Accounts for this year were not accepted by the District Meeting of 1864. See MMS Box 159: Minutes of the St. Vincent District, 1864. Cf. MMS Box 229 (File 1864) No. 25: Hurd to the General Secretaries, March 11, 1864.

62. *The Times,* November 3, 1863. Letter by "Observer".

63. Box 229 (File 1863) No. 67: Bleby to Boyce, July 25, 1863.

64. Bleby complained bitterly that Hoole was inclined to support underhand activity. See MMS Box 229 (File 1863) No. 127: Bleby to Hoole, December 25, 1863; Cf. No. 12: Bleby to Boyce, February 24, 1863, where he complained of being snubbed by certain persons at the Mission House.

65. MMS Box 229 (File 1863) No. 63: Bleby to Boyce, July 9, 1863; cf. No. 67: Bleby to Boyce, July 25, 1863; also (File 1862) No. 81; Padgham to Hoole, October 9, 1862.

66. *The Times,* April 14, 1865; also Minutes of the Assembly, April 11, 1865.

67. Minutes of the Assembly, October 31, 1865. The division on this occasion was fifteen in favour and eight against. Earlier in the year a similar resolution was passed by a margin of 12 to 5 but this was rejected by the Council. See Minutes of the Assembly, April 25, 1865; Cf. MMS Box 230 (File 1865) No. 31: Hurd to the General Secretaries, May 25, 1865.

68. MMS Box 159: Minutes of the St. Vincent District, 1864.

69. G. Smith, *History,* II, 696, cf. E. Halevy, *The Triumph of Reform, (1830–1841).* London: Ernest Benn, 1961, p. 154.

70. Smith, *History,* III, 203–220. As the name implies, the Society aimed at separation of Church and State.

71. O. Chadwick, *The Victorian Church, Part II.* 2nd. edn., London: A & C Black, 1970, pp. 427–430. See also A. C. Carpenter, *op. cit.,* p. 341.

72. Buckingham and Chandos to West Indian Governors, Downing St., November 30, 1868. The Act is 31 and 32 Victoria, c. 120: An Act to

Relieve the Consolidated Fund from the Charge of the Salaries of Future Bishops, Archdeacons, Ministers and Persons in the West Indies. These documents are enclosed in the Minutes of the Assembly for January 26, 1869.

73.   See Grenville to Rawson, Downing St., June 11, 1870; and Kimberly to Longden, January 6, 1871. Longden was Governor of Trinidad, and Rawson was directed to use that letter as a guide.

74.   For these arrangements see A. Caldecott, *The Church in the West Indies.* London, 1898, pp. 134–147.

75.   Regrettably, the newspaper issues no longer exist, and we only know of the arguments through quotations by one of the contestants.

76.   See the Governor's message to the Assembly contained in the Minutes of the Assembly, July 25, 1871.

77.   This was in his address to the Legislature, which was reported in *The Times* of January 18, 1863. Cf. *The Times,* February 28, 1871, where in paragraph 19 of his speech, the Governor indicated that the British Government would not interfere with the methods used or the details.

78.   The message is contained in the Minutes of the Assembly for July 25, 1871.

79.   C. O. 28/212: Rawson to Granville, April 17, 1870 (No. 51). In this despatch, Rawson gave another reason for the delay – he wanted to visit Grenada first.

80.   The Governor's message and the petition from the Rev. J. Y. Edghill are both embodied in the Minutes of the Assembly for September 27, 1870.

81.   The bill was read a first time on October 25, and passed the Assembly on November 1. In the Council, it was read a first time on November 4, and passed on November 8. See the Council and Assembly Minutes for those dates. For the text of the Act, see *The Official Gazette,* October 27, and November 7, 1870.

82.   The accolade appeared in an editorial of *The Times* dated October 8, 1870.

83.   This information appeared in a letter from Edghill, expressing the thanks of the Moravians. See *The Times,* November 12, 1870.

84.   See Rawson to Kimberley, December 3, 1870. The unsigned despatch, obviously a draft, was dated January 12, 1871.

85.   According to the *Barbados Almanac,* 1870, pp. 47 and 52, the Established Church had 25 633 members, the Moravians 1795, and the

Methodists 3 115. These figures would give a more accurate picture than the censuses which tend to put everyone not declared otherwise as belonging to the Established Church.

86. See the Minutes of the Assembly, January 31, 1871; cf. *The Official Gazette,* February 6, 1871.

87. See MMS Box 231 (File 1870). Hurd to Boyce, September 24, 1870. In another letter some time previously, Hurd indicated that many of the missionaries were opposed to concurrent endowment. MMS Box 231 (File 1869): No. 51: Hurd to Boyce, November 8, 1869.

88. *The Times,* October 8, 1870. In his despatch of December 3, 1870, Governor Rawson warned of opposition to any grant to the Methodists.

89. See Minutes of the Assembly, February 14, April 18 and May 16, 1871.

90. Henry Pilgrim was one of the representatives for the city; Thomas Gill was one of those for St. Thomas.

91. See Minutes of the Assembly, July 11, 1871.

92. Minutes of the Assembly, August 15 and November 7, 1871. The second reading of the bill in Council was postponed in October. See Minutes of the Assembly, October 24, 1871.

93. See *The Times,* January 18, 1871.

94. MMS Box 231 (File 1869) No. 51: Hurd to Boyce, November 8, 1869.

95. *The Times,* July 14, 1875. The letter, signed NONCONFORMIST, was published at the time of Rawson's departure from the island. Cf. MMS Box 231 (File 1876) No. 15: Hammond to Punshon, April 29, 1876, where the injustice of the arrangement was condemned.

96. While the addresses of the Council and Assembly may contain some flattery, it cannot be assumed that everything said in them was untrue. For these addresses, see the *Official Gazette,* November 25, 1875.

97. See *The Times,* November 24 and December 1, 1875. In the course of his reply, the Governor told of his having travelled day and night across Europe in order to cast his vote in a crucial debate at Westminister in favour of the Church of England.

98. For the Methodists' Address and the Governor's reply, see *The West Indian,* February 25, 1876. Cf. *The Official Gazette,* February 21, 1876.

99. Minutes of the Assembly, June 8, 1880. Cf. *The Official Gazette,* June 14 and July 19, 1880.

CHAPTER 6

1. Findlay and Holdsworth, I, 278, 335.

2. For the Jamaican experience, see Findlay and Holdsworth, II. 104–114; cf. Turner, *Slaves and Missionaries,* pp. 179–191.

3. Trinidad Duplicate Despatches, (T.D.D.) Vol. 3, No. 254: Woodford to Bathurst, August 1, 1817, enclosing Minutes of the Council, April 20, 1811.

4. Minutes of the Council, February 9 and August 24, 1815, and February 22, 1816, enclosed with T.D.D. 3. 254 as above.

5. H. Cnattingius, *Bishops and Societies,* p. 148; Reece and Clarke-Hunt, *Barbados Diocesan History,* p. 36.

6. Findlay and Holdsworth, II, 143.

7. See Appendix VII for a list of clergy in areas where Methodists had difficulty.

8. For Phelp's correspondence on the matter, see MMS Box 139, No. 164: Phelp to Beecham, Speightstown, September 30, 1837; also No. 130: Phelp to Beecham, May 25, 1837.

9. MMS Box 137 (File 1835), No. 143: Aldis to the Missionary Committee, November 20, 1835.

10. MMS Box 141 (File 1845), No. 10: Francis Whitehead to Beecham, Providence, February 6, 1845.

11. MMS Box 139 (File 1837), No. 130: Phelp to Beecham, May 25, 1837.

12. MMS Box 141 (File 1843), No. 25: Fidler to the Committee, April 27, 1843.

13. There is only one copy of *The Times* in existence, and that is in the H. A. Vaughan collection at the Barbados Department of Archives. That copy, however, is closed as it is in poor condition. Bleby's pamphlet was called "True and False Apostles". Scraps from both sides appear in newspaper extracts from *The West Indian,* in the Public Library Microfilms, Bs. 37.

14. See *The Times,* March 20, 1863.

15. This is from a letter dated July 17, 1862, by "A Minister of the Church of England". The source of the extract is not indicated. Bs. 37.

16. Letter by "A Methodist" dated July 8, 1862. From Bs. 37.

17. Letter supposedly from John Wesley to Henry Bleby, captioned "A VOICE FROM THE GRAVE!" These letters sought to remind Bleby

that the Wesleys never intended separation from the Church of England. In Bs. 37.

18. These criticisms appeared in two letters by "A WHITE LAYMAN" in *The Times,* March 20, 1863, and April 24, 1863, both in Bs. 37.

19. MMS Box 229 (File 1862), No. 81: Padgham to Hoole, October 9, 1862.

20. *The Times,* July 3, 1863.

21. *The Times,* July 10, 1863.

22. For Bleby's views on the laws relating to this matter, see *The Times,* July 14 and 21, 1863.

23. *The Times,* July 28, 1863.

24. The Bishop's letter was dated July 20, and Bleby's acceptance July 22.

25. On this point see *Barbados Diocesan History,* p. 47, the penultimate paragraph of which gives an apt assessment of Mitchinson's pronouncements. See also Kortright Davis, *Cross and Crown,* pp. 142f.

26. "Charge delivered in St. Michael's Cathedral, Bridgetown, Barbados, by John Lord Bishop of Barbados at his Visitation of that Island on March 5, 1874, being the First Year after his Consecration". Oxford and London, 1874. By the term "Catholic" the Bishop meant the "universal" church, especially as it was before the Reformation. The Moravian Church is held to have evolved from the church in ancient Moravia, a province of Czechoslovakia. Both Davis pp. 127f. and Kingsley Lewis, *op. cit.,* pp. 78f. refer to this charge without any comment as to its implications for church relations. This section of the Charge, as cited in the *Barbados Diocesan History* is inaccurate. See p. 44 of the History.

27. This somewhat inane statement by Lewis fails to do justice to the significance of Mitchinson's comments. Lewis, *op. cit.,* p. 79.

28. Charge, p. 29. A correspondent in *The Agricultural Reporter,* May 2, 1879, noted that Mitchinson had created disharmony in the religious climate in the island.

29. From the Liverpool Minutes, section 24. See Peirce, *op. cit.,* p. 783.

30. Liverpool Minutes, section 3. Peirce, *op. cit.,* p. 780.

31. A. F. Wells, "Fraternal Organizations" in *Encyclopaedia Britannica.* 1968 Edition. James Hastings, Ed. *Encyclopaedia of Religion and Ethics,* Edinburgh: (T. & T. Clarke), 1974, Vol. 6 "Freemasons" and Vol. 8 "Oddfellows".

32. MMS Box 141 (File 1844), No. 68: Branston to the Gen Secs., November 24, 1844. Branston, who was then the resident missionary at James

Street, had Austin and Thomas in mind. For Hamilton's role, see Box 141 (File 1844), No. 38: Fidler to the Gen Secs., June 19, 1844. For the general course of the dispute see *The Liberal* of September 6, 13, 17, 20, 24, 27; October 1, 4, 15, 1845; and April 8, 18, 1846.

33.   MMS Box 141 (File 1844), No. 38: Fidler to the General Secretaries, June 19, 1844. Cf. (File 1845), No. 5: Fidler to the Gen. Secs. January 8, 1845; No. 35: Fidler, Branston and Whitehead to the General Secretaries, May 8, 1845; No. 43, Fidler et al to the Gen. Secs., June 17, 1845.

34.   For the allegations of Warrenism see MMS Box 141 (File 1844), No. 38: Fidler to the Gen. Secs., June 19, 1844; and (File 1845), No. 35: Fidler et al. to the Gen. Secs., May 8, 1845. The barest sketch of the issue of Dr. Warren ist to be found in Owen Chadwick, *The Victorian Church,* Pt. 1, A & C Black, 1966, p. 377. Cf. R. F. Wearmouth, *op. cit.,* pp. 231–289 for further details. In Jamaica, where a plea for a more liberal policy was made in the early 1830's, it was also described as Warrenism. See Findlay & Holdsworth, II. 334.

35.   MMS Box 141 (File 1844), No. 38: Fidler to the Gen. Secs., June 19, 1844.

36.   MMS Box 141 (File 1844), No. 68: Edward Branston to the Gen. Secs., James Street, November 24, 1844.

37.   MMS Box 129, No. 1 Untitled Doc 'ment. Section entitled "Leaders and Leaders' Meetings".

38.   MMS Box 141 (File 1847), No. 11: Hurd to Beecham, March 9, 1847.

39.   MMS Box 141 (File 1845), No. 5: Fidler to the Gen. Secs., Bay St., January 8, 1845. Cf. No. 45: Fidler to the Gen. Secs., June 24, 1845, in which he claimed that the most intelligent females and the best educated approved the limitation.

40.   MMS Box 141 (File 1844), No. 38: Fidler to the Gen. Secs., June 19, 1844. Cf. (File 1845), No. 35: Fidler, Branston and Whitehead to the Gen. Secs., May 8, 1845, where those being tried before the Leaders' Meeting protested the failure of the missionaries to summon the female leaders.

41.   MMS Box 141 (File 1845), No. 43: Fidler to the Gen. Secs., June 17, 1845.

42.   MMS Box 141 (File 1845), No. 45: Fidler to the Gen. Secs., June 24, 1845.

43.   MMS Box 141 (File 1846), No. 98: George Ranyell to the Secs., December 19, 1846.

44.   *Ibid.*

45.   MMS Box 141 (File 1847), No. 11: Hurd to Beecham, March 9, 1847.

46. MMS Box 141 (File 1847), No. 29: John Corlett to the Gen. Secs., June 24, 1847.

47. *Ibid.*

48. W. J. Gardner, *History of Jamaica*, (1873), London: Frank Cass and Co. Ltd., Repr., 1971, p. 357.

49. Maynard, *op. cit.,* p. 52.

50. F. A. Hoyos, *Barbados,* p. 135f. for Prescod; see Swithin Wilmot, "Baptist Missionaries and Jamaican Politics, 1838–54", in K. O. Lawrence, Ed., A Selection of Papers Presented at the Twelfth Conference of the Association of Caribbean Historians, pp. 48–51.

51. George Belle, "The Abortive Revolution of 1876 in Barbados", *Journal of Caribbean History,* Vol. 18, 1984, pp. 12, 26.

52. Findlay and Holdsworth, II. 331.

53. E. Williams, *Documents on British West Indian History, 1807–1833.* Port of Spain: Trinidad Publishing Co., 1952, Nos. 375, 376, and 380.

54. For biographical material on both men, see Kingsley Lewis, *op. cit.,* pp. 59–76.

55. See W. G. Sewell, *The Ordeal of Free Labour in the West Indies.* London, 1862, Chap. VII, "Social Distinctions in Barbados".

56. J. Gilmore, "Church and Society in Barbados, 1824–1881", in W. K. Marshall, (Ed.) *Emancipation II: A Series of Lectures to Commemorate the 150th Anniversary of Emancipation.* Bridgetown, 1987, p. 15.

57. Cnattingius, *op. cit.,* p. 149.

58. MMS Box 231 (File 1871), No. 56: Hurd to Boyce, November 8, 1871.

59. See MMS Box 143 (File 1853), No. 109: Bannister to the Committee, December 10, 1853; and Box 230 (File 1867), No. 19: Horsford to Hoole, May 2, 1867.

60. MMS Box 155: Minutes of the St. Vincent and Demerara District, 1852. Griffith appears on the list of stations for 1854, appointed to Biabou in St. Vincent. For the case of Walter Garry, see John A. Parker, *A Church in the Sun.* London: Cargate Press, 1959, p. 80.

61. MMS Box 155: Minutes of the St. Vincent and Demerara District, 1854.

62. MMS Box 157: Minutes of the St. Vincent and Demerara District, 1858. These circumstances were mentioned when his candidature was discussed. The Minutes also described him as having unblemished reputation, serious deportment, and deep piety.

63.   MMS Box 228 (File 1859), No. 3: "Address to the Rev. James E. Chase", dated December 1858. Chase was initially posted to Tobago. In an appended note, Henry Hurd described the author of the Address as a former member of his Theological Class, whom he regretted not having put forward for the ministry.

64.   This idea was referred to in MMS Box 142 (File 1849), No. 11: Corlett to the Secretaries, March 10, 1849, and was also challenged in Box 229 (File 1864), No. 69: Heath to Hoole, June 24, 1864. It was generally current with respect to the needs of the coloureds and blacks.

65.   This institution was founded in 1834 to train ministers, and was the cause of considerable controversy. For information on this, see G. Smith, *History,* III, 230–245.

66.   MMS Box 158: Minutes of the St. Vincent and Demerara District, 1863.

67.   J. Horsford, *op. cit.,* pp. 65, 72, 453f., 461 and 471.

68.   MMS Box 230 (File 1867), No. 14: Horsford to Hoole, March 13, 1867.

69.   MMS Box 230 (File 1867), No. 19: Horsford to Hoole, May 2, 1867.

70.   MMS Box 230 (File 1867), No. 29: Horsford to Hoole, June 25, 1867.

71.   The estimates for the salaries of the clergy of the Established Church are taken from Blue Books, 1867, pp. 148–159.

72.   Lewis, *op. cit.,* p. 73 seems to attribute debts to Moore, but Moore only went to Mt. Tabor in 1871.

73.   MMS Box 230 (File 1867), No. 19: Horsford to Hoole, May 2, 1867.

74.   MMS Box 231 (File 1871), No. 56: Hurd to Boyce, November 8, 1871. In this letter, Hurd quoted one from Chase to himself complaining about the inequality.

75.   MMS Box 230 (File 1867), No. 23: Hurd to the Gen. Secs., May 10, 1867, where the writer also admitted that the term "Native" implied inferiority and should be discontinued. Also, Box 231 (File 1872), No. 37: Hurd to the Gen. Secs., December 28, 1872.

76.   MMS Box 230 (File 1867), No. 23: Hurd to the Gen. Secs. May 10, 1867.

77.   MMS Box 550: Minutes of the Missionary Committee, April 25, 1867.

78.   *Ibid.*

79.   MMS Box 230 (File 1867), No. 19: Horsford to Hoole, May 2, 1867.

80.   MMS Box 230 (File 1867), No. 23: Hurd to the Gen. Secs., May 10, 1867. Hurd went on to say that the families of both men were united by

marriage, a union he regarded as detrimental to peace. Cf. (File 1865), No. 72: Hurd to Boyce, December 11, 1865.

81. MMS Box 231 (File 1869), No. 23: Horsford to Hoole, May 10, 1869. In the *Official Gazette*, January 25, 1870, it was announced that Horsford had been licensed by the Bishop Coadjutor to assist Archdeacon Cummins at Holy Trinity Church, Port of Spain, Trinidad.

82. MMS Box 231 (File 1869), No. 31: Hurd to Boyce, June 25, 1869.

83. MMS Box 161: Report of the Second Barbados Circuit, 1869. The Report was signed by Charles Buzza and Richard Wrench, the latter of whom was subsequently dismissed for immorality. Despite claiming that there was great increase after Horsford's departure, the Report showed an increase of only nine members.

84. MMS Box 231 (File 1876), No. 14: Genge to Boyce, April 29, 1876. The punctuation is somewhat awry, but the text is quoted as it stands.

85. MMS Box 232 (File 1883), No. 40: Parker to Osborn, August 24, 1883; No. 52: Parker to Osborn, October 27, 1883. Also (File 1884), No. 11: Parker to Johnson and Anton, March 28, 1884.

86. MMS Box 232 (File 1883), No. 48: Parker to Osborn, September 29, 1883.

87. MMS Box 232 (File 1883), No. 60: Parker to Osborn, December 26, 1883, No. 52: Parker to Osborn, October 27, 1883.

88. MMS Box 232 (File 1883), No. 59: Parker to Osborn, November 29, 1883.

89. MMS Box 232 (File 1883), No. 40: Parker to Osborn, August 24, 1883; No. 52: Parker to Osborn, October 27, 1883; and (File 1884), No. 11: Parker to Johnson and Anton, March 28, 1884. Both of the ministers were senior to Parker, as were others in the District.

90. Reece and Clark-Hunt, *op. cit.,* p. 127.

91. S.P.G. Report, 1870, pp. 44, 46; of the decision on a Province see the 1873 Report, p. 30.

92. Abstract of the Journal, together with the Constitution, Canons and Resolutions of the Provincial Synod of the West Indies, Jamaica, 1883, pp. 30f., Article 1. Cf. "Constitution, Canons and Resolutions of the Provincial Synod of the Church of England in the West Indies, 1887", p. 10, Articles 1 and 12.

93. Maynard, *op. cit.,* p. 139 on Codrington College, and pp. 144–146.

94.   Findlay and Holdsworth, II. 445f.

95.   MMS Box 230 (File 1867), No. 19: Horsford to Hoole, May 2, 1867.

96.   MMS Box 162: Minutes of the St. Vincent District, 1872.

97.   MMS Box 162: Minutes of the St. Vincent District, 1873.

98.   MMS Box 163: Minutes of the St. Vincent District, 1875. See also Findlay and Holdsworth, II, 460f.

99.   MMS Box 550: Minutes of a Special Committee on Mr. Osborn's proposed visit to the West Indies, held on October 18, 1878.

100.   MMS Box 164: Minutes of the St. Vincent District, 1879. The District meeting made a strong protest in 1880 against a letter from the Committee to Chairman Sykes, which seemed to impute poor organisation to the ministers.

101.   MMS Box 232 (File 1879), No. 18: Wright to Osborn, June 9, 1879.

102.   MMS Box 164: Minutes of the St. Vincent District, 1879. See Findlay and Holdsworth, II, 446f. where the proposals have been attributed, wrongly it seems, to Osborn. It is quite likely that, in the discussions, some of his views and those of the Districts would have been similar.

103.   MMS Box 550: Minutes of the Committee, September 17, 1879: and for the adjourned meeting, September 27, 1879.

104.   MMS Box 165: Minutes of the St. Vincent District, 1881.

105.   Findlay and Holdsworth, II, 450f. On pp. 460f. it seems clear that there was a depletion of the English staff on the establishment of the Conference. They cite a minister who expressed horror at a District having "only two ordained English Ministers in it".

106.   Findlay and Holdsworth, II. 448–449; 457.

107.   For further details of the plan, see Appendix VIII.

108.   The full texts of the Resolutions are as follows:

        1.   That this meeting whilst recognising the desirability of a West Indian Conference, and pledging itself to put forth every effort to prepare the way for one, desires to press on the Missionary Committee and the Conference its firm conviction that the time has not yet come for such a step – that it would be very detrimental to our work here – and that it would greatly militate against the object which the Committee have in view to press this radical change prematurely upon this part of the mission field.

2.   That in the judgment of this Meeting the time has fully come for forming a West Indian Conference, and this meeting earnestly requests that the Committee make the necessary preliminary arrangements for such a Conference.

3.   That this meeting deeply sympathize with the Committee in their determination to form a West Indian Conference, and while we would put no obstacle in the way we ask for full information respecting the details of the scheme.

109.   Findlay and Holdsworth, II. 419 on Chambers' position; p. 429 on Richardson's.

110.   MMS Box 553: Minutes of the Conference, 1883, "General Statements". The details of the scheme are in the same document.

112.   *The West Indian,* October 10, 1884.

113.   See Appendix IX for the full list of topics.

BIBLIOGRAPHY

A. *Guides or References*

Chandler, M.J. *A Guide to Records in Barbados.* Oxford: Basil Blackwell, 1965.

Cundall, F. *Bibliography of the West Indies.* New York: Johnson Reprint Corporation, 1972.

Guiseppi, M.S. *Guide to the Contents of the Public Record Office.* 2 Vols. London: HMSO, 1963.

Gt. Britain. H.M. Manuscript Commission. *Record Repositories in Great Britain.* 3rd. edition. London: H.M.S.O., 1968.

Handler, J.S. *A Guide to Source Materials for the Study of Barbados History, 1627–1834.* Carbondale and Edwardsville: Southern Illinois University Press, 1972

Hewitt, A.R. *Union List of Commonwealth Newspapers in London, Oxford and Cambridge.* London: Institute of Commonwealth Studies, 1960.

Hewitt, A.R. *Guide to Resources for Commonwealth Studies in London, Oxford, and Cambridge.* London: Athlone Press, 1957.

Ingram, K.E. *Manuscripts relating to Commonwealth Caribbean Countries in United States and Canadian Repositories.* London: Caribbean Universities Press, 1975.

Ragatz, L.J. *A Guide for the Study of British Caribbean History, 1763–1834.* Washington: American Historical Association, 1932.

B. *British Parliamentary Papers (B.P.P.)*

Report from the Select Committee on West India Colonies together with the Minutes of Evidence, Appendix and Index 1842. B.P.P., Colonies : West Indies I.
Shannon: Irish University Press, (I.U.P.) 1968.

Papers relating to the Slave Population of the West India Colonies and the Abolition of the Slave Trade. Vol. XVIII.
Session 4 Feb. – 19 July 1823.
B.P.P., Slave Trade 65, I.U.P., 1969

Return of the Slave Population in the West India Colonies.
1824 (424) Vol. XXIV.

Acts of Colonial Legislatures, 1818–23.
1824 (160) Vol. XXIII.
B. P. P., Slave Trade 66, I.U.P., 1969

No. 113: Slaves in the West Indies III. Further Papers, being, Return to an Address for communications received by the Governor of Barbados, relative to the demolition of the Methodist chapel there, and the expulsion of Mr. Shewsbury the Methodist missionary.

No. 127: Slaves in the West Indies IV. Further Papers relating to the same subject. B.P.P., Slave Trade 67, I.U.P., 1969.

Papers and Returns Relating to the Slave Population in the West Indies 1826.
1826 (353) XVIII.
B. P. P., Slave Trade 70, I.U.P., 1969

Further Papers Relating to the Slave Populations of British Possessions in the West Indies and South America.
1826 Vol. XXIX.
B.P.P., Slave Trade 71, I.U.P., 1971

Papers outlining the Measures adopted by Great Britain for improving the Condition of the Slave Population. 1826–27. Vol. XXV.

Papers Relating to the Religious Instruction of Slaves in the West Indies.
1826–27 Vol. XXVI.
B.P.P., Slave Trade 73, I.U.P., 1969.

Papers outlining the Measures adopted by His Majesty's Government for im-
    proving the condition of Slaves in British Possessions. 1828 Vol. XXVII.
    B.P.P., Slave Trade 76, I.U.P., 1969.

Returns from all Slave Colonies belonging to the British Crown. 1831–32 (660)
    Vol. XLVII.
    B.P.P., Slave Trade 80, I.U.P., 1969.

Papers in Explanation of the Measures adopted by Her Majesty's Government
    for giving Effect to the Act for the Abolition of Slavery. 154.11 Pt. V(2)
    Barbados and British Guiana.
    B.P.P., Slave Trade 85, I.U.P., 1968

C. *Public Records, Barbados*

Barbados Blue Books   1833 – 1883.

Report of the Commission on Education, 1875.

Report of the Commission on Poor Relief, 1878.

D. *Methodist Records*

Synod Minutes – West Indies, 1822 to 1884 SOAS Boxes 148 to 166.

Correspondence – West Indies, General, 1830 – 1857.
        Boxes 129 – 143.
      – St. Vincent with Demerara, 1858 – 1867.
        Boxes 228 – 230.
      – St. Vincent, 1868 – 1890, Boxes 231 – 232.

St. Vincent and Demerara District Minute Book, 1848 – 1859
    Public Library Microfilm Bs. 51.

St. Vincent Annual Society Reports, 1853 – 1855.
    Public Library Microfilm Bs. 54.

Bethel Society Friendly Society Accounts, 1844 – 1853.
    Public Library Microfilm Bs. 54.

St. Vincent and Demerara District Minute Book, 1827 – 1839;
    Chapel Accounts, 1832 – 1846; Circuit Accounts, 1840 – 1865.
    Public Library Microfilms Bs. 52.

Bethel Society Reports and Accounts, 1873 – 1891.
    Public Library Microfilm, Bs. 54.

E. *Newspapers*

Barbados Mercury, 1783 – 1789.

Barbados Mercury and Bridgetown Gazette, 1805 – 1825

The Liberal, 1837 – 1859.

The West Indian, 1876 – 1885.

The Official Gazette, 1867 – 1883.

Barbados Times, 1863 – 1876.

Barbados Agricultural Reporter, 1870.

Barbados Herald, 1878 – 1883.

F. *Secondary Works*

Abbey, C.T. & Overton, J.H. *The English Church in the Eighteenth Century.*
    London, 1878,

Augier, F.R. and Gordon, S. *Sources of West Indian History.* London: Longmans,
    1967.

Bayley, F.W.N. *Four Years' Residence in the West Indies.* London, 1832.

Beckles, H. *Black Rebellion in Barbados.* Barbados: Antilles Publications, Barbados, 1984.

_____. "Emancipation by Law or War? Wilberforce and the 1816 Barbados Slave Rebellion". David Richardson (Ed.) *Abolition and Its Aftermath.* London: Frank Cass and Co. Ltd., 1985, 80–104.

Beecham, J. *An Essay in the Constitution of Wesleyan Methodism.* London, 1851.

Bennett, J.H., jr. *Bondsmen and Bishops.* Berkeley: University of California Press, 1958.

Bickford, J. *An Autobiography of Christian Labour in the West Indies, Demerara, Victoria, New South Wales, and South Australia, 1838–1888.* London, 1890.

Brathwaite, E. *The Development of Creole Society in Jamaica, 1770 – 1820.* Oxford: Clarendon Press, 1978.

Bready, J.W. *England Before and After Wesley.* London: Hodder and Stoughton, 1938.

Burchell, W.F. *Memoir of Thomas Burchell.* London, 1849.

Burns, A. *History of the British West Indies.* Revised Second Edition. London: Allen and Unwin, 1965.

Caldecott, A. *The Church in the West Indies.* London, 1898.

Campbell, C.C. "Towards an Imperial Policy for the Education of Negroes in the West Indies after Emancipation", *Jamaican Historical Review,* VIII (1967): 68–102.
_____. "Denominationalism and the Mico Charity Schools in Jamaica, 1835–1842", *Caribbean Studies,* 10.4 (1970): 151–172.

_____. "Social and Economic Obstacles to the Development of Popular Education in Post Emancipation Jamaica, 1834–1865", *Journal of Caribbean History,* 1 (1970): 57–88.

Chadwick, O. *The Victorian Church.* 2nd. Edition. Pts. 1 & II. London: A & C. Black, 1970.

Cnattingius, H. *Bishops and Societies.* London: S.P.C.K., 1952.

Coleridge, H. N. *Six Months in the West Indies in 1825.* 1832. New York: Negro Universities Press, 1970.

Coleridge, W.H. *Charges Delivered to the Clergy of the Diocese of Barbados and the Leeward Islands.* London, 1835.

Cox, E.L. *Free Coloureds in the Slave Societies of St. Kitts and Grenada.* Knoxville: University of Tennessee Press, 1984.

Craton, M. *Sinews of Empire.* London: Temple Smith, 1974.

Curtis, S.J. *History of Education in Great Britain.* 7th Edition. London: Tutorial Press Ltd., 1968.

Davis, K. *Cross and Crown in Barbados.* Frankfurt am Main: Verlag Peter Lang, 1983.

Davy, J. *The West Indies Before and Since Slave Emancipation.* 1854. London: Frank Cass, 1971.

Dickson, W. *Letters on Slavery.* London: 1879.

_____. *Mitigation of Slavery* 1814. New York: Negro Universities Press, 1970.

Dixon, J. *Methodism in its Origin, Economy and Present Position.* New York, 1843.

Dorner, A. *History of Protestant Theology,* Vol. II 1871. New York: AMS Press, 1970.

Findlay, G.G. & Holdsworth, W.W. *The History of the Wesleyan Methodist Missionary Society.* 5 Vols. London: The Epworth Press, 1921.

Fraser, L.M. *History of Trinidad.* Vol. I 1891, Vol.II 1896. London: Frank Cass, 1971.

Furley, O.W. "Moravian Missionaries and Slaves in the West Indies", *Caribbean Studies,* 5.2 (1965): 3–16.

Gardner, W.J. *A History of Jamaica* (1873). London: Frank Cass, 1971.

Gibbes, B. "The Establishment of the Tenantry System in Barbados", Marshall, W.K. (Ed.) *Emancipation II: Aspects of Post Slavery Experience in Barbados.* Barbados: Department of History, U.W.I. and National Cultural Foundation, 1987, 23–45.

Gilmore, J.T. "Church and Society in Barbados, 1824-1881", *Emancipation II: Aspects of Post-Slavery Experience in Barbados.* Barbados: Department of History, U.W.I. and National Cultural Foundation, 1987, 1–22.

_____. "The Rev. William Harte and Attitudes to Slavery in Early Nineteenth Century Barbados", *Journal of Ecclesiastical History,* 30.4 (1979): 461–474.

Goodridge. S.S. *Facing the Challenge of Emancipation.* Barbados: Cedar Press, 1981.

Gordon, S.C. *A Century of West Indian Education.* London: Longmans, 1963.

_____. *Reports and Repercussions in West Indies Education.* London: Caribbean University Press/Ginn, 1968.

Goveia, E.V. *Slave Society in the British Leeward Islands at the End of the Eighteenth Century.* 1965. Westport, Conn.: Greenwood Press, 1980.

Green, W.A. *British Slave Emancipation.* Oxford: Clarendon Press, 1976.

_____. "The Apprenticeship in British Guiana, 1834–1838". *Caribbean Studies,* 9.2 (1969): 44–66.

Halevy, E. *History of the English People in the Nineteenth Century:*
Vol. I: *England in 1815.* London: Ernest Benn Ltd., 2nd Edn., 1964.

Vol. 3: *The Triumph of Reform* (1830–1841). London: Ernest Benn, 1961.

Vol. 4: *Victorian Years (1841–1895).* London: Ernest Benn Ltd., 1961.

Hall, D. "The Flight from the Estates Reconsidered: the British West Indies, 1838-1842". *Journal of Caribbean History,* 10 & 11 (1978): 7–24.

Hamilton, B. *Barbados and the Confederation Question, 1871–1885.* London: Crown Agents for Overseas Governments and Administrations, 1956.

Hamilton, J.T. & K.G. *History of the Moravian Church, The Renewed Unitas Fratrum, 1722–1957.* Bethlehem, Pennsylvania: Moravian Church in America, 1901.

Handler, Jerome. *The Unappropriated People.* Baltimore: Johns Hopkins University Press, 1974.

Harlow, V. & Madden, F. *British Colonial Development,* 1774–1834. Oxford: Clarendon Press, 1953.

Harricharan, J.T. *The Catholic Church in Trinidad, 1498–1852.* Port of Spain: Inprint Caribbean, 1981.

Hinton, J.H. *Memoir of William Knibb.* London, 1849.

Holder, H.E. *A Short Essay on the Subject of Negro Slavery.* London, 1788.

Horsford, J. *A Voice from the West Indies.* London, 1856.

Howse, E.M. *Saints in Politics.* London: Allen and Unwin, 1971.

Hughes, R. "The Origins of Barbados Sugar Plantations and the Role of the White Population in Sugar Plantation Society", Thompson, A.O. (Ed.) *Emancipation I: A Series of Lectures to Commemorate the 150th Anniversary of Emancipation.* Barbados: Department of History, U.W.I. and National Cultural Foundation, 1984, 26–32.

Hutton, J.E. *A History of Moravian Missions.* London: Moravian Publication Office, 1922.

Jakobsson, S. *Am I not a Man and a Brother?* Uppsala: Gleerup, 1972.

Klingberg, F.J. *Codrington Chronicle.* Berkeley: University of California Press, 1949.

————. *The Anti-Slavery Movement in England.* 1926. Hamden, Conn.: Archon Books, 1968.

————. "The Lady Mico Charity Schools in the British West Indies, 1835–1842", *Journal of Negro History,* 24 (1939): 291–344.

Knapland, P. *James Stephen and the British Colonial System, 1813–1847.* Madison: University of Wisconsin Press, 1953.

Knight, F.W. *The Caribbean.* New York: Oxford University Press, 1978.

Knox, R. *Enthusiasm* 1950. London: Collins Liturgical Publications, 1987.

Lawton, G. *John Wesley's English.* London: Allen & Unwin, 1962.

Lewis, G.K. *Main Currents in Caribbean Thought.* Baltimore: Johns Hopkins University Press, 1983.

Lewis, K. *The Moravian Missions in Barbados, 1816–1886.* Frankfurt am Main: Verlag Peter Lang, 1985.

Levy, C. *Emancipation, Sugar and Federalism: Barbados and the West Indies, 1833–1876.* Gainsville: University Presses of Florida, 1980.

_____. "Barbados: The Last Years of Slavery, 1823–1833", *Journal of Negro History,* 44 (1959): 308–345.

_____. "Slavery and the Emancipation Movement in Barbados, 1650–1833", *Journal of Negro History,* 55 (1970): 1–12.

Lobdell, Richard. "Patterns of Investment and Sources of Credit in the British West indian Sugar Industry, 1838- 97", *Journal of Caribbean History,* 4 (1972): 31–53.

Long, Edward. *History of Jamaica.* 3 Vols. 1774. London: Frank Cass, 1970.

Lucas, C.P. *A Historical Geography of the British Colonies.* 5 Vols. Vol. II, *The West Indian Dependencies.* Oxford: Clarendon Press, 1905.

Manning, H.T. *British Colonial Governments after the American Revolution, 1782–1820.* 1933. Hamden, Conn.: Archon Books, 1966.

Mannix, D.P. & Cowley, M. *Black Cargoes.* London: Longmans, Green, 1962.

Marshall, W.K. "Amelioration and Emancipation (with Special Reference to Barbados)", Thompson, A.O. (Ed.). *Emancipation I: A Series of Lectures to Commemorate the 150th Anniversary of Emancipation.* 1984, 72–87.

Martin, R.M. *History of the Colonies of the British Empire.* 1843. London: Dawson's of Pall Mall, 1967.

Mathieson, W.L. *British Slavery and its Abolition, 1823–1838.* 1926. New York: Octagon Books, 1967.

Maynard, G.O. *History of the Moravian Church Eastern West Indian Province.* Port of Spain, Trinidad: Yuille's Printerie, 1968.

Millette, James. *The Genesis of Crown Colony Government.* Trinidad: Moko Enterprises, 1970.

Moister, W. *The West Indies Enslaved and Free.* London, 1883.

_____. *Memorials of Missionary Labours in Western Africa and the West Indies.* London, 1850.

Murray, D.J. *The West Indies and the Development of Colonial Government, 1801–1834.* Oxford: Clarendon Press, 1965.

Nimkoff, W.F. & M.F. *A Handbook of Sociology.* 5th Edn. London: Routledge & Kegan Paul, 1968.

Northcott, C. *Slavery's Martyr.* London: Epworth Press, 1970.

Paget, H. "The Free Village System in Jamaica", *Apprenticeship and Emancipation.* Dept. of Extra Mural Studies, U.W.I., n.d., 45–58.

Palmer, C. *Human Cargoes.* Chicago: University of Illinois Press, 1981.

Parker, J.A. *A Church in the Sun.* London: Cargate Press, 1959.

Pascoe, C.F. *Two Hundred years of the S.P.G.* London: Society for the Publication of the Gospel, 1901.

Patterson, Orlando. *The Sociology of Slavery.* London: Granada Publishing, 1973.

Parrinder, E.G. *African Traditional Religion.* 3rd. Edition. London: Sheldon Press, 1976.

Peirce, W. *The Principles and Polity of the Wesleyan Methodists.* London, 1873.

Pinckard, G. *Notes on the West Indies.* 3 Vols. London, 1806.

Raboteau, A.J. *Slave Religion.* London: Oxford University Press, 1980.

Ragatz, L.J. *The Fall of the Planter Class in the British Caribbean, 1763–1833.* 1928. New York: Octagon Books, 1971.

Reece, J.E. & Clark-Hunt, C.G. *Barbados Diocesan History.* London: The West India Committee, 1925.

Riviere, W.E. "Labour Shortage in the British West Indies After Emancipation", *Journal of Caribbean History,* 4. (1972): 1–30.

Rupp, E.G. *Religion in England, 1688–1791.* Oxford: Clarendon Press, 1986.

Schomburgk, R.H. *The History of Barbados.* 1848. London: Frank Cass, 1971.

Sewell, W.G. *The Ordeal of Free Labour in the West Indies.* 1862. London: Frank Cass, 1968.

Sheridan, Richard. *An Era of West Indian Prosperity, 1750–1775. Chapters in Caribbean History.* London: Caribbean University Press, 1973.

Sherlock, P.M. *West Indian Nations.* Kingston: Jamaica Publishing House, 1973.

Shrewsbury, J.V.B. *Memorials of the Rev. William J. Shrewsbury.* 2nd. Edition, London, 1868.

Shrewsbury, William J. *Sermons Preached on Several Occasions in the Island of Barbados.* London, 1825.

Smith, G. *History of Wesleyan Methodism.* London, 1861.

Southey, Capt. Thomas. *Chronological History of the West Indies.* 3 Vols. 1827. London: Frank Cass, 1968.

Sturge, J. & Harvey, T. *The West Indies in 1837.* 1838. London: Frank Cass, 1968.

Substance of the Debate in the House of Commons, June 23, 1825, on Mr. Buxton's Motion, Respecting the Destruction of the Methodist Chapel in Barbados.

Sutton-Moxley, J.H. *An Account of a West Indian Sanatorium and a Guide to Barbados.* London, 1886.

Thome, J.A. & Kimball, J.H. *Emancipation in the West Indies.* 1838. New York: Arno Press, 1969.

Thompson, E.P. *The Making of the English Working Class.* London, 1965.

Titus, Noel. *The Church and Slavery in the English Speaking Caribbean.* Barbados: Caribbean Group for Social and Religious Studies, 1983.

Troeltsch, E. *The Social Teaching of the Christian Churches.* 2 Vols. New York: Harper Torchbooks, 1960.

Trollope, A. *The West Indies and the Spanish Main.* 1860. London: Frank Cass, 1968.

Turner, G. *The Constitution and Discipline of Wesleyan Methodism.* London, 1841.

Turner, M. *Slaves and Missionaries.* Chicago: University of Illinois Press, 1982.

Wallbridge, E.A. *The Demerara Martyr.* 1848. New York: Negro Universities Press, 1969.

Walvin, J. (Ed.) *Slavery and British Society, 1776–1846.* London: Macmillan, 1982.

_____. "Recurring Themes: White Images of Black Life During and After Slavery", *Slavery and Abolition,* 5.2 (1984) 118–140.

Watson, K.S. *The Civilised Island. Barbados, A Social History, 1750–1816.* University of Florida, Ph.D. Thesis, 1975. Barbados: Caribbean Graphics, 1979.

Watson, R. *A Defence of the Wesleyan Methodist Missions in the West Indies.* London, 1817.

Watts, M. *The Dissenters.* Oxford: Clarendon Press, 1978.

Wearmouth, R.F. *Methodism and the Working-Class Movement in England, 1800–1850.* London: Epworth Press, 1947.

Whiteley, J.H. *Wesley's England.* 4th Edition. London: The Epworth Press, 1954.

Whyte, Millicent. *A Short History of Education in Jamaica.* London: Hodder and Stoughton, 1983.

Williams, Colbert. *The Methodist Contribution to Education in the Bahamas.* Gloucester: Allan Sutton, 1982.

Williams, Eric. *From Columbus to Castro.* London: Andre Deutsch, 1970.

Williams, Eric. *Documents on British West Indian History, 1807–1833.* Port of Spain: Trinidad Publishing Co., 1952.

Wilmot, Swithin. "Baptist Missionaries and Jamaican Politics, 1838–1854", Lawrence, K.O. (Ed.) *A Selection of Papers Presented at the Twelfth Conference of Caribbean Historians,* 1980, 45–62.

Wilson, Bryan. *Religious Sects.* London: World University Library, 1970.

Wood, Donald. *Trinidad in Transition.* London: Oxford University Press, 1968.

G. *Theses and Unpublished Papers*

Blouet, Olwyn. "Education and Emancipation in Barbados, 1823–1846: A Study in Cultural Transference", Ph.D. Thesis, University of Nebraska, 1977.

Campbell, C.C. "The Development of Primary Education in Jamaica, 1835–1865". M.A. Thesis, London, 1963.

Campbell, C.C. "The Development of Education in Trinidad, 1834–1870". Ph.D. Thesis, U.W.I., 1973.

Dayfoot, A.C. "The Shaping of the West Indian Church." Th.D. Thesis, Emmanuel College, Victoria University, Canada, 1982.

Goodridge, R. "The Development of Education in Barbados, 1818–1860." M.Ed. Thesis, University of Leeds, 1966.

Marshall, W.K. "The Ex-Slaves as Wage Labourers on the Sugar Estates in the British Windward Islands, 1838–1846." U.W.I., Cave Hill Seminar Paper, 197–?

Marshall, W.K. & Gibbs, Bentley. "The Establishment of a Peasantry in Barbados, 1840–1920." U.W.I. Seminar Paper, Cave Hill, 1974.

McCarthy, C.R. "The Imperialist Movement in the Introduction of Popular Education in Barbados, 1823–1876" M.Ed. Thesis, University of Alberta, 1983.

Watson, K. "Slave Resistance in Barbados: the Eighteenth Century–Acquiescence or Resilience?" U.W.I. Seminar Paper, Mona, February 1983.

Williams, Fay. "The Work of the Anglican Church in Education in Jamaica, 1826–1845.", U.W.I., M.A. Research Paper, 1987.

APPENDICES

APPENDIX 1

QUESTIONS TO BE ANSWERED BY ALL CANDIDATES FOR ADMISSION

1.   Have you been baptized?

2.   By whom were you baptized?

3.   Have you been married?

4.   By whom were you married?

5.   Are you living with your husband or wife?

6.   Were you ever in Society before?

7.   What was the cause of your exclusion?

8.   Is that cause removed?

9.   Do you keep holy the Sabbath Day?

10.   Do you labour at all on that day?

11.   Do you buy or sell on that day?

12.   Why do you wish to join our Society?

13.   How long have you had that wish?

14.   By what means was that wish produced?

APPENDIX 1 (Continued)

15.   How often do you attend prayers?

16.   How long is it since you began to attend?

17.   Where do you live?

18.   Are you free?

19.   Have you any children, and do they come to Sunday School?

20.   Have you heard or read our rules?

21.   Will you keep those rules?

22.   Do you send your children or any young people under your care to the market on Sunday?

23.   Are any of your children living with your consent with a husband or wife without being married?

24.   Do you hinder your daughter who is married from properly attending to her husband?

25.   Will you always speak the truth and hate lying?

26.   Will you pray with your Family every day, if you can?

27.   Are you living in peace and love with every body?

28.   Have you nothing in your heart against any body at all?

29.   Are you in Debt?

Source: MMS Box 129: No. 1. This document has no title, and is merely a compendium of Methodist practice. The relevant section is entitled "On the Admission and Exclusion of Members," Clause 12.

APPENDIX II

METHODIST MEMBERSHIP AND ATTENDANCE FIGURES,
1822–1883.

Year	MEMBERSHIP Barbados	District	ATTENDANCE Barbados	District
1822	75	4726		
1823	90	4926		
1824	100	5131		
1825	75	5724		
1826	101	6314		
1827	108	6924		
1828	121	7173		
1829	129	6982		
1830	178			
1831	263	6538		
1832	383	6051		
1833	480	5857		
1834	587	6312		
1835	698	7184		
1836	905	2794		
1837	1056	2895		

APPENDIX II (Continued)

| Year | MEMBERSHIP | | ATTENDANCE | |
	Barbados	District	Barbados	District
1838	1331	3129		
1839	1350	3150		
1840	1352	3175		
1841	1323	3208		
1842	1470	3242	4550	10400
1843	1564	3396	4695	10145
1844				
1845				
1846	1877	13548	5450	31648
1847	2014	13852	5880	32380
1848	2134	14001	6000	32680
1849	2259	13576	6130	28755
1850	2416	13327	6165	29888
1851	2700	12893	7300	33550
1852	3045	12988	9500	35882
1853	3709	13227	9500	35726
1854	4046	13716	10200	35230
1855	4011	13624	10400	35850
1856	3653	13998	10400	36400
1857	3445	14016	8400	27413

APPENDIX II (Continued)

Year	MEMBERSHIP		ATTENDANCE	
	Barbados	District	Barbados	District
1858	3259			
1859	3404	13350	9640	34448
1860				
1861				
1862	3089	12302		37992
1863	2935	8568 *	10521	26941
1864	1909			
1865	1977	7078	9650	25720
1866	2153			
1867	2245	7244	9900	25820
1868	2694	8082		
1869	2723	8394	10730	26790
1870	2881	8808	10830	27890
1871	2819	8813	11630	28490
1872	2597	8557	11130	27190
1873				
1874	2380	8421	11000	26330
1875	2280	8456	10706	27706
1876		8386	11100	27450
1877	2051	8435	10175	27255

APPENDIX II (Continued)

Year	MEMBERSHIP		ATTENDANCE	
	Barbados	District	Barbados	District
1880	2039	8446	11800	32300
1881	2163	8538	11700	37400
1882	2061	8880	12500	34500
1883	1939	12254	8000 **	28295 **

Notes:

(1)   "Membership" refers to the number of those who were full members, and "Attendance" to the aggregate of those who attended the various chapels.

(2)   Figures under "Barbados" give the aggregates of members or attendants at all chapels in the island. Those under "District" give corresponding figures for the District(s) to which Barbados belonged.

(3)   From 1822–1835 Barbados was part of the St. Vincent District which included Demerara. From 1836 to 1845 the island was part of the Demerara District. From 1846 to 1862, Barbados was part of the St. Vincent and Demerara District. From 1863 to 1883, Barbados was part of the St. Vincent District.

(4)   Because of deficient records, there are some missing figures.

*   Attendance figures for Biabou in St. Vincent are missing.

** These figures are incomplete.

Source: Annual District Minutes and Circuit Reports, 1823–1883. Returns were submitted annually by each Circuit to the District Meeting.

APPENDIX III

DAY AND SUNDAY SCHOOL STUDENTS, 1826–1883

Year	DAY SCHOOLS		SUNDAY SCHOOLS	
	Barbados	District	Barbados	District
1826			73	1031
1827			358	1156
1828			299	1220
1829			265	1205
1830			384	
1831			160	
1832			394	1297
1833			509	1377
1834			428	2016
1835			1170	3047
1836			880	1820
1837	334	484	1355	2106
1838	673	777	1626	2230
1839	632		1952	
1840	311	674	1174	1911
1841				
1842	438	750	1479	2039

APPENDIX III (Continued)

Year	DAY SCHOOLS		SUNDAY SCHOOLS	
	Barbados	District	Barbados	District
1843	46	659	1237	1844
1844				
1845				
1846	415	2738	960	4512
1847	256	2911	968	4433
1848	322	2951	1500	4471
1849	260	2961	1636	4874
1850	1054	4104	1446	5236
1851	1244	4416	1701	5175
1852	1344	4718	1800	5478
1853	1256	4726	893	4457
1854	947	4326	800	3921
1855	997	3801	1263	4306
1856	696	3578	1370	4940
1857	817	4594	1569	6094
1858				
1859	1420	5712	1538	4966
1860				
1861				
1862	1447	4921	1492	4909

APPENDIX III (Continued)

Year	DAY SCHOOLS		SUNDAY SCHOOLS	
	Barbados	District	Barbados	District
1863	1355	3167	1432	3040
1864				
1865	912	2656	871	2193
1866				
1867	1362	3360	1203	2923
1868				
1869	1029	3157	1163	3619
1870	1249	3262	991	3330
1871				
1872	1558	3445	1184	3765
1873				
1874	1621	4342	1579	3902
1875	2155	5449	1068	3630
1876	1305	4266	1341	3835
1877	1864	5752	1010	4101
1878				
1879	2230	6252	764	4194
1880	2354	6348	826	3816
1881	2028	5122	804	3793

APPENDIX III (Continued)

Year	DAY SCHOOLS		SUNDAY SCHOOLS	
	Barbados	District	Barbados	District
1882	2234	5654	951	3942
1883	2210	8661	994	5576

Notes:

(1)   As in Appendix II, the figures under "Barbados" and "District" give the aggregate for the island and the District(s).

(2)   From 1826 to 1835, Barbados was part of the St. Vincent District which included Demerara.

(3)   From 1836 to 1845, Barbados was part of the Demerara District. From 1846 to 1862, Barbados was part of the St. Vincent and Demerara District. From 1863 to 1883, Barbados was part of the St. Vincent District.

(4)   Because of deficient records, there are some missing figures.

Source: Annual District Minutes and Circuit Reports, 1823–1883. Returns were submitted annually by each Circuit to the District Meeting.

APPENDIX IV

METHODIST CIRCUIT REVENUE, 1840–1845

Year	Class and Ticket (£)	Total Revenue (£)	Class and Ticket as % of Total
1840	327.15.2 1/2	841.4.11	39
1841	309.16.4	878.19.4 1/2	35
1842	373.16.4	978.2.2	38
1843	401.11.8 1/2	1072.2.10 1/2	37
1844	462. 0.11 1/2	907.19.10	51
1845	701.19.6 1/2	992.19.1 1/2	51

Source: Barbados Chapel Accounts, 1832–1846, Records of the Methodist Church, Microfilm Bs. 52 at the Barbados Public Library.

APPENDIX V

HEADS OF REVENUE AND EXPENDITURE
MAIN SOURCES OF REVENUE

Chapel Account	Circuit Account
Pew Rents	Class Money
Monthly Collections	Ticket Money
	Yearly Collection
	Missionary Meeting

MAIN AREAS OF EXPENDITURE

Chapel Account	Circuit Account
Candles	Quarterages
Repairs to Chapel	Stationery
New Pews, etc.	Fuel
	Medicines
	Furniture

Source: Barbados Circuit and Chapel Accounts, 1832–1846, Records of the Methodist Church, Microfilm Bs. 52 at the Barbados Public Library.

APPENDIX VI

COMPARISON OF PUBLIC FUNDING OF CHURCHES.

YEAR	ESTAB. CHURCH (£)	MORAVIANS (£)	METHODISTS (£)	R.C (£)
1871	8761.15.1 1/2	400	700	50
1872	12289.6.3	400	700	50
1873	10591.9.4	400	700	50
1874	10661.15.6	400	700	50
1875	10467.19.8	400	700	50
1876	10601.19.8	400	700	50
1877	10232.6.0	400	700	50
1878	10342.9.11	400	700	50
1879	10514.0.6	400	700	50
1880	10568.16.10	400	700	50
1881	9920.11.7	400	700	50
1882	9562.11.1	400	700	50
1883	10493.13.2 1/2	400	700	50

Source: Barbados Blue Books: 1871, p C 4; 1872, p. C 4; 1873, p. C4; 1874, p. C4; 1875, p. C4; 1876, p. C4; 1877, p. C4; 1878, p. C8; 1879, p. C4; 1880, p. C4; 1881, p. C4; 1882, p. C4; 1883, p. C4.

APPENDIX VII

CLERGY OF THE ESTABLISHED CHURCH WORKING IN AREAS OF CONFLICT*

CHRIST CHURCH

C.C. Gill	Rector	1833 – 59	Cod.	Coll.	1829
Abraham Reece	"	1859 – 69	"	"	1835
F.B. Grant	"	1869 – 71	"	"	1830
H.W. Moore	"	1876 – 82	"	"	1836
W. Eversley	Vicar		"	"	1841
	St. Bartholomew				

ST. PETER

W.D. Sealy	Rector	1834 – 39			
W.M. Payne	"	1839 – 77	"	"	1829
G.M. Frederick	"	1877 – 97	"	"	1850

ST. JAMES

G.F. Maynard	"	1833 – 48			
Charles Lawson	"	1848 – 60	"	"	1850?
P.B. Austin	"	1860 – 75			

ST. JOHN

J.H. Gittens	"		"	"	before 1829
A.H. Bishop	"		"	"	1843
E.McG. Sealy	"		"	"	1859
E.P. Smith	Vicar		"	"	1813
	St. Mark				

APPENDIX VII (continued)

ST. PHILIP

R.F. King	Rector	1831–75	Asst. Master Cod. Grammar School
P.B. Austin	"	1875 –	

* Those clergy who were trained at Codrington College are indicated with the dates of their matriculation where that is known.

Source: Codrington College Matriculation Register 1830 to Present.

APPENDIX VIII

ABSTRACT OF THE PLAN FOR WEST INDIAN CONFERENCES

There were to be two *Annual* Conferences: The Western Conference to comprise the Jamaica and Haiti Districts, the Eastern Conference to comprise the Antigua, St. Vincent and British Guiana Districts. Both Annual Conferences were to be affiliated to the English Yearly Conference.

There was to be a General Conference affiliated to the English Yearly Conference.

The West Indian Conferences were to "keep and uphold the doctrines of Wesleyan Methodism ... and observe and maintain the general rules and usages of Wesleyan Methodism."

Disciplinary action against ministers of any rank by the West Indian Conferences did not require confirmation or approval by the Yearly Conference.

The General Conference had the right to nominate a President, but the Yearly Conference had the right of appointment.

The President of the General Conference had the same powers and duties with respect to ministers and institutions as the President of the Yearly Conference.

Each Annual Conference was to elect a Vice-President.

The General Conference had sole power of legislation for the West Indies, and full power and oversight of West Indian Methodism.

APPENDIX VIII (Continued)

The duties of the General Conference involved the following:

1.   Introduction of the President appointed by the 'Yearly Conference,' election of Secretary, and appointment of the other officers of the Conference.

2.   Report of number of Members and state of the Societies; plans and means for the promotion of directly aggressive and Missionary work.

3.   General supervision of Connexional Literature, and official Ministerial appointments which may be necessary in connection therewith.

4.   Questions affecting the conduct of public worship.

The Annual Conference had responsibility for ministerial appointments, and for supervision of Methodist work in each conference.

APPENDIX IX

EXTRACT FROM *THE WEST INDIAN,* OCTOBER 10, 1884

"TOPICS"

1st Topic   The West Indian Conference means that our Church becomes
                self-governing.
                                    Revd. J.R. Tull

2nd   "   The West Indian Conference means that our Churches must
                soon become self-supporting, and be no longer dependent on
                British Charity
                                    Revd. C. Denham

3rd   "   The organization of West Indian Methodism means that we are
                to establish and support Missions, that we may fulfil the voca-
                tion and perform the duty of a Church to the Lord and to our
                fellow-men.
                                    Rev. W. Lavender

4th   "   The West Indian Conference needs the fervent prayers, the act-
                ive energies, and the Christian liberality of all who are connec-
                ted with our Churches out here, and of those who are in sym-
                pathy with us.
                                    Rev. G. Irvine

5th   "   The West Indian Conference means that our intelligent Godly
                laymen shall take an active part in the work of Methodism in
                Circuits, District Meetings and Conferences.
                                    Rev. J. Allan Campbell

APPENDIX IX (Continued)

6th "   Inasmuch as "the right man in the right place" is a necessity for successful christian work, as well as for secular pursuits, the Methodists of the West Indies must pray that the Conference may have wisdom, and courage to carry this out independent of all personal considerations.

Rev. A.H. Aguilar

7th "   The West Indian Conference means that greater efforts than have ever yet been made must be put forth to raise up a suitable, efficient Ministry, and they become self-perpetuating.

Rev. J.C. Richardson

APPENDIX X

LIST OF WEST INDIAN MINISTERS IN THE ST. VINCENT DISTRICT

Year Recruited	Name	Island of Origin	Complexion
1848	W.P. Garry*	Grenada	Coloured
1853	Gilbert Irvine*	Tobago	,,
1853	W.H. Griffith	,,	,,
1856	J.C. Richardson*	St. Maarten	White
1858	J.E. Chase*	Barbados	Coloured
1868	J.C. Johnson	,,	,,
1868	J.A. Campbell*	Grenada	,,
1870	J.R.F. Tull*	Barbados	,,
1871	A.H. Anguilar*	Jamaica	,,
1872	W.H. Sammy	Demerara	,,
1874	T.A. Franklin	St. Eustatius	Coloured
1877	J.P. Owens*	Barbados	,,
1877	J. Licorish	,,	,,
1878	J.S. Thompson	Jamaica	Black
1879	Simon Bacchus	St. Vincent	,,
1879	T.H. Bayley	Barbados	White
1880	D.W. Bland	Demerara	Coloured
1883	E.D. Jones	Barbados	White
1883	J.E. Payne	,,	Coloured

* These worked in Barbados.

No coloured minister was appointed to James Street.

Source: MMS Box 228 (File 1883): Parker to Osborn, September 6, 1883, enclosure.

INDEX